Anonymous

List of Christian and Monuments

Anonymous

List of Christian and Monuments

ISBN/EAN: 9783337385019

Printed in Europe, USA, Canada, Australia, Japan

Cover: Foto ©Lupo / pixelio.de

More available books at **www.hansebooks.com**

Christ[illegible]

AN[illegible]

ARCHÆOL[illegible]

[illegible]TED AND PU[illegible]

CONTENTS.

			Page.
Preface	...	... ...	v
Addenda et Corrigenda		... ...	vii

NORTH-WESTERN PROVINCES.

I.—Meerut Division.

				Page
Dehra Dún	District	(Nos. 1-6)	... ...	2-4
Ditto	"	(Nos. 532 & 533)	... ...	170
Sahāranpur	"	(Blank).		
Muzaffarnagar	"	(Ditto).		
Meerut	"	(Nos. 7-40)	... ...	5-16
Ditto	"	(Nos. 534-537)	... ...	170-171
Bulandshahr	"	(No. 41) ...	... ...	17
Aligarh	"	(Nos. 42-51)	... ...	18-25
Ditto	"	(Nos. 538-543)	... ...	171-172

II.—Agra Division.

				Page
Muttra	District	(Nos. 52-68)	... ...	26-29
Ditto	"	(No. 544)	... ...	173
Agra	"	(Nos. 69-78)	... ...	29-32
Do.	"	(Nos. 545-556)	... ...	173-177
Farukhabad	"	(Nos. 79-86)	... ...	32-35
Ditto	"	(Nos. 557-566)	... ...	177-179
Mainpuri	"	(Nos. 87-90)	... ...	35
Etáwah	"	(Nos. 91-93)	... ...	36-37
Etah	"	(No. 94)	... ...	37

III.—Rohilkhand Division.

				Page
Bareilly	District	(Nos. 95-105)	... ...	38-44
Ditto	"	(No. 567)	... ...	180
Bijnor	"	(Blank).		
Budaun	"	(Ditto).		
Moradabad	"	(No. 568)	... ...	180
Shâhjahánpur	"	(Nos. 106 & 107)	... ...	44-45
Ditto	"	(No. (569)	... ...	180
Pilibhit	"	(Blank).		

IV.—Allahabad Division.

				Page
Cawnpore	District	(Nos. 108-158)	... ...	46-71
Ditto	"	(Nos. 570-578)	... ...	181-183
Fatehpur	"	(Nos. 159 & 160)	... ...	72
Ditto	"	(No. 579)	... ...	183
Bánda	"	(Nos. 161-166)	... ...	73-75
Ditto	"	(No. 580)	... ...	183
Hamirpur	"	(Nos. 167-192)	... ...	75-79
Allahabad	"	(Nos. 193-210)	... ...	79-84
Ditto	"	(No. 581)	... ...	184
Jhánsi	"	(Nos. 211-214)	... ...	84-87
Jalaun	"	(Nos. 215-220)	... ...	88-89
Ditto	"	(No. 582)	... ...	184

V.—Benares Division.

				Page
Benares	District	(Nos. 221-233)	... ...	90-94
Ditto	"	(Nos. 583-586)	... ...	185

V.—Benares Division—(*concld.*).

			Page.
Mirzapur	District	(Nos. 239-341)	94-113
Ditto	„	(Nos. 587-599)	186-188
Jaunpur	„	(Nos. 342-366)	113-117
Gházipur	„	(Nos. 367-371)	118-119
Ballia	„	(*Blank*).	

VI.—Gorakhpur Division.

Gorakhpur	District	(Nos. 372-388)	120-123
Basti	„	(Nos. 389-391)	123-124
Azamgarh	„	(Nos. 392-402)	124-127

VII.—Kumaun Division.

Naini Tal	District	(Nos. 403-408)	128-130
Almora	„	(Nos. 409 & 410)	130-131
Garhwál	„	(*Blank*).	

OUDH.

VIII.—Lucknow Division.

Lucknow	District	(Nos. 411-523)	132-163
Unao	„	(*Blank*).	
Rae Bareli	„	(*Ditto*).	
Sitapur	„	(No. 524)	164
Hardoi	„	(Nos. 525-528)	164-165
Kheri	„	(No. 529)	165-166

IX.—Fyzabad Division.

Fyzabad	District	(*Blank*).	
Gonda	„	(No. 530)	167
Bahraich	„	(No. 531)	167
Sultánpur	„	(*Blank*).	
Partábgarh	„	(*Ditto*).	
Bara Banki	„	(*Ditto*).	

PREFACE.

The List of Obituary Monuments and Epitaphania of historical or archæological interest in the North-Western Provinces and Oudh, contained in this volume, has been prepared in the form prescribed by the Government of India, Home Department (Ecclesiastical), Resolution No. $\frac{1\ Eccl.}{57}$, dated Calcutta, the 28th February 1893. The information here furnished regarding these Christian monuments is based partly on personal knowledge and partly on the official returns prepared by the Divisional and District Officers in compliance with the instructions issued by the Local Government in the Public Works Department Resolution No. C. $\frac{4844}{1478}$ W.A., dated Naini Tal, the 11th October 1893. No pains have been spared by the compiler to make this list of Epitaphs and Monumental Inscriptions as comprehensive and in as full detail as possible, in order to secure new information respecting the early European settlers, factors, writers and others who spent their lives in this country and helped in laying the foundations of the British Indian Empire. No tomb or memorial tablet has been excluded on account of its recent date, if otherwise of interest; for many important events of the British rule in this country, on which these "Chronicles of the Tomb" shed new light, such as, for instance, the great Indian Mutiny, &c., are of comparatively recent occurrence.

With a view to preserve from unmerited oblivion the hitherto forgotten biographies of India, short obituary sketches and memoirs have been given of the most distinguished men in the Annals of Indian History,—men who, at the sacrifice of their lives, have gradually raised the British Indian Empire to its present state of stability and eminence by consolidating its Government, ameliorating the conditions of its subjects, and embracing their spiritual and temporal happiness through the education of its people and the protection of their rights and liberties from the encroachments of invading and cruel enemies. These great men have passed away from the stage on which they have shone so conspicuously, and it is the object of this obituary to perpetuate, cherish and embalm their memory, which becomes doubly dear from the consideration that they have fought, bled and devoted their entire lives and energies to promoting the glory of their country and the good of the people over whom Providence has willed that they should rule.

The list comprehends events connected with a long series of years, viz., from about A.D. 1627, the first formation of the British and Dutch settlements at Agra (*see* entry No. 545*ff*.), down to A.D. 1857-58, the dark period of the great Indian rebellion, and it includes a great number of memorial tablets, monumental inscriptions and short obituary sketches. Who will deny that the sight of a mere monument has not repeatedly inspired martial enthusiasm, the flame of patriotism or the emulation of genius in the youthful breast? *Siste viator, heroem calcas* has awakened ardour in the minds of all who have perused the memorial tablet. How much more, then, is not a memoir of the great actions of illustrious men, in every department of usefulness, calculated to arouse attention and induce the like endeavour? To every class and grade of society, the manifestation that there is no station of life wherein the good and honest men may not have their names and deeds imperishably recorded, will become at once apparent.

LUCKNOW MUSEUM:
The 4th September 1895.

A. FÜHRER,
Archæological Surveyor, N.-W. P. and Oudh.

ADDENDA ET CORRIGENDA.

Page 10, entry No. 24. *for* tell *read* fell.

Page 24, entry No. 50.—*For* Lieutenant and Adjutant William Menth *read* Lieutenant and Adjutant William Meulh.

Page 26, entry No. 52.—*Read* second paragraph of *Note* as follows :—The Commander-in-Chief, in addressing the Governor-General on the occasion of this battle, describes it as "appearing to have been as severe, attended with as complete success, and achieved by gallantry and courage as ardent, as had marked the conduct of any army, &c."

Page 28, entry No. 67, *Note.—For* George Hessing *read* John William Hessing (*see* entry No. 74).

Page 29, entry No. 69.—*Add* the following *Note* :—Major-General Sir John Withington Adams entered the service in 1780; he was present at the battle fought with the Rohillas (*see* entries 104 and 105), under Sir R. Abercrombie in 1794; in 1799 he was present at the battle of Mallivelli; under General Harris at the storming and capture of Seringapatam, and at the taking of several Forts. In 1809 he commanded his regiment, attached to the force under Major-General St. Leger, on the banks of the Sutlej; in 1813 he commanded the field force in Rewah and captured by storm the fort of Entauri, for which he received the thanks of Government. In 1815 he was made a Companion of the Bath and obtained the command of the Kumaun Province; in 1816 he was selected to command the Nagpur Subsidiary Force; in 1817 he commanded the 5th Division of the Army of the Dekkan. In 1818 he totally defeated the army of the Peshwa at Soni, and afterwards took by storm the strongly fortified city of Chanda. In 1826 Brigadier-General Adams, C.B., commanded the reserve at the siege of Bhartpur, which concluded his active services in the field. He was appointed to the command of the Sirhind Division on the 3rd May 1828, promoted to the rank of Major-General by Brevet in 1830, and subsequently made a Knight Commander of the Bath, and resigned the command, having completed his tour on the staff, on the 17th April 1835. Major-General Sir John Adams was greatly beloved by all who were under his command or associated with him during his long and glorious military career in India. His consideration for others and the real active benevolence of his heart: such were the qualities which made him beloved by all. It is well known that the Natives were sincerely and devotedly attached to him, and that they fondly styled him *Baba Adams*. He never turned a deaf ear to a complaint or tale of sorrow, and was not only liberal in actual donations, but on every occasion soothed the sorrows he could not altogether alleviate, by a tender sympathy, and showed that he felt another's woes.

Major-General Sir John W. Adams died on the 9th March 1837, and his remains were interred in the Subathu Cemetery. The following epitaph marks the grave:—"Sacred to the memory of Major-General Sir John Withington Adams, G.C.B., who, after a distinguished career of 57 years in India in the service of the Honourable East India Company, departed this life on the 9th March 1837, in the 74th year of his age.

"This tomb is erected over his remains in commemoration of his private virtues.

"Agra contains the monument of his public services."

Page 29, entry No. 69. *After* Sir John W. Adams, G.C.B., *add* "died 1837."

Page 30, entry No. 74, *Note.—Add*: compare also *Note* to entry No. 552.

Page 32, entry No. 81, *read:* "Sacred to the memory of Lieutenant-Colonel Tudor Tucker, of the late 9th Bengal Light Cavalry; John Moore Jones, Esq., of the Uncovenanted Service; and &c."

Page 35, entry No. 85. *For* Scared *read* Sacred.

Page 44, entry No. 105, *Note.—For* see entry No. 284 *read* see entry No. 305.

Page 66, entry No. 140.—*Add* the following *Note*:—Captain Stuart Beatson, who died of cholera on the 19th July 1857, was buried near the camp at the north-west corner of the station, beyond Nawâbgang; where his tomb serves not only as a memorial of himself, but as an historical reminiscence of Havelock's position. Stuart Beatson died in the prime of life; and there seems little doubt, had he lived, his clear head and high spirit would have carried him to great distinction.

Page 147, entry No. 469. *For* Homberg *read* Homburg.

LIST

OF

CHRISTIAN TOMBS OR MONUMENTS

of Archæological or Historical Interest and their Inscriptions

IN THE

NORTH-WESTERN PROVINCES AND OUDH.

List of Christian Tombs or Monuments in the Meerut Division possessing historical or archæological interest.

Serial number.	Name of Cemetery, Churchyard, or Church.	Where situated (giving exact situation as far as possible).	District.	Tomb or Monument to the memory of—	Inscription on Tomb or Monument.	Inscription on slabs or pillars placed in churches or chapels.	Remarks. Tombs on road-sides, or battle-fields (furnishing information as in columns 3, 4, 5 and 6).
1	2	3	4	5	6	7	8
1	Landour Cemetry.	To the north-west of Lal-tiba.	Debra Dún.	Tomb of Captain G. Bolton, died 1828.	Sacred to the memory of Captain George Bolton, H. C.'s 2nd European Regiment, who after some months of painful suffering departed this life on the 13th of June in the year of the Lord 1828, aged 40. His virtuous and amiable disposition rendered him generally beloved in life and lamented in death. This memorial is erected by his afflicted widow as the last earthly tribute of affection and respect to an indulgent and affectionate husband.		
2	Ditto ...	Ditto ...	Ditto ...	Tomb of Captain J. R. Graham, died 1830.	Sacred to the memory of John Richard Graham, Esq., late a Captain of the 5th Regiment of Bengal Light Cavalry. This monument is erected by his brother officers as a mark of their esteem and regard for the character of one universally beloved for his many good and amiable qualities. He died on the 30th day of May A. D. 1830, aged 29 years.		
3	Ditto ...	Ditto ...	Ditto ...	Tomb of Mrs. S. M. Raikes, died 1835.	Sacred to the memory of Sophia Mary Raikes, the fondly beloved wife of Charles Raikes of the Bengal Civil Service. She departed this life on the 10th April 1835, in the 19th year of her age. Those who in agony, but in humility deplore her loss deem not her death premature, for through the mercies of that Saviour in whom she trusted she was already meet for immortality; her rare personal and mental endowments were but the blossoms of the tree whose fruits were Christian purity and holiness.		

		May those who now mourn her on earth be made partakers with her in the resurrection of the Blessed !		
Ditto ...	Monument to the memory of Lieut-Col. T. Maddock, died 1841.	Erected by the Officers of the 10th Regiment N. I. to the memory of their esteemed and much valued friend and Commandant the late Lieutenant Colonel T. Maddock, who departed this life on the 14th day of October 1841, *æt.* 58. During a command of 12 years, his undeviating kindness and the warm interest ever displayed towards all under him, secured to Colonel Maddock the love and respect of his Regiment by the officers and men of which his worth was justly appreciated and his death keenly deplored. *Requiescat in pace !*		
Ditto ...	Tomb of Sir Charles H. Farrington, died 1828.			(5) Near Jharipáni Bazar, on the 3rd milestone of the Rajpur-Mussooree-Landour road. (6) Sacred to the memory of Charles Henry Farrington, Bart., late Captain His Majesty's 31st Regiment, who departed this life 20th day of March 1828, in the 35th year of his age.
Ditto ...	Two small monuments, one in memory of Sir R. R. Gillespie, and the officers, non-commissioned officers and soldiers who fell at the capture of the Kalanga Fort in 1814, and the other in memory of Bhalbhadra Singh Thápa and the gallant Gorkháli defenders of the fort.			(5) Kalanga monuments, on a low hill about 3½ miles north-east of Dehra, opposite the 6th furlong of mile 110, Meerut-Roorkee-Landour road, at a distance of about ½ mile, on the right hand. (6) I—*(a) On the west side.* To the memory of Major-General Sir Robert Rollo Gillespie, K.C.B., Lieutenant O'Hara, 6th N.I., Lieutenant Gosling, Light Battalion, Ensign Fothergill, 17th N. I., Ensign Ellis, Pioneers, killed on the 31st October 1814; Captain Campbell, 6th N.I., Lieutenant Luxford, Horse Artillery, Lieutenant Harington, His Majesty's 53rd Regiment, Lieutenant Cunningham, 13th N.I., killed on

the 27th November, and of the Non-Commissioned Officers and men who fell at the assault.

I.—(*b*) *On east side.*—Troops engaged: detachments Horse and Foot Artillery, 100 men of the 8th Royal Irish Light Dragoons who were dismounted and led to the assault by Sir R.R. Gillespie, His Majesty's 53rd Regiment.

5 Light Companies from Corps in Meerut.
1st Battalion, 6th N. I.
1st ditto 7th N. I.
Ditto 13th N. I.
Ditto 17th N. I.
7th Native Cavalry.
1 Risalah of Skinner's Horse.

I.—(*a*) *On west side.*—On the highest point of the hill above this tomb stood the fort of Kalanga. After two assaults on the 31st October and 27th November, it was captured by the British troops on the 30th of November 1814 and completely razed to the ground.

II.—(*b*) *On east side.*—This is inscribed as a tribute of respect for our gallant adversary Bulbudder, Commander of the Fort, and his brave Gurkhas, who were afterwards, while in the service of Runjit Singh, shot down in their ranks to the last man by the Afghan Artillery.

St. John's Church Cemetery, Meerut Cantonment.	On the south-west side, near the west gateway.	Meerut.	Tomb of Veterinary-Surgeon John Phillips and Charles John Dawson and Mrs. Eliza Dawson, killed in 1857.	EAST SIDE— Sacred to the memory of John Phillips, Veterinary-Surgeon, 3rd Bengal Cavalry, murdered during the Mutiny at Meerut on 10th May 1857. This tomb is erected by George Carmichael Smyth, Colonel of the Regiment, in token of affection and regard. Oh tell me, hope and faith, Is there no resting-place, From sorrow, sin and death. Is there no happy spot, Where mortals may be blest, Where grief may find a balm, And weariness a rest. Faith, hope and love, Best boons to mortals given, Waved their bright wings And whispered, 'yes,' in Heaven. WEST SIDE— This tablet was erected by Colonel G. Carmichael Smyth, 3rd Bengal Cavalry, to the memory of his friend Charles John Dawson, Veterinary-Surgeon, Bengal Cavalry, and Eliza, his wife, both murdered at Meerut on 10th May 1857.
Ditto ...	Ditto ...	Ditto ...	Tomb of Colonel Finnis, 11th Regiment, Native Infantry, killed 1857.	A PLAIN HEADSTONE WITH THE FOLLOWING INSCRIPTION :— To the memory of John Finnis, Colonel, 11th Regiment, Native Infantry, 10th May 1857, aged 33 years.
Ditto ...	Ditto ...	Ditto ...	Tomb of Captain and Mrs Macdonald and three children, 20th Native Infantry, killed 1857.	A PLAIN HEADSTONE ON WHICH IS THE FOLLOWING INSCRIPTION :— Sacred to the memory of Donald Macdonald, Captain, 20th Regiment, Native Infantry, who was killed by his own men on the 10th May 1857, aged 35 years, and Louisa Sophia, his wife, aged 30 years, who was barbarously murdered the same night, while trying to make her escape with her three infants from her burning house to the European Lines. Awake and stand up to judge My quarrel; avenge Thou my case, My God and Lord. *Psalm XXXV—33.* I am the resurrection and the life. He that believeth in Me, though he were dead, yet shall he live. *John XI—35.*

List of Christian Tombs or Monuments in the Meerut Division possessing historical or archæological interest—(continued).

Serial number.	Name of cemetery, churchyard, or church.	Where situated (giving exact situation as far as possible).	District	Tomb or Monument to the memory of—	Inscription on Tomb or Monument.	Inscription on slabs or pillars placed in churches or chapels.	Remarks. Tombs on road-sides, or battle-fields (furnishing information as in columns 3, 4, 5 and 6).
1	2	3	4	5	6	7	8
10	St. John's Church Cemetery, Meerut Cantonment.	South-west end.	Meerut...	Memorial tablets to Captain Sir George and Lady Parker, 74th Native Infantry, died 1850 and 1857.	1st Marble Tablet— Sacred to the memory of Gertrude Lady Parker, wife of Captain Sir George Parker, Bart., 74th Regiment, Native Infantry, who departed this life on 12th May 1850, aged 26 years. Deeply and sincerely regretted by all who knew her. 2nd Marble Tablet— Sacred to the memory of Sir George Parker, Bart., Captain, 74th Native Infantry, who died of sunstroke in the trenches at Cawnpore in the month of July 1857. They shall hunger no more neither Thirst any more neither shall The sun light on them nor any Heat. *John VI—47.*		
11	Ditto ...	Ditto ...	Ditto ...	Tomb of Captain Coxen, died 1857.	*A plain headstone.*—Sacred to the memory of Captain Edward Coxen, for 31 years Paymaster to the 1st Battalion, 60th Royal Rifles, who died at Meerut on the 14th February 1857, aged 77 years. He served at Flushing throughout the Peninsular War, at Waterloo, and in the campaign of 1848-49 and received three medals and 12 clasps. Erected by the Officers of the 1st Battalion, 60th Royal Rifles.		
12	Ditto ...	Ditto ...	Ditto ...	Major-General N. Penny, C.B., killed 1858.	*A new stone cenotaph, very handsomely carved.*—Sacred to the memory of Major-General N. Penny, C.B., Commanding the Meerut Division. Born at Weymouth, Dorsetshire, on the 12th March 1790; killed at the head of		

					his column in a skirmish with the enemy, near the village of Kakirowlee* in Rohilcund, on the morning of the 30th April 1858 after a service of 51 years. His precious remains were brought into Meerut through the kind exertions of Captain E. J. Simpson, Assistant Commissary-General. Say yet to the righteous that it shall be well with him. *Thes. 3rd chapter, part of 10th verse.* Them also which sleep in Jesus will God bring with him. *Thes. 4th chapter, part of 11th verse.*		*NOTE.—Kakrâlâ in the Budaon district.
13	Ditto ...	North-east side, near principal gateway.	Ditto ...	Memorial column in memory of Sir R. R. Gillespie, K.C.B., killed 1814.	*On slab at base of pillar, facing west.* VELLORE—CORNELLIS—PALIMBANG. Sir R. R. Gillespie, K.C.B., Djocjocarta, 31st October 1814. KALANGA. *On slab at base of pillar, facing east.* Repaired in 1862 by his old Corps, the 8th King's Royal Irish Hussars.		NOTE.—This monument is a large column, 50 feet high, with square base of pakká masonry, and pakká plastered. The first three words are inscribed on a scroll and the remainder on a funeral urn; both are in bas-relief on the same slab.
14	Ditto ...	Ditto ...	Ditto ...	Tomb of Major-General Hardyman, C. B., died 1821.	In this spot are deposited the remains of Major-General B. Hardyman, C.B., late in command of the 2nd Division in Lord Lake's Field Force (late of 17th Foot), 1816. He departed this life on 28th November 1821, in the 55th year of his age; greatly and deservedly regretted by all who knew him, but by none more than the Officers of His Majesty's 17th Foot, who raised this monument as a small but sincere token of the high esteem and regard in which his memory is held by a Corps, which he so long and so happily commanded.		NOTE.—A large cenotaph of pakká masonry with a marble inscription tablet.
15	Ditto ...	Near the well	Ditto ...	Monument in memory of Major-General Sir David Ochterlony, Bart., G.C.B., died 1825.	NORTH SIDE OF TOMB, ON A MARBLE SLAB FIXED IN THE TOMB— Major-General Sir David Ochterlony, Baronet, G.C.B., born February 12th, 1758, died July 14th, 1825.		NOTE.—A large cenotaph of ornamental brick work. A memorial column at Calcutta commemorates the high respect in which Sir David Ochterlony was held, and even to this day the reputation he won for generosity and goodness during fifty years of Indian work remains fresh in the minds of many as his best monument.

List of Christian Tombs or Monuments in the Meerut Division possessing historical or archæological interest.—(continued).

Serial number.	Name of cemetery, churchyard, or church.	Where situated (giving exact situation as far as possible).	District.	Tomb or Monument to the memory of—	Inscription on Tomb or Monument.	Inscription on slabs or pillars placed in churches or chapels.	Remarks. Tombs on road-sides or battle-fields (furnishing information as in columns 3, 4, 5 and 6)
1	2	3	4	5	6	7	8
16	St. John's Church Cemetery, Meerut Cantonment.	Near west gate of Cemetery.	Meerut ...	Tomb of Mr. Vincent Tregear, Department of Public Instruction, killed 1857.	On upper marble slab— Sacred to the memory of Vincent Tregear of the Department of Public Instruction, who was killed by the mutineers at Meerut on 10th May 1857, aged 48 years; also Eliza Hannah, his widow, who died at Meerut on the 3rd June 1880, aged 60 years. Lord all pitying Jesus blest, Grant them their eternal rest.		
17	Ditto ...	Ditto ...	Ditto ...	Tomb of Lieut. W. Pattle, 20th Native Infantry, died 1857.	A plain stone slab— William Pattle, Lieutenant, 20th Regiment, Native Infantry, born 21st June 1832, was killed in the Mutiny at Meerut on 10th May 1857.		
18	Ditto ...	Ditto ...	Ditto ...	Tomb of David H. Henderson, Lieutenant, 20th Native Infantry, killed 1857.	A plain stone slab— Sacred to the memory of David Henry Henderson, Lieutenant, Bengal Native Infantry, who was killed during the Mutiny at Meerut on the 10th May 1857, aged 31 years. The Lord gave and the Lord hath taken away. Blessed be the name of the Lord.		
19	Ditto ...	Near the east gate.	Ditto ...	Monument in memory of Major Lumsden, Deputy Commissary-General, died 1816.	*A marble slab fixed in the masonry floor of the cenotaph in front of the stone altar—* Sacred to the memory of Major Lumsden, late Deputy Commissary-General to the Bengal Forces, who died 30th September 1816, in the 32nd year of his age. This monument is erected by his afflicted widow, who though she mourned her early separation from one in every way calculated to inspire her with the most lasting affection, and thus to form the greatest earthly happiness, humbly hopes through the merits of		Note.—The monument is a large brick masonry cenotaph, with a stone altar inside; it is used as a chapel and vestry.

					that "Great Redeemer" in whom he trusted, to meet again in the realms of peace and joy. Where God shall wipe away all tears from their eyes, and where shall be no more deaths, neither sorrow nor crying. *Rev. XXI—4.*
20	Ditto ...	Near the west gate.	Ditto ...	Tomb of Assistant-Surgeon S. Moore, 6th Dragoon Guards, died 1857.	Sacred to the memory of Stewart Moore, Esq. Assistant-Surgeon, H. M.'s 6th Dragoon Guards (Carbineers), who died at Meerut, on the 2nd June 1857, of wounds received in action with the mutineers at Ghazi-ud-din Nagar, on the 31st May 1857, aged 26 years. This tomb was erected by his brother officers as a token of their sincere regard.
21	Ditto ...	Ditto ...	Ditto ...	Tomb of Mrs. Chambers, killed 1857.	Sacred to the memory of Charlotte, the beloved and deeply lamented wife of R. W. Chambers, Captain, 11th N.I., who died on the 10th May 1857, an innocent victim of the murderous insurrection of 1857. Jesus said unto her, "I am the resurrection and the life, He that believeth in me, though he were dead, yet shall he live." *John X—25.*
22	Ditto ...	Near south-east gate corner of cemetery.	Ditto ...	Cenotaph of Lieutenant Luxford, B. H.A., died 1814.	ON A MARBLE SLAB FIXED IN THE BACK WALL:— Sacred to the memory of Lieut. John B. B. Luxford of the Bengal Horse Artillery, who fell mortally wounded in the attack of Fort Kalunga on the 27th, and died on the 30th November 1814, aged 22 years. This cenotaph is erected by his brother officers in testimony of their affection and esteem.
23	Ditto ...	Ditto ...	Ditto ...	Tomb of Captain James Hunter, 26th N. I., died 1917.	ON A MARBLE SLAB IN THE BACK WALL:— Sacred to the memory of Captain James Hunter, of the 26th N. I., who departed this life, 8th December 1817, aged 39 years.

List of Christian Tombs or Monuments in the Meerut Division possessing historical or archæological interest—(continued.)

Serial number.	Name of Cemetery, Churchyard, or Church.	Where situated (giving exact situation as far as possible).	District.	Tomb or Monument to the memory of—	Inscription on Tomb or Monument.	Inscription on Slabs or Pillars placed in Churches or Chapels.	Remarks. Tombs of road-sides or battle-fields (furnishing information as in columns 3, 4, 5 and 6).
1	2	3	4	5	6	7	8
24	St. John's Church, Meerut Cantonment.	South-east side.	Meerut...	Memorial tablet in memory of Lieutenant Swetenham, 16th Lancers, killed 1846.		Sacred to the memory of Henry D. Swetenham, Esq., Lieutenant in Her Majesty's 16th Lancers, who fell at the battle of Aliwal, 28th January 1846, in the hour of victory, whilst charging the enemy's batteries, *anno ætatis* 27. This tablet is erected by his brother officers as a token of esteem and affection.	
25	Ditto ...	Ditto ...	Ditto ...	Memorial tablet in memory of Lieutenant-Colonel Robert Arnold, 16th Lancers; Captain W. Hilton; Lieutenant D. Jowerarity.		Sacred to the memory of Lieutenant-Colonel Robert Arnold, 16th Lancers, Brigadier, commanding the Bengal Cavalry of the Army of the 'Indus,' who died at Kabul, 20th August 1839; also of Captain William Hilton, drowned in crossing the river Jhelum on the 11th December 1839; and of Lieutenant David Jowerarity barbarously murdered at Kandahar, 18th May 1839. This tablet is erected by the Regimental Officers and men as a record of their affection and esteem for their commanding officer, and respect for the memory of their deeply lamented comrades.	
26	Ditto ...	North-east side.	Ditto ...	Memorial tablet in memory of Brigadier-General W. I. Edwards, His Majesty's 14th Regiment, and Captain H. B. Armstrong of the same corps, killed 1826.		Sacred to the memory of Brigadier-General W. I. Edwards, His Majesty's 14th Regiment, and Captain H. B. Armstrong of the same corps, who in the successful assault of the fortress of Bharatpur on the morning of the 8th July 1826, fell on the ramparts in the gallant discharge of his duty, General Edwards leading the left column of attack. This tablet is erected by their brother officers.	

27	Ditto ...	North-west side.	Ditto ...	Memorial tablet in memory of the non-commissioned officers and soldiers, 14th Regiment, Foot, who fell at the storming of the Fort of Bhartpur in 1825.		Sacred to the memory of those gallant soldiers, Non-Commissioned Officers and Privates of His Majesty's 14th Regiment of Foot, who fell or who subsequently died of wounds received during the siege and at the storming of the fortified town and fortress of Bhartpur, under the personal command of His Excellency the Right Hon'ble Stapleton Lord Combermere, G. C. B., Commander-in-Chief of British India, in the latter end of December 1825 and on the memorable 18th January 1826. SERGEANTS. W. Livingstone. B. Lewis. R. Childs. J. Gray, serving as Quarter-Master Sergeant. D. Crew. W. Weston, 11th Native Infantry. W. Reynolds. J. Byron. J. Belcher. T. Sagg. T. Fryer. J. Haugh. T. Smith. F. Gibbs. L. Woods. W. Thomas. W. Handcock. J. Abbots. T. Watsons. R. Jermyer. P. Dalton. R. Wood. CORPORALS. J. Rowner. W. Endicote. J. Evans. P. Symes. J. Carthy. J. Hammerton. T. Springham. J. Horne. PRIVATES. R. Byron. J. Watt. R. Jiffe. J. Mauldo. J. Pulpit. J. Dickens. T. Turner. W. Irons. A. Bennett. H. Wells. G. Kerr. J. King. While darkness veiled the vaulted sky, In solemn silent march they trod, Eager to shout their battle cry, And prompt to war for Britain and for God. And when the earthquake signal shock, Gave angry summons to advance, And firm and stern as planted rock, Each hero braved the hostile lance: Remember, soldiers, nothing could uphold The warrior spirit like the hope of Heaven; And wouldst thou bear thyself with front as bold, Believe in Him in whom thy sins forgiven, He shall support thee in more awful scenes, When louder trumpets' clang shall rouse their ear, When Nature's universal wreck is seen, And saints victorious shout, and sinners sink with fear.	

List of Christian Tombs or Monuments in the Meerut Division possessing historical or archæological interest—(continued).

Serial number.	Name of cemetery, churchyard, or church.	Where situated (giving exact situation as far as possible).	District.	Tomb or Monument to the memory of—	Inscription on Tomb or Monument.	Inscription on slabs or pillars placed in churches or chapels.	Remarks. Tombs on road-sides, or battle-fields (furnishing information as in columns 2, 4, 5 and 6).
1	2	3	4	5	6	7	8
						This tablet here inscribed with the sanction of Major-General Sir Thomas Reynell, K.C.B. (whose division and under whose immediate charge His Majesty's 14th Regiment had the honor to do their duty), is placed as a mark of esteem and of faithful remembrance by their surviving comrades.	
28	St. John's Church, Meerut Cantonment.	North-west side.	Meerut...	Memorial tablet in memory of Lieut. R. B. Gwitt, died 1845, and Lieut. W. Y. Beale, 10th Foot, killed 1846.		Sacred to the memory of Lt. Richard Brandram Gwitt of Her Majesty's 10th Regiment of Foot, who died at Meerut on the 3rd June 1845; also to the memory of Lieut. Walter Young Beale, Her Majesty's 10th Regiment of Foot, who fell in action gallantly leading on his company to the attack of the trenches at 'Sobraon' on the 10th February 1846. This tablet is erected by their brother officers as a token of the regard they felt for them and regret at their loss.	Note.—The victory at Sobraon broke and scattered the Sikh army and resulted in the establishment of a British Protectorate at Lahore and the incorporation in the British dominions of all the country, hill and plain, situated between the Beas and the Sutlej.
29	Ditto ...	Ditto ...	Ditto ...	Memorial tablet in memory of Lieut.-Colonel Grant Gerrard, 1st Bengal Fusiliers, killed 1857.		Sacred to the memory of Lieut.-Colonel John Grant Gerrard, 1st Bengal Fusiliers, who was killed in action whilst gallantly leading on to victory the movable column which he commanded against the Jodhpur Legion, at Narnaul near Delhi, November 17th, 1857, aged 48 years.	
30	Roman Catholic Cathedral, Sirdhana.	Inside the Mortuary Chapel.	Ditto ...	Tomb of Her Highness Joanna Zeb-un-nissa, or Samru Begam, died 1836.	Sacred to the memory of Her Highness Joanna Zeb-un-nissa, styled "the distinguished of Nobles and beloved daughter of the State," who quitted a transitory court for an eternal world, revered and lamented by thousands of her devoted subjects, at the Palace of	...	Note.—This famous lady was one of the most remarkable personages of her time: a woman of exceptional beauty and talent, and asserted by some historians to have been the daughter of a decayed Mughal nobleman. In 1767, she married Walter Reinhardt, alias Sombre, or "Sombre" (see entry No. 75), according to the rites of the Muhammadan Faith. After his death at Agra

		Sirdhana on the 27th of January 1836, aged nearly ninety years. Her remains are deposited underneath in this Cathedral built by herself. To her powerful mind, her remarkable talent, and the wisdom, justice, and moderation with which she governed for a period exceeding half a century he to whom she was more than a mother, is not the person to award the praise; but in grateful respect to her beloved memory is this monument erected by him who humbly trusts she will receive a crown of glory that fadeth not away. DAVID OCHTERLONY DYCE SOMBRE. (Besides this, there is an Urdu epitaph to the same effect.)	
Ditto ...	Tomb of Her Highness Babu Begam Julia Anne, died 1815.	Sacred to the memory of Her Highness Babu Begam Julia Anne, relict of the late Nawab Muzaffar-ud-daulah Louis Balthazar Reynaud, and daughter of the late Captain Louis Anthony Lefevre and Anne, who departed this life Wednesday, A.M., XVIII October A.D. MDCCCXV. Aged forty five years. This tomb is dedicated by her afflicted daughter and son-in-law.	...
Ditto ...	Memorial tablet to the memory of Julia Anne, the wife of Colonel Dyce, died 1820.		Sacred to the memory of Julia Anne, (Begam Sahiba), the wife of Colonel G. A. D. Dyce, and daughter of the late Nawab Muzaffar-ud-Daulah and Julia Anne, who departed this life Tuesday, A. M., June XIII A.D. MDCCCXX at Delhi. Aged XXXI years and V months. She was a tender mother, a sincere friend, and an affectionate spouse; to the distressed and unfortunate, a kind and liberal benefactress; her heart the seat of patience

List of Christian Tombs or Monuments in the Meerut Division possessing historical or archæological interest—(continued).

Serial number.	Name of cemetery, churchyard, or church.	Where situated (giving exact situation as far as possible).	District.	Tomb or Monument to the memory of—	Inscription on Tomb or Monument.	Inscription on Slabs or Pillars placed in churches or chapels.	Remarks. Tombs on road-sides, or battle fields (furnishing information as in columns 3, 4, 5 and 6).
1	2	3	4	5	6	7	8
						and sympathy; loved and respected by all, who knew her, and in death deeply regretted. But now she is dead, can I bring her back again? I shall go to her; but she will not return to me! *2nd Sam. Ch. 12, V. 23rd.* This stone is inscribed by her disconsolate husband.	
33	Roman-Catholic Cathedral, Sirdhana.	Inside the Mortuary Chapel	Meerut...	Tomb of David Ochterlony Dyce Sombre, died 1851.	Sacred to the memory of David Ochterlony Dyce Sombre of Sirdhana, who departed this life in London 1st July 1851. His remains were conveyed to his Native country, (in conformity with his wishes, in the year 1867, and are deposited in the vault beneath, near those of his beloved and revered benefactress, Her Highness the Begam Sombre. He was born at Sirdhana, 18th December 1808, and married 26th September 1840, the Honorable Mary Anne Jervis, daughter of Edward Jervis-Jervis, Viscount St. Vincent of Meaford in the county of Stafford.	...	NOTE.—This union was a most unhappy one, and led to an appalling law suit known as the "Dyce Sombre case," the record of which fills ten bulky volumes, whose perusal, however, is not uninteresting, especially that part of the evidence which treats of life at Sirdhana. In 1862, Mr. Dyce Sombre's widow, married George Cecil, third Lord Forester. In 1886, Lady Forester lost her second husband, and she herself died on the 7th March 1893.
34	Roman-Catholic Cemetery, Sirdhana.	Right side of the Sirdhana and Ekrika road, near Sirdhana town.	Ditto ...	Tomb of Major Gotlieb Koine, died 1821.	Sacred to the memory of Major Gotlieb Koine, Native of Poland, born Sunday, 25th December A.D. MDCCXLV., died Sunday, P.M. II. September, MDCCCXXI, who was in the service of Her Highness Begam Sombre for 50 years, the last 32 of which as Collector of Bhudhana. He lived and died with the reputation of an honest man and a pious Christian. The memory of the just is blessed. The righteous shall be had in everlasting remembrance.		

Ditto ...	Ditto ...	Tomb of Captain Manuel Pereira Oballo, died in 1815.	Sacred to the memory of Captain Manuel Pereira Oballo, Begam Sombre's service, who departed this life the 25th December 1815, aged 80 years.
Ditto ...	Ditto ...	Tomb of Colonel Louis Claude Paethod, died 1819.	Sacred to the memory of Colonel Louis Claude Paethod, Commandant of Her Highness Begam Sombre's Brigade, who departed this life Wednesday, A.M., 13th January 1819, aged 78 years.
Ditto ...	Ditto ...	Tomb of Mrs. Anne Lefevre, wife of Captain Louis Lefevre, died 1818.	To the memory of Anne, relict of the late Captain Louis Lefevre, who departed this life Saturday, A. M., January III, A.D. MDCCCXVIII. Age 76 years.
Ditto ...	Ditto ...	Tomb of Captain Rommel, died 23rd Muharram, A. H. 1231, or Sunday, the 19th July 1816.	مزار متبرک یادگاری کپتان رومال صاحب آنکه ازین جهان فانی به ملک جاودانی بتاریخ بیست سوم محرم سنه ۱۲۳۱ هجری وصال نمود
Ditto ...	Ditto ...	Tomb of Julia Anne, wife of George Alexander David Dyce, Bahadur Muzaffar Jang, daughter of Nawab Zafar Yab Khan Bahadur and Julia Bahu Begam, step-grand-daughter of Samru Begam; born 2nd Rabi'-ul-awwal A. H 1203 (19th November 1789), died Ramazan 1235 (13th June 1820).	بیت بجز گیاه نه پوشد کسی مزار مرا که قبر پوش غریبان همین گیا بست ——— این مرقد مطهر آرامگاه عصمت نواب تقدس احتجاب صاحب بیگم نبیره شمرو صاحب بهادر زوجه ظفر الدوله جارج الکساندر داود دیس بهادر مظفر جنگ بنت نواب ظفریاب خان بهادر از بطن جولیانا عرف بهوبیگم که بتاریخ دوم شهر ربیع الاول سنه ۱۲۰۳ هجری ولادت یافته و غره رمضان سنه ۱۲۳۵ هجری مطابق سنه ۱۸۲۰ع شب سه شنبه ازین دار فنا بدار البقا شتافته عیسی علیه السلام فرمودند که تا روز قیامت هر کسی بر من ایمان آرد اگر میرد زنده باشد

List of Christian Tombs or Monuments in the Meerut Division possessing historical or archæological interest.—(continued).

Serial number.	Name of cemetery, churchyard, or church.	Where situated (giving exact situation as far as possible).	District.	Tomb or Monument to the memory of—	Inscription on Tomb or Monument.	Inscription on Slabs or Pillars placed in Church or Chapels.	Remarks. Tombs on Road-sides, or Battle-fields (furnishing information as in columns 2, 4, 5 and 6).
1	2	3	4	5	6	7	8
40			Meerut...	Two monuments to the memory of the officers and men who fell in action with the Mutineers at the Hindan river in 1857.			(3) At Mauza Beonja Khaera on the right side of the road from Ghaziabad to Delhi are two monuments standing in a masonry enclosure, 14 yards square, with an outer mud band fenced with prickly pear. (a) *Larger monument of Agra sandstone is fenced by four iron standposts and a chain, and has inscriptions on four sides as follows:—* On West Face— *Celer et audax.* Erected by the 60th Rifles in memory of— Captain F. Andrews, Sergeant W. McPherson, Corporal T. O'Meaghe, Private J. Daring. On South Face— Private S. J. Gainty, " D. Tomnisson, " H. Armitage, " J. Scriven, " P. Quirk, " A. Edmond, " J. Casey, who were killed near this spot in action with the mutineers of the Bengal Army on the 30th and 31st May 1857.

							On East Face— And of— Sergeant R. Hackett, Corporal J. Sherry, " J. Moore, Private J. Lehane, who died of sunstroke during the fight. They all belonged to the 1st Battalion, 60th Rifles, and were buried here. On North Face— And also of— Ensign W. H. Napier, who was wounded on the 31st May and died at Meerut on the 4th June 1857. (b) *This sacred monument consists of a horizontal stone, with another headstone, the whole enclosed by an iron railing.* *The headstone facing west has the following inscription :—* In memory of— 1st Lieutenant Henry George Perkins, Bombardier Bernard Horan, Rough Rider Patrick O'Neil, Gunner John Riley of the 2nd Troop, 1st Brigade, Bengal Horse Artillery, who fell in action with the mutineers at the Hindan river on the 31st May 1857, nobly doing their duty. This monument is erected by their Commanding Officer Colonel H. Tombs in token of esteem and regret.
41	Bulandshahr Cemetery.	First in the second row to the left, facing the gate of the cemetery.	Bulandshahr.	Tomb of Lieutenant Duncan Charles Home, killed 1857.	In memory of Lieutenant Duncan Charles Home, Bengal Engineers, aged 29 years, who was killed by the explosion of a mine when engaged in destroying the Fort of Malagarh on the 1st October 1857. As leader of the Forlorn Hope, which on the 21st September 1857 successfully attacked the Cashmere Gate, Delhi, he was awarded the first Victoria Cross given in India.		

List of Christian Tombs or Monuments in the Meerut Division possessing historical or archæological interest—(continued).

Serial number.	Name of cemetery, churchyard, or church.	Where situated (giving exact situation as far as possible).	District.	Tomb or Monument to the memory of—	Inscription on Tomb or Monument.	Inscription on slabs or pillars placed in churches or chapels.	Remarks. Tombs on road-sides, or battle-fields (furnishing information as in columns 3, 4, 5 and 6).
1	2	3	4	5	6	7	8
42	...	...	Aligarh...	Tomb of Captain Thomas Smith, died 16th Nov. 1816.			(3) Near the Fort gate at Tappal in the Khair tahsil of the Aligarh district are five tombs, but only two have inscriptions on them. Tomb No. I.—This tomb is in fair order, a few slight repairs are required in replacing some bricks that have come out and plastering. The inscription on the head-stone is quite legible; but it is not sufficiently protected from the weather, and some of the letters are wearing away. The tomb is that of Captain Thomas Smith who commanded the Begam Samru's troops at Tappal at the beginning of this century. The inscription runs:— مرقد طامس اسمتهه صاحب که بتاریخ بست و دوم ذی الحجه سنه ۱۲۱۱ هجری نبوی مطابق هژدهم نوامبر سنه ۱۸۱۶ ع لعسو بست ویلیج دوات حیات سپرد Tomb No. II—This tomb is situated to the south of Captain Thomas Smith's. There is no inscription on it, though there are remains of what might have been a head-stone at A, the west of the grave.

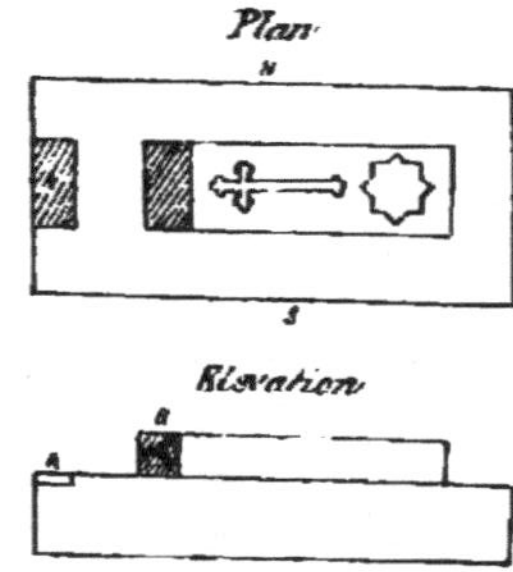

The grave is reported to be that of the wife of the Officer Commanding the Begam's Troops at Tappal, who committed suicide about 60 years ago. Part of the masonry has been broken at the places marked A and B on the plan; but otherwise the tomb is in good order.

Tomb No. III.—This tomb is in very bad repair, and will fall down in a few years if not looked after, as all the bricks from the foundation have gone, and the superstructure is holding itself together as best it can.

List of Christian Tombs or Monuments in the Meerut Division possessing historical or archæological interest—(continued).

Serial number.	Name of cemetery, churchyard, or church.	Where situated (giving exact situation as far as possible).	District.	Tomb or Monument to the memory of—	Inscription of Tomb or Monument.	Inscription of slabs or pillars placed in churches or chapels.	Remarks. Tombs on road-sides, or battle-fields (furnishing information as in columns 3, 4, 5 and 6).
1	2	3	4	5	6	7	8
			Aligarh...				Plan 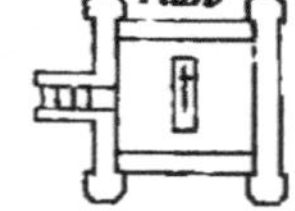 Elevation  No information could be got on the spot as to who is buried in it. The inscription which is very much obliterated, and a facsimile of which is given below—

					 appears to be partly in French. In the Urdu inscription, which is almost illegible, one line is very clear; giving the date, 9th Rabi' us-Sani 1115 Hejira, or the 24th July 1713. The line runs as follows:— بتاریخ ۹ ربیع الثانی سنه ۱۱۱۵ هجری
...	Ditto.	Tomb of Major R. Nairn, killed in 1803.			At Rathbanpur, in tahsil and parganah Sikandra Rao, is a tomb with the following inscription:—"Here lieth the remains of Major Robert Nairn, who, in command of the 6th Regiment, Bengal Native Cavalry, fell at the siege of Kachora on 13th March 1803."
...	Ditto.	Tomb of officers and men killed at Mandrak in 1857.			In Háthras Town is a monument with no inscription, situated in Mr. Bellon's compound, requiring plaster and iron curbs of 1 foot long with bolts and nuts. This tomb contains the remains of the officers and men killed at Mandrak on the Aligarh-Agra road on 24th August 1857. (*Vide* No. 51 in the List).

List of Christian Tombs or Monuments in the Meerut Division possessing historical or archæological interest—(continued.)

Serial number.	Name of Cemetery, Churchyard, or Church.	Where situated (giving exact situation as far as possible.	District.	Tomb or Monument to the memory of—	Inscription on Tomb or Monument.	Inscription on slabs or pillars placed in churches or chapels.	Remarks. Tombs on road-sides or battle-fields (furnishing information as to columns 3, 4, 5 and 6).
1	2	3	4	5	6	7	8
45	...	...	Aligarh ...	Tomb of Mr. S. A. Nichterlein, killed 1857.			At Sásni in pargana Háthras are three tombs, two without inscriptions. One close to the Police station has the following record:— Sacred to the memory of Samuel Anderson Nichterlein, much lamented, and the only son of John Nichterlein of Mandrak Factory, who was massacred by a band of rebellious villagers at Savamsee village during the Mutiny of 1857-58, on the 21st May, A. D. 1857, aged 33 years.
46		...	Ditto ...	Tomb of Mrs. C. S. L. Westroys, died 1827.			At Mendoo, in tahsil and pargannah Háthras, are two tombs:— (a) Sacred to the memory of Clarissa Sophia Louisa, the wife of George Westroys, who departed this life at Mendoo, on Monday, the 21st May, A.D. 1827, aged 27 years. (b) Sacred to the memory of Eliza, the infant daughter of Clarissa Sophia Louisa and George Westroys, who departed this life at Mendoo on Thursday, the 7th of June, A. D 1827, aged one month and 28 days.
47	...	...	Ditto ...	Monument to the officers and men who fell at Ganghiri, in 1857.			(3) At Kanohi-Ganghiri, in tahsil Atrauli, is a monument erected to the officers and men who were killed fighting against the rebels in 1857. The monument is situated in the ravines on the left bank of the Nim Nadi; on the site of the engagement, the ravines have been cutting back somewhat apparently; but as the cultivation comes close to the monument, and the cultivators protect the edges of

				their fields, there is not much fear of their cutting back sufficiently far to endanger the monument. It bears the following inscription:— (6) In memory of the brave men who fell in the hour of victory at Gangiri on 14th December 1857, and whose mortal remains rest here upon the field of battle: George Wardlow, Captain; John Hudson, Lieutenant; Sydney Vyse, Lieutenant; Joseph Barnett, Private; Robert Chapman, Private; Walter Coser, Private; Allen Eastwood, Private: all of H. M.'s 6th Dragoon Guards (Carabineers), and John Dyson, Private; Henry Trampton, Private, of H. M.'s 9th (Queen's) Lancers.
Ditto ...	Tomb of Mary Ann Burrowes, died 1827.			(3) At Barlah in tahsil Atrauli, is a tomb with the following inscription:— (6) Sacred to the memory of Mary Ann, daughter of Charles and Mary Burrowes. Born 2nd August 1827, died 8th July 1828. The lovely babe beneath this tomb was cut off in the bud. But she in Paradise will bloom and ever live with God.
Ditto ...	Tomb of Monsieur Julien Hamulin, died 1801.			At Aligarh, in the compound of the Dispensary, are eight tombs, but only one has an inscription. Nothing is known about them beyond what the inscription, which is only very partially legible, gives. It runs:—Monsieur Julien Hamulin 1801.
Ditto ...	Monument to the officers and men who were killed in storming the Fort of Aligarh in 1803.			(3) Near the East Indian Railway crossing at Aligarh, stands a monument to the officers and men who were killed in storming the Fort of Aligarh under Lord Lake. There were formerly two inscriptions on the upright, the front being in English, Urdu and Hindi, and the back in English only. The English inscription was renewed in 1892 at the request of the Lieutenant-

List of Christian Tombs or Monuments in the Meerut Division possessing historical or archæological interest—(concluded).

Serial number.	Name of cemetery, churchyard, or church.	Where situated (giving exact situation as far as possible).	District.	Tomb or Monument to the memory of—	Inscription of Tomb or Monument.	Inscription on slabs or pillars placed in churches or chapels.	Remarks. Tombs on road-side, or battle-fields (furnishing information as in columns 3, 4, 5 and 6).
1	2	3	4	5	6	7	8
							Governor and put up in the fort. It runs :— To THE MEMORY OF the undermentioned gallant Officers, H. M.'s 76th Regiment of Foot : Captain Ronald Cameron. Lieutenant Michael Bayling Fleming. Lieutenant John Brown. Lieutenant and Adjt. Frederic Wm. St. Aubin. Lieutenant Arthur Cuthbert Campbell, who were killed during the Assault in which the strong Fortress of Aligarh defended by a numerous and well appointed Garrison fell to the superior energy of British valour and British spirit on the 4th Sept. A. D. 1803. Also of Lieutenant and Adjutant William Menth ; Lieutenant John Henry Hurd, of H. M.'s 76th Regiment of Foot, who lost their lives nobly fighting in their country's cause during the memorable victory afterwards gained over the army of Dowlat Rao Scindia near Laswarry in Hindustan by the British Forces under the Command of General Lake on the 1st November A. D. 1803. This monument was erected by brother officers.
51	...		Aligarh...	Monument to the officers and men who were killed near Mandrak in 1857.			(3) Near the 3rd mile-stone from Aligarh, on the Aligarh-Delhi-Agra road, stands a monument with the following inscription :—

(6) Near this spot fell the undermentioned gallant officers and men, on 24th August 1857, fighting in the defence of their Government against a large body of rebels who had come from the town of Koel, and were repulsed by a small force under Major Montgomery, 15th Bengal Native Infantry:

Ensign Henry Lewin Marsh, 16th Bengal Native Infantry. Mr. John O'Brien Tandy, Merchant Volunteer, and Robert Lockhart, 2nd Company, 5th Battalion, Bengal Artillery.

Corporal William Armstrong.
Private Nicholas Fitzgerald.
Patrick Leving
} 3rd Bengal European Infantry.

Their mortal remains lie buried at Hatras.

(*Vide* entry No. 44).

List of Christian Tombs or Monuments in the Agra Division possessing historical or archæological interest.

Serial number.	Name of cemetery, churchyard, or church.	Where situated (giving exact situation as far as possible).	District.	Tomb or Monument to the memory of—	Inscription on Tomb or Monument.	Inscription on Slabs or Pillars placed in churches or chapels.	Remarks. Tombs on road-sides, or battle-fields (furnishing information as in columns 3, 4, 5 and 6).
1	2	3	4	5	6	7	8
52	Cantonment Cemetery, Muttra.	North of Sadr Bazar.	Muttra ..	Tomb of Major General H. Frazer, died 1804.	Sacred to the memory of Major-General Henry Frazer of His Majesty's 11th Regiment of Foot, who commanded the British Army at the battle of Deig, on the 13th November 1804, and by his judgment and valour achieved an important and glorious victory. He died in consequence of a wound he received when leading on the troops and was interred here on the 25th of November 1804, in the 40th year of his age. The Army lament his loss with the deepest sorrow; his country regards his heroic conduct with grateful admiration. History will record his fame and perpetuate the glory of his illustrious deed.		Note.—The epitaph in column 6 is sufficient evidence that General Frazer's tomb may be considered historical. The Commander-in Chief in addressing the Governor-General on the occasion of this battle, describes it as "appearing to have been as severe, attended with as complete success, and achieved by gallantry and courage as ardent, has had marked the conduct of any army, entitling all engaged to the thanks and admiration of their country."
53	Ditto ...	Ditto ...	Ditto ...	Tomb of Lieutenant W. Boyd, died 1804.	Sacred to the memory of Lieutenant William Boyd, of the 15th Regiment of Bengal Native Infantry, who was wounded at the battle of Deig on the 13th of November and departed this life on the 26th of the same month A.D. 1804. Weep not for those that die in the Lord, For they rest from their labours.		
54	Ditto ...	Ditto ...	Ditto ...	Tomb of Major General John Smith, died 1806.	Sacred to the memory of Major-General John Smith of His Majesty's Service, Commanding Officer in the Field, who departed this life, 6th August 1806, aged 41 years. In testimony of their high opinion of his public character and conduct and of their sincere respect and regard for his private virtues, this monument was erected by the unanimous subscription of the Hon'ble Company's Officers and staff of the station of Muttra.		

Ditto ...	Ditto ...	Tomb of Colonel R. Wood, died 1808.	In memory of Colonel Robert Wood of His Majesty's 17th Infantry, who departed this life 18th July 1808.		
Ditto ...	Ditto ...	Tomb of Major Charles Ryder, died 1821.	Sacred to the memory of Major Charles Ryder, of the 3rd Regiment, Light Cavalry, who departed this life on the 7th day of May in the year of our Lord 1821. Deeply lamented by his brother officers and the men of the Regiment.		
Ditto ...	Ditto ...	Tomb of Brigadier-General R. Frith, died 1819.	In memory of Brigadier-General Richard Frith, 8th Regiment, Light Cavalry, and Commanding the Agra and Muttra Frontiers, who departed this life 26th July 1819, aged 63 years.		
Ditto ...	Ditto ...	Monument to the memory of Major-General R. M. Dickens, died 1808.	Sacred to the memory of Major-General Richard Mark Dickens, H. M.'s 34th Regiment of Foot, who departed this life on the 29th of April 1808, aged 45 years.		
Ditto ...	Ditto ...	Tomb of Lieutenant F. C. Ellison, died 1815.	Sacred to the memory of Lieutenant F.C. Ellison, late of the VII Regiment, Native Cavalry, who departed this life November XXII, MDCCCXV, aged XXXII years.		
Ditto ..	Ditto ...	Tomb of Lieutenant F. Dibdin, died 1826.	Sacred to the memory of Lieutenant Francis Dibdin, 5th Regiment, Light Cavalry, who departed this life at Muttra, on the 16th of October 1826, aged 26 years. This monument was erected by his brother officers as a mark of their esteem for him while living and of their sorrow for his loss.		
Ditto ...	Ditto ...	Tomb of Lieutenant W. Kerr, died 1819.	Sacred to the memory of Lieut. William Kerr of the 2nd Battalion, 12th Regt., Native Infantry, who died on the 18th November 1819, aged 26 years. In testimony of their regard and esteem for the deceased, the officers of his corps have erected this monument.		

List of Christian Tombs or Monuments in the Agra Division possessing historical or archæological interest.—(continued).

Serial number.	Name of cemetery, churchyard, or church.	Where situate (giving exact situation as far as possible).	District.	Tomb or Monument to the memory of—	Inscription on Tomb or Monument.	Inscription on Slabs or Pillars placed in churches or chapels.	Remarks. Tombs of Road-sides, or Battle-fields (furnishing information as in columns 2, 4, 5 and 6).
1	2	3	4	5	6	7	8
62	Cantonment Cemetery, Muttra.	North of Sadr Bazar.	Muttra ...	Tomb of Lieutenant J. Mansfield, died 1827.	Sacred to the memory of Lieutenant James Mansfield, 1st Regiment, Native Infantry, who departed this life on the 24th of November 1827, much regretted by the whole Corps, aged 32 years. This monument is erected by his brother officers.		
63	Ditto ...	Ditto ...	Ditto ...	Tomb of Mr. D. H. Crawford, C. S., died 1838.	Sacred to the memory of Douglas Hadow Crawford of the Bengal Civil Service, who was born on 5th April 1816 and died beloved by all who knew him on 2nd June 1838.		
64	Ditto ...	Ditto ...	Ditto ...	Tomb of Captain A. F. Dingwall, died 1830.	Sacred to the memory of Captain A. F. Dingwall, XIX Bengal Native Infantry, died 16th December, A. D. 1830, aged 39 years.		
65	Ditto ...	Ditto ...	Ditto ...	Tomb of Ensign A Moore, died 1809.	Sacred to the memory of En. A. Moore, 17th Regiment, Native Infantry, died 6th July 1809, aged 21 years.		
66	Ditto ...	Ditto ...	Ditto ...	Tomb of Lieutenant J. Morris, died 1814.	To the memory of Lieutenant J. Morris, I. B. 5 N. R., who died regretted by the whole corps, 12th August 1814.		
67		Sutherland gardens, near the Sadr Bazar, Muttra.	Ditto ...	Tomb of Colonel Sutherland, died 1804.	In memory of Robert Sutherland, Colonel in Maharaja Daulat Rao Sindhia's Service, who departed this life on the 20th July 1804, aged 36 years. Also in remembrance of his son, C. P. Sutherland (a very promising youth), who died at Hindia, on the 14th of October 1801, aged 3 years.		NOTE.—Colonel Robert Sutherland of Maharaja Sindhia's Service was according to Mr. Keene (*Handbook to Agra*), the Governor of the Agra Fort at the time of its capitulation to Lord Lake on the 18th October 1803. It is clear from the narrative of Major Thorn, one of the officers of the investing force, that this is a mistake and that the actual Governor was George Hessing. Colonel Sutherland was, however, on account of his British origin, released from the confinement in which all their European officers had been placed by the mutinous garrison and was sent to treat with Lord Lake for a capitulation. He died at Muttra in July

					of the following year. One son is buried with him. Another (J. W.) was in 1871, a Justice of the Peace for the county of Surrey. Colonel Sutherland's tomb, an obelisk of greyish red sandstone, some 30 feet high, is in good repair. It may be considered a local monument of the British conquest of this district and should be maintained in good order.
Outside the ruins of the old Collector's Office, near the Sadr Bazar, Muttra.	Ditto ...	Tomb of Lieutenant P. H. C. Burlton, killed 1857.	Sacred to the memory of Lieutenant P. H. C. Burlton, 67th Native Infantry, who was shot by a detachment of his regiment and of the 41st Native Infantry near this spot on the 30th May 1857. This tomb is erected by his brother officers.		NOTE.—Lieutenant P. H. C. Burlton commanded the Treasury Guard of the Bengal Native Infantry at Muttra, in 1857. Being considered unsafe at Muttra the treasury was loaded in tumbrils in front of the Collector's Office, with a view to its immediate removal to Agra. When Mr. Burlton gave the order to march the guard mutinied and shot him. He was several days later buried on the spot where he fell and a neat tomb which is in good repair was afterwards erected over his grave. Mr. Burlton was the only European murdered in this district during 1857. His tomb has an historical interest in connection with the great mutiny and should be preserved.
Cantonment gardens, Agra.	Agra ...	Monument to the memory of Major General Sir John W. Adams, G. C. B.	Seringapatam, Rewah, Pindari War, Nagpur, Seonie, Entouri, Chandah. In honour of Major-General Sir John Adams, G. C. B., his European and Native friends and admirers of the Bengal Army erect this column. During a distinguished service of 56 years, his eminent military capacity and judgment, his just and general feelings and his demeanour, ever courteous and kind, secured him the respect, love, and veneration of all classes, and more especially of the Bengal Sepoys.		
Agra Fort.	Ditto ...	Memorial tablet to the Hon'ble Sir John Strachey.	In grateful commemoration of services rendered to posterity by the Hon'ble Sir John Strachey, G. C. S. I., to whom, not forgetting the enlightened sympathy and timely care of others, India is mainly indebted for the rescued and preserved beauty of the Taj Mahal and other famous monuments of the ancient art and history of these Provinces formerly administered by him. This tablet is placed by order of his friend the Earl of Lytton, Viceroy and Governor-General of India, A. D. 1880.		

List of Christian Tombs or Monuments in the Agra Division possessing historical or archæological interest—(continued).

Serial Number.	Name of Cemetery, Churchyard, or Church.	Where situated (giving exact situation as far as possible).	District.	Tomb or Monument to the memory of—	Inscription on Tomb or Monument.	Inscription on slabs or pillars placed in churches or chapels.	Remarks. Tombs on road-sides, or battle-fields (furnishing information as in columns 3, 4, 5 and 6).
1	2	3	4	5	6	7	8
71	Fort Cemetery, Agra.	Near Amar Singh gate.	Agra ...	Tomb of Lieutenant J. K. Henderson Lamb, died 1857.	In memory of John Henderson Lamb, Lieutenant of the Bengal Artillery, died on the 24th August 1857, of wounds received in action on the 5th July 1857. Death swallowed up in victory.		
72	Ditto ...	Ditto ...	Ditto ...	Tomb of Captain Burlton, died 1857.	Sacred to the memory of Francis Morin Hastings Burlton, Captain, 52nd Regiment, Bengal Native Infantry, and Commandant, 2nd Cavalry, Gwalior Contingent, son of Colonel William Burlton, C. B., Commissary General, Bengal Army, died in the Agra Fort in the year of the Black Indian Mutiny 1857, from wounds received in action.		
73		Agra Fort.	Ditto ...	Tomb of Mr. John Russel Colvin, died 1857.	In memory of John Russel Colvin, born May 29th, 1807, died in this Fort, September 9th, 1857. Lieutenant-Governor of the North-Western Provinces, India.		
74	Roman-Catholic Cemetery, Agra.	Adjoining boundary of Civil Courts on the west.	Ditto ...	Domed tomb of Colonel J. W. Hessing, died 1803.	John William Hessing, late a Colonel in the service of Maharaja Daulat Rao Sindhia, who, after sustaining a lingering and very painful illness for many years with a tone of Christian fortitude and resignation, departed this life, 21st July 1803, aged 63 years, 11 months, and 5 days. As tribute of their affection and regard this monument is erected to his beloved memory by his disconsolate widow, Anne Hessing, and afflicted sons and daughters, George William Hessing, Thomas William Hessing and Magdalene Sutherland. He was a native of Utrecht in Holland		NOTE.—This cemetery is the earliest Christian cemetery in Northern India and dates from the time of the Emperor Akbar Shah; in it lie buried the remains of the early Catholic missionaries as well as of some famous men known to Indian history, viz., Colonel John Hessing, Walter Reinhardt, "Le Sombre," or General Samru, the descendants of Prince John Philip Bourbon of Navarre, who married Akbar's sister-in-law, Lady Juliana, and others. Unfortunately most of the inscriptions on the tombstones are either completely destroyed by exposure to the weather or partly illegible; those still readable are either in Portuguese, or Armenian, or French, or Italian. The following epitaphs are of interest:— Episcopus Zachar from Tabrez, died A.D. 1618 Padre Lanfranki S. J. „ „ 1634 „ Antonio Machado S. J. „ „ 1636

		and came out to Ceylon in the Military service of the Dutch E. I. Company in the year 1757, and was present at the taking of Candia by their troops. Five years afterwards he returned to Holland and came out again to India in the year 1763, and served under the Nizam of the Deccan. In the year 1784, he entered into the service of Madho Rao Sindhia and was engaged in the several battles that led to the aggrandizement of that Chief and wherein he signalized himself so by his bravery as to gain the esteem and approbation of his employer, more particularly at the battle of Bhondagaon near Agra in the year 1787, which took place between this Chief and Nawab Ismael Beg, when he then became a Captain, and was severely wounded. On the death of Madho Rao Sindhia in 1793, he continued under his successor, Daulat Rao Sindhia, and in 1798 he attained to the rank of Colonel and immediately after to the command of the Fort and City of Agra, which he held to his death.		,, Joseph de Castro ,, ,, ,, 1668 ,, Antonio Conques ,, ,, ,, 1686 ,, Paulo de Mattos ,, ,, ,, 1664 ,, Marco Antonio Santoss ,, ,, ,, 1684 ,, Francisco de Cruz ,, ,, ,, 1742 ,, Abel Sperger ,, ,, ,, 1761 Of the Armenian inscriptions three are of the early part of the XVII century, eighteen of the XVIII, and about forty of the beginning of the present century.
Ditto ...	Monument to the memory of Walter Reinhard, or General Samru, died 4th May 1778.	Aqui jazo Walter Reinhard morreo aos 4 de Mayo no Anno de 1778.		NOTE.—This mausoleum, still in good repairs, is a handsome octagonal building surmounted by a low dome. The epitaph, very roughly carved in bold letters, is in Portuguese; there is also a Persian chronogram in very flowery style to the same effect. Walter Reinhardt, a native of Strassburg or of Trèves, took service as a sailor with the French, and as a soldier with the British. Finally he drifted to India, where he attached himself to Mir Kásim, the Nawáb of Bengal, and was responsible for the murder of the British residents at Patna in the year 1763. He obtained large grants of land, and married Zeb-un-nissa Begam. He was nicknamed "Le Sombre" on account of his swarthy complexion and sombre cast of his countenance, which the Natives corrupted into Samrú, and when he died in 1778 as the Civil and Military Governor of Agra, his widow became famous as the Begam Samrú (*see* entry No. 30).
Ditto ...	Tomb of Paulo Frederic, killed at the siege of Kama, 2nd October 1792.	Ici repose le corps de Paulo Frederic, tué aux siége de Kama, le 3, Octobre 1792.		

List of Christian Tombs or Monuments in the Agra Division possessing historical or archæological interest—(continued).

Serial number.	Name of cemetery, churchyard, or church.	Where situated (giving exact situation as far as possible).	District.	Tomb or Monument to the memory of—	Inscription on Tomb or Monument.	Inscription on slabs or pillars placed in churches or chapels.	Remarks. Tombs on road-sides, or battle-fields (furnishing information as in columns 3, 4, 5 and 6).
1	2	3	4	5	6	7	8
77	Roman-Catholic Cemetery, Agra.	Adjoining boundry of Civil Courts on the west.	Agra ...	Tomb to the memory of General Perron's four sons, died 1793.	Here lie interred the four children of General Perron, Commanding 3rd Brigade, in the Service of Maharajah Sindiah, A.D. 1793. Ici reste les corps de 4res enfans de General Perron, dans le service de Maharaja Sindiah, A. D. 1793.		NOTE.—Besides the English and French inscriptions, there are two epitaphs in Urdu and Hindi to the same effect. General Perron served under Mádhava Ráo Sindhia against the English; he was "a man of plain sense, of no talent, but a brave soldier," as General Count de Boigne—a brilliant adventurer—described him to Grant Duff.
78	R. C. Cathedral Cemetery, Agra.	Native City	Ditto ...	Tomb of Father Joseph Tieffenthaler, died 1785.	Pater J. Tieffentali, obiit Lacnoi 5 Jul. 1785.		NOTE.—Father Joseph Tieffenthaler, Ex-Jesuit and Missionary Apostolic, was born at Bolzano in Tyrol, landed in India in 1743, lived and laboured at Lucknow from 1760 until his death on the 5th July 1785, his mortal remains being conveyed to Agra. He is the author of *Descriptio Indiae*, the first Gazetteer of India ever attempted and published in French by Jean Bernoulli at Berlin in 1786 in his "Description Historique et Géographique de l'Inde," Vols. 1-3, 4to.
79	Fort Cemetery, Farukhabad.	On the banks of the river Ganges in the Fort.	Farukhabad.	Tomb of Lieutenant C. J. M. Macdowell, European Bengal Fusiliers, killed 1859.	To Lieutenant C. J. M. Macdowell, 2nd European Bengal Fusiliers, killed in action against the rebels at Shamshabad 27th January 1859, whilst second in command of Hudson's Horse. Erected by his brother officers as a slight token of their sincere esteem.		
80	Ditto ...	Ditto ...	Ditto ...	Tomb of Captain E. Claydon, Native Regiment, died 1799.	To the memory of Captain E. Claydon, 5th Native Regiment, who departed this life the 16th of November 1799, aged 46 years.		
81	Ditto ...	Ditto ...	Ditto ...	Tomb of Lieutenant-Colonel Tudor Tucker, Bengal Cavalry; Mr. John Moore Jones and Sub-Conductor John Ashern, killed 1857.	Sacred to the memory of Lieutenant-Colonel Tudor Tucker of the Bengal Light Cavalry; John Moore Jones, Esq., of the * * * (*illegible*); and Sub-Conductor John Ashern, Army Clothing Department, all of whom fell on the 28th and 29th of June 1857, whilst nobly defending the Fort at Fatehgarh against an overwhelming number of mutinous sepoys.		

82	Ditto ...	Ditto ...	Ditto ...	Tomb of Lieutenant Thomas Macfie, died 1794.	Here lies the body of Lieutenant Thomas Macfie, who departed this life on the 8th July 1794, in the 35th year of his age. Deeply lamented by all to whom his amiable manner and many virtues were known.		
83	Ditto ...	Ditto ...	Ditto ...	Tablet to the memory of Samuel Skardon, died 1788.	To the memory of Mr. Samuel Skardon, who died October 30th, 1768, aged 57 years. This tomb was erected by his friend, Captain Richard Ramsawy.		
84	Fatehgarh Church-yard.	On Parade ground near the European Infantry Barracks.	Ditto ...	Monument in the form of a memorial cross over a well in which lie the bodies of those murdered in 1857.	(FRONT.) Erected by the Government, North-Western Provinces, to the memory of the residents of Futtehghur in the year of Our Lord 1857, who perished in the troubles of that period. The bodies of some lie in the well beneath; of others the resting place is unknown; yet not one of them is forgotten before God. The Lamb which is in the midst of the throne shall feed them and shall lead them unto living waters, and God shall wipe away all tears from their eyes. (BACK.) Colonel and Mrs. Goldie and three daughters; Mr. and Mrs. Thornhill, C.S., two children and Nancy Lang, Servant; Revd. Mr. and Mrs. Fisher and child; Doctor and Mrs. Heathcote and two children; Lieutenant and Mrs. Monckton, R.E., and child. Miss Stuart. MERCHANTS. Mr. and Mrs. Sutherland, two daughters and one boy. Mr. and Mrs. Ives and daughter. Sergt. and Mrs. Roach and two children. Mr. and Mrs. Gibson and two children. MISSIONARIES. Mr. and Mrs. Campbell and two children. Mr. and Mrs. Johnston. Mr. and Mrs. Macmullen. Mr. and Mrs. Freeman. ——— Mr. and Mrs. Palmer, Deputy Magistrate, and nine children, Miss Finlay. Mr. and Mrs. Kew & family, Post-Master. Miss Kew; Mr. and Mrs. Sheils, School-Master and two children.		

Fatehgarh Church-yard.	On Parade ground near the European Infantry Barracks.	Farukhabad	Monument in the form of a memorial cross over a well in which lie the bodies of those murdered in 1857.	RIGHT SIDE— 10th Native Infantry. Col. and Mrs. Smith, Major Munro, Major Phillott, Captain Phillomore, Lieutenant Simpson, Lieutenant and Mrs. Fitzgerald and child. Lieutenant Swetenham. Lieut. Henderson. Ensign Eckford, Ensign Byrne. Mr. Wrixen (Senior). Mr. Wrixen (Junior). Sergeant Redman, wife and two children. ——— Captain Vibart, 2nd Cavalry. Sergeant Best, wife and three children. Pensioners Mr. and Mrs. Bosco. Mr. Faulkner and family. ——— Mr. Alexander. Mr. and Mrs. Cuise. Mr. and Mrs. Elliott and five children. Two Misses Ray. Mr. and Mrs. Joyce and four children. Mr. and Mrs. Brierly, Dhoukal Pershad and family. LEFT SIDE— Colonel and Mrs. Tucker, three children, Miss Tucker and Miss Humphreys. Mr. and Mrs. Lowis, C.S., and two children. Major and Mrs. Robertson, child and Miss Thomson. Doctor and Mrs. Maltby, Mr. E. James, Assistant Opium Agent. INDIGO PLANTERS. M. T. H. Churcher. Mr. and Mrs. J. M. Jones and child, Mr. and Mrs. Maclean.

		GENERAL CLOTHING AGENCY. Mr. and Mrs. Jones, brother-in-law and four children. Conductor and Mrs. Ashern. Conductor and Mrs. Bohan and nine children. Mr. Anderson and mother. Mr. and Mrs. Madden and family. Mr. Finlay and family. Mr. and Mrs. Cawood and two children. Mr. and Mrs. Macklin, Head-Clerk, Collector's Office, and eight children. Mrs. Shepherd and family, Mr. and Mrs. Catania, Inspector of Post Offices. Mr. Macdonald and family. Mr. Bellington. Persecuted but not forgotten.		
Farukhabad	Tomb of Surgeon Thomas Hamilton, died 1788.			(3) Situated at the north corner of Collector's Kacheri compound, Farukhabad, tomb of Thomas Hamilton, Esq., Head Surgeon. The tomb is raised on a large terrace, about 24 feet square and 6 feet high. (6) Scared to the memory of Thomas Hamilton, Esq., Head Surgeon, who died 12th August A. D. 1788, aged about 50 years. The monument is erected by Major S. Farmer, Executor.
Ditto ...	Tomb of Lieutenant-Colonel John Guthrie, died 1803.	...	...	(3) Situated in a mango grove to the north-east of the old Thatia mud Fort in tahsil Tirwa of the Farukhabad district, tomb of Lieutenant-Colonel John Guthrie. The tomb is a plain square masonry platform with a stone slab let into one side, bearing the following inscription :— (6) Sacred to the memory of Lieutenant-Colonel John Guthrie of Kilmarnock in Scotland, a Peer of the Moghal Empire. He was born the 6th of March 1749, and departed this life on the 18th October, in consequence of a wound received at the assault on Fort Thatia, 30th September, 1803.

List of Christian Tombs or Monuments in the Agra Division possessing historical or archæological interest—(continued).

Serial number.	Name of cemetery, churchyard, or church.	Where situated (giving exact situation as far as possible).	District.	Tomb or Monument to the memory of—	Inscription on Tomb or Monument.	Inscription on slabs or pillars placed in churches or chapels.	Remarks. Tombs on road-sides, on battle-fields (furnishing information as in columns 3, 4, 5 and 6).
1	2	3	4	5	6	7	8
87	Mainpuri Cemetery.	In Nagla Sansarpur, a mile north-east of St. Paul's Church, Mainpuri.	Mainpuri,	Tomb of Captain Alcock, murdered 1844.	On marble slab:— Here lies the mortal remains of Captain Richard Ponsonby Alcock, 46th Native Infantry, and Assistant Quartermaster-General of the Army, who was murdered in this district on the 26th October 1844.		Note.—Captain Alcock was murdered by dacoits by mistake, it is believed, for the Magistrate of the District.
88	Saint Paul's Church yard, Mainpuri.	Near Collector's Kacheri.	Ditto ...	Tomb of Richard Wilkinson Fayrer, murdered 1857.	In memory of Richard Wilkinson Fayrer, Esq., who fell treacherously murdered by his own men when commanding on duties a detachment of Oudh Irregular Cavalry near Mainpuri on the 1st June 1857. Aetas 23.		
89	Ditto ...	To the south-east of Collector's Kacheri.	Ditto ...	Tomb of Lieutenant George Douglas Barber, killed 1857.	Lieutenant George Douglas Barber, Adjuant, 2nd Oudh Irregular Cavalry. He was killed by the men of his own Regiment while on detached command near Mainpuri on the 1st June 1857. Born June 9th, 1819.		
90	Ditto ...	Ditto ...	Ditto ...	Tomb of Captain Fletcher F.C. Hayes, killed 1857.	Fletcher F. C. Hayes, M.A., Captain of 62nd Regiment, Bengal Native Infantry, and Military Secretary to Sir Henry Lawrence, K.C.B., at the commencement of the great Indian Mutiny. He was treacherously slain near Mainpuri on the 1st June 1857, while in the discharge of an important duty for which he had volunteered.		Note.—Captain Fletcher Hayes was a man of great capacity and great courage; an erudite scholar; an accomplished gentleman; in the prime of his life and the height of his daring.
91		Near the fort and village of Pharha on the left bank of the Jumna river.	Etáwah,	Tomb of Lieutenant William Jennings Firebrace, died 1846.	Sacred to the memory of William Jennings Firebrace, Lieutenant, Her Majesty's 21st Fusiliers, aged 23 years, who died on the 10th October 1846, on the left bank of the Jumna near the village and fort of Pharha on his way to Calcutta. This monument was erected by his brother officers as a mark of their esteem and regard.		

92	Etáwah Cemetery.	No. 3 in block B.	Ditto ...	Tomb of Captain Charles James Doyle, killed 1858.	Sacred to the memory of Charles James Doyle, who was killed in action at Harchandpore in the Etáwah district on the 8th December 1858, aged 29 years.		
93	Etáwah Church.	...	Ditto ...	Memorial tablet in memory of Captain James Charles Doyle, killed 1858.	...	Sacred to the memory of Charles James Doyle, who fell leading a small band against overwhelming numbers of savage foes at the battle of Harchandpore, December 8th, 1858. True-hearted, generous and gentle as he was brave. His companions in arms have erected this tablet in remembrance of their lost friend; thankful amid their grief that he died as became a Christian hero; fighting only in his Company's cause, beloved and respected by all his comrades and at peace with God.	
94		At Chhaoni near Kásganj.	Etah ..	Tomb of Mr. Alan Gardner, eldest son of Colonel William Linnæus Gardner, died 1828, aged 29 years.	Alan Gardner died XXX January 1828.		NOTE.—The handsome marble mausoleum contains only this meagre and laconic inscription: those on the other tombs having become effaced, if they ever existed. Colonel William Linnæus Gardner, born in 1770, of a noble Irish family, ran away from home and entered the Maratha service, in which he highly distinguished and enriched himself. In the war with Nepál in 1815, when the incompetence of our Generals was bringing disgrace on the British name, Colonel Gardner was offered command of the force destined to occupy Kumaun. In this expedition he was completely successful, reducing Almora; and in conjunction with his brother, the Hon'ble E. Gardner—resident at Khatmandu putting an end to the war. He married a daughter of the royal family of Kebh, and establishing himself at Chhaoni in the Etah district, lived in princely splendour. By gift, purchase or as farmer, Colonel Gardner held a large portion of Etah, and on his death, on the 29th July 1835, was succeeded by his second son, W. James Gardner, who ran away with a daughter of the King of Delhi, to whom he was subsequently married. Mr W. Gardner died at Chhaoni on the 14th June 1845, and was buried in the marble mausoleum there, beside his father. He left issue, Sulaiman Shikoh, commonly known as Munna Sahib, James *alias* Hinga Sahib; William Lennis; Sikandar Shikoh; and Jahangir Samuel; but his own extravagance, and the dissensions that arose among his children regarding the distribution of his property, combined with the utmost prodigality in his establishment, has alienated the noble possessions once belonging to the family. For ten-and-a-half years preceding the Mutiny the estates were mortgaged to a Farukhabad banker, and have since, in a great measure, passed away from the family.

Sacred to the memory of—

D. Robertson, Esq., Judge of Bareilly.
G. D. Raikes, Esq., Sessions Judge.
Dr. J. M. Hay, Civil Surgeon.
Dr. Hansbrow, Superintendent, Central Jail.
Dr. Buck, Principal of the College.
G. Wyatt, Esq., Deputy Collector.
Mr. J. Beeb.
Mr. Watts.
Miss Watts.
Brigadier H. Sibbald, C.B., Commanding in Rohilkhand.
Sergeant Staples, Artillery.
Ensign R. G. Tucker, 68th Regiment, Native Infantry.
Quartermaster Sergeant Henry, 68th Regiment, Native Infantry.
Major H. C. Pearson, 18th Regiment, Native Infantry.
Captain T. C. Richardson, 18th Regiment, Native Infantry.
Captain H. B. Hathord, 18th Regiment, Native Infantry.
Lieutenant H. R. Stewart, 18th Regiment, Native Infantry.
Lieutenant J. C. Dyson, 18th Regiment, Native Infantry.
Quartermaster Sergeant Cross and child, 18th Regiment, Native Infantry.
Mr. A. Fenwick, Commissioner's Office.
Mr. and Mrs. Alone and two children, Commissioner's Office.
Mr. S. G. Nicholas, Commissioner's Office.
Mr. and Mrs. Phelan and four children, Collector's Office.
Mr. and Mrs. Davis and two children, Collector's Office.
Sergeant Warrell, Jail Establishment.

NOTE.—These victims were slaughtered by the express order of Khan Bahadur Khan, the heir of the famous Rohilla chief, Hafiz Rahmat Khan, and many of them after having been brought into his presence.

						Mr. Cruisor, Jail Establishment. Mr. J. Bolst. Miss Bolst. Mr. Lawrence. Mr. and Mrs. Aspinall and two children. Mrs. Aspinall, Senior. Mr. R. Richie. Mr. Taynoe. Sub-Conductor Cameron, Engineering Department. Mr. Cameron and two children. These are they which came out of great tribulation.—*Rev.* vii, 14. Blessed are ye when men shall revile you and persecute you and say all manner of evil against you falsely for My sake.—*Matt.* v, 11. He that loseth his life for My sake shall find it.—*Matt.* x, 39. This tablet and chancel windows were erected in memory of the abovenamed persons, who were murdered at Bareilly in June 1857. A.D. | 1863.	
96	New Cemetery, Bareilly.	North-east corner.	Ditto ...	Tomb of Brigadier H. Sibbald, Bengal Army, killed 1857.	In memory of Brigadier Sibbald, C.B., Commanding in Rohilkhand and Kumaun; murdered, after upwards of 51 years' service, by the mutineers of the Bareilly Brigade, on the 31st May 1857 in the 68th year of his age. This tomb is erected in token of affectionate remembrance by his widow and children.	...	
97	Christ Church, Bareilly.	To the left of main entrance.	Ditto ...	Tablet in memory of George Davy Raikes, C.S., killed 1857.	...	Sacred to the memory of George Davy Raikes, Esq., of the Bengal Civil Service, who was killed at Bareilly by the rebels on the day of the outbreak, May 31st, 1857, aged 39 years. This tablet is erected to his memory by his bereaved widow, Margaret Julia Raikes. Be ye also ready; for in such hour as ye think not the Son of Man cometh.—*Matt.* xxiv, 44.	
98	Christ Church compound, Bareilly.	South-east...	Ditto ...	Tomb of Dr. John Macdowall Hay, killed 1857.	John Macdowall Hay, May 31st, 1857, aged 39 years.		

List of Christian Tombs or Monuments in the Rohilkhand Division possessing historical or archæological interest—(continued).

Serial number.	Name of cemetery, churchyard or church.	Where situated (giving exact situation as far as possible).	District.	Tomb or Monument to the memory of—	Inscription on Tomb or Monument.	Inscription on slabs or pillars placed in churches or chapels.	Remarks. Tombs on road-sides or battle-fields (furnishing information as in columns 3, 4, 5 and 6).
1	2	3	4	5	6	7	8
99	Christ Church compound, Bareilly.	South-east ...	Bareilly ...	Tomb of James Thomason, Lieutenant-Governor of the North-Western Provinces, died 1853.	Here lie the remains of James Thomason, late Lieutenant-Governor of the North-Western Provinces. Died September 21st, A.D. 1853, aged 49 years. This grave was restored A.D. 1858. The souls of the righteous are in the hand of God: neither shall any grief hurt them.		Note.—This tomb was destroyed in the beginning of June 1857 by Khan Bahadur Khan, the rebel viceroy of Rohilkhand, in order to build with the materials, after the manner of the princes of the house of Timur, a mausoleum for himself.
100	Highland Cemetery, Bareilly.	...	Ditto ...	Monument to the Sergeants of the 42nd Royal Highlanders, who fell in the Mutiny Campaigns.	Sacred to the memory of the Sergeants, 42nd Royal Highlanders, who fell in the Campaigns of the Mutiny or died of disease in India during the years 1858-59, viz.— George McCullock, died at Lucknow, 9th April 1858. James Fraser, killed at Rooyah, 15th April 1858. John Reed, died at Sandeelah, 19th April 1858. David Daly Leigh, died at Shâhjahânpur, 1st May 1858. Thomas Ridley, died at Fatehgarh, 3rd May 1858. Alexander Leitch, died at Allahabad, 21st May 1858. John McMillan, died at Bareilly, 22nd May 1858. John Hiddle, died at Bareilly, 31st May 1858. Robert Blackie, died at Moradabad, 14th June 1858. Thomas Adams, died at Bareilly, 1st July 1858. George Scott, died at Moradabad, 19th July 1858. Duncan Macpherson, died at Bareilly, 11th August 1858. Robert Thompson, died at Naini Tal, 21st September 1858.		

					George Fraser, died at Bareilly, 6th October 1858. Andrew Landles, killed, Maylahghât, 15th January 1859. James Hunter, drowned in the Ganges, 21st July 1859. George Rankin, died at Naini Tal, 4th August 1859. Robert McNair, died at Bareilly, 1st September 1859. This stone is erected as a token of affectionate remembrance by their surviving comrades.		
101	Ditto ...		Ditto ...	Monument to the Non-Commissioned Officers and men of No. 8 Company of the 42nd Royal Highlanders, who fell in the Mutiny Campaigns.	No. 8 Company, XLII Royal Highlanders. To the memory of the under-mentioned Non-Commissioned Officers and men of the above Company and Regiment, who died in the service of their Queen and country :— Lce.-Corpl. Ar. Mackie, Private A. McKay, Gd. Spence, Josh. Brates, Jn. Hepburn } Killed or died of their wounds, received at Rooyah, 15th April 1858. Hugh McKenzie, 12th April 1858, James Barnes, 2nd May ,, Alexander Burgess, 12th June ,, Walter Swanson, 29th August ,, } Died at Lucknow. James Wright, 22nd April, died at Aliganj. John Todd, 7th July 1858, died at Naini Tal. John March, 2nd September 1858, died at Naini Tal. Sergeant John Hiddue, 31st May 1858. Private Alexander Cormack, 29th June 1858. Private John Ceronan, 4th October 1858. Corporal William Sheldon, 10th July 1859. Private James Napier, 18th August 1859. Alexander Shaw, 31st August 1859. E. McPherson, 8th March 1860. } Died at Bareilly.		

102	Highland Cemetery, Bareilly.		Bareilly ...	Monument to the Non-Commissioned Officers and men of No. 2 Company, 42nd Royal Highlanders.	Sacred to the memory of the under-mentioned Non-Commissioned Officers and men of No. 2 Company, 42nd Royal Highlanders:— Private Alexander McDonald, died 28th November 1857. James McNair, died 30th November 1857. William McKane, died 3rd December 1857. John Dickson, died 7th December 1857. David Teirnant, died 1st February 1858. Thomas Bell, died 18th April 1858. Sergeant John Reid, died 19th April 1858. Private Duncan McIntyre, died 23rd April 1858. Alexander Wilson, died 25th April 1858. Andrew Buchanan, died 5th May 1858. Corporal Donald McLardy, died 24th May 1858. Private Robert McKay, died 26th June 1858 This is erected by Captain Fraser, Commanding the Company, as a token of respect.
103	Cantonment Cemetery, Bareilly.	Near entrance gate.	Ditto ...	Monument to the Non-Commissioned Officers and men of the Light Company of the 42nd Royal Highlanders.	Sacred to the memory of the under-mentioned Officers, Non-Commissioned Officers, and men of the Light Company, 42nd Royal Highlanders, killed or died in India in the service of their country, from November 1857 to August 1860:— Lieutenant A. I. Brambly, killed 15th April 1858. Lance-Corpl. R. Holans, 11th March 1858. Private P. Doyle, killed, 11th March 1858. T. Monteith " 18th " " A. Brodie " 15th April 1858. J. Dunn " 28th " " D. Hennessey " 30th " " D. McInnes died " 27th " " T. Smith " 8th May "

					D. Lawson „ 25th August „ W. Haynes „ 2nd September „ R. Anderson „ 10th „ „ C. Layan „ 24th October „ C. Gates „ 26th „ „ Sergeant W. Taylor, died 21st June 1860. Private D. Morrison, died 11th July „ Drummer A. Morrison, died 21st August 1860. Erected by the Company.		
104	...	...	Ditto ...	Tombs of four British Officers, killed in action on the 26th October 1794.	...	...	(3) Near Mauza Sitniya, close to Fatehganj West, in tahsil Bareilly, are the tombs of four British officers killed in action with the Rohillas. (5) Here lie the bodies of Captain Norman Macleod, Lieutenant William Hinkeman, Lieutenant William Odell, and Lieutenant Joseph Richardson, of the 13th Battalion Native Infantry, killed near this place in the action of 26th October 1794. درین جا لاش‌های کپتان نارمن میکلود لفتننت ولیم هنکسمن ولیم ادل جوزف رچاردسن سرداران در پلٹن سپاهیان سیزدهم که نزدیک همین جا در جنگ بتاریخ بست و ششم اکتوبر سنه ۱۷۹۴ع یکهزار هفتصد نود و چهار عیسوی کشته شدند دفن اند NOTE.—A brigade of British troops under Sir Ralph Abercrombie completely routed the Rohillas under Ghulam Muhammad and brought their dominion to an end; the loss on the British side being 600 men and 14 Officers (see entry No. 105). Najib Khan and Buland Khan, two Rohilla chiefs, were slain in the battle.
105	...	...	Ditto ...	Monument to the British troops who fell in action against the Rohillas in 1794.		...	(3) On some rising ground south-east of the village of Fatehganj West or Bhitaura, in tahsil Bareilly, stands a memorial to the British troops who fell in the engagement of 24th October 1794, between the British and the Rohillas. It is a large obelisk of red sandstone slabs, and stands in a small but shady walled enclosure, which is entered by a Roman archway.

Monument to the British troops who fell in action against the Rohillas in 1794.	...	...	(5) At its base on the side facing the road is engraved the following inscription:—Erected by order of the Governor-General in Council, in memory of Colonel George Burrington, Major Thomas Bolton, Captain Norman Macleod, Captain John Maubey, Captain James Mordaunt, Lieutenant Andrew Cummings, Lieutenant Edward Wells, Lieutenant William Hinksman, Lieutenant J. Richardson, Lieutenant John Plumer, Lieutenant Y. Z. M. Birch, Lieutenant W. Odell, Lieutenant Edward Baker, Lieutenant-Fireworker James Tilfer, and the European and Native Non-Commissioned Officers and privates who fell near this spot in action against the Rohillas, October the 24th, A.D. 1794. NOTE.—At Chunár in the Mirzapur district exists a slab bearing the same inscription (see entry No. 2941); even the arrangement of the lines is the same. Chunár tradition says that the stone was ordered for some place up country, but never sent there, the reason obviously being a crack which obliterates one or two letters on the left side. The slab now at Fatehganj must have been sent instead, and sent in all probability from Chunár.
Monument to the memory of victims of the Mutiny of 1857 at Sháhjahánpur.	I. H. S. *(On west side.)* This monument is erected by the friends and relatives of those honored and beloved ones whose names are here inscribed, who yielded up their lives unto death, through the violence of a lawless and fanatical insurrection at this station on the 31st day of May A.D. 1857.		

107	St. Mary's Church, Sháhjahánpur.	...	Sháhjahánpur.	Tablet to the memory of victims of the Mutiny of 1857.	To the care of two poor natives, residents of this city, they owe a grave on this spot and in God their Saviour, we trust, they have found a place. Lord Jesus receive my spirit. Lord lay not this sin to their charge. *(On south side.)* Henry Hawkins Bowling, Surgeon, 28th Regiment, B. N. I., aged 43. Captain Marshall James, 28th B. N. I., aged 37. *(On east side).* The Reverend John MacCallam, aged 45. Mordaunt Ricketts, B.C.S., Magistrate and Collector of this district, aged 30. Arthur Chester Smith, Esquire, B.C.S., aged 22, and only and beloved son of the late E. Peploe Smith, Esquire, B.C.S., and Harriet, his wife. *(On north side).* John Robert LeMaistre, clerk in the Magistrate's Office, aged 42 years.	Sacred to the memory of the undermentioned officers of the 28th Regiment, N.I., who perished in the performance of their duty at the hands of the mutinous sepoys in 1857:— Captain M. James, killed at Sháhjahánpur, 31st May 1857. Captain I. H. Guise, killed at Benares, 4th June 1857. Captain H. W. L. Sneyd, killed } " O. Lysaght, " } " M. M. Salmon, " } Lieutenant A. Key, " } " C. A. Robertson, " } " C. F. Scott, " } At Aurangabad, 10th June 1857. " W. W. Pitt, " } " G. W. Rutherford " } " T. I. H. Spens, " } " C. E. Scott, " } " P. D. Johnston, " } Surgeon H. H. Bowling, killed at Sháhjahánpur, 31st May 1857. *Also*— Mrs. Bowling, killed } " Lysaght, " } " Scott, " } At Aurangabad, 10th June 1857. " Key, " } " Scott, " } The noble army of martyrs praise Thee.	

List of Christian Tombs or Monuments in the Allahabad Division possessing historical or archæological interest.

Serial number.	Name of Cemetery, Churchyard, or Church.	Where situated (giving exact situation as far as possible).	District.	Tomb or Monument to the memory of—	Inscription on Tomb or Monument.	Inscription on slabs or pillars placed in churches or chapels.	Remarks. Tombs on road-sides, or battle-fields (furnishing information as in columns 3, 4, 5 and 6).
1	2	3	4	5	6	7	8
108	All Souls' Memorial Church, Cawnpore.	In Cantonments.	Cawnpore,	Monument to the memory of Christian people killed during the Mutiny of 1857.			Note.—The Memorial Church was erected at a cost of about £18,000 on the site of General Wheeler's entrenchment, and serves as a monument to those who fell at or near Cawnpore during the disturbances of 1857-58. It is built in the Lombardo-Gothic style of architecture, and constructed of red brick faced with buff sandstone. Its roofs are groined and covered externally with corrugated iron. The floor of the nave and transept is paved with marble and that of the chancel with Minton's tiles. The principal feature in the western façade is the rose-window over the entrance, while the windows at the eastern end, which is apsidal, are enriched with stained glass memorials to the victims of the great rebellion. Other less striking records of bravery and death exist in the 14 memorial tablets which cover the walls.
109	Ditto ...	East wall ...	Ditto ...	Fourteen tablets in memory of persons murdered at Cawnpore between 6th June and 15th July 1857, erected by the Government of the North-Western Provinces.		To The Glory of God and in memory of more than a thousand Christian people who met their deaths hard by between 6th June and 15th July 1857. These tablets are placed in this the Memorial Church, All Souls, Cawnpore, by The Government, N.-W. Provinces. Staff: Major-General Sir H. Wheeler, K.C.B. Lady Wheeler and daughters. Lieutenant G. R. Wheeler, 1st N.I., A.-D.-C. Lieutenant Colonel E. Wiggens, 52nd N.I., D.J.A.G. Mrs. Wiggens. Major W. Lindsay, A.A.C. Mrs. Lindsay and daughters. Ensign C. and Mrs. Lindsay. Brigadier-General Jack, C.B. Mrs. Jack.	

			Tablet No. 2.		Captain Sir G. Parker, 74th N.I., Cantonment Magistrate. Captain Williamson, 71st N.I., D.A.C.G. Mrs. Williamson and child. *Bengal Artillery.* Major C. Larkins, wife, and children. Lieutenant C. Dempster, wife, and children. Lieutenant B. Ashburner. " J. Martin. " St. G. Ashe. " J. A. H. and Mrs. Eckford. 2nd Lieutenant C. M. W. Sotheby. " F. W. Burney. Assistant Surgeon D. McAuley, M.D. Hospital-Steward W. Hefferan. Assistant Apothecary W. Slaney. 63 Non-Commissioned Officers and men, besides women and children. *Bengal Engineers.* Captain F. Whiting. Lieutenant B. C. Jervis. *32nd Light Infantry.* Captain J. Moore, wife, and children. Lieutenant F., Mrs., and Miss Wainwright. Ensign E. C. and Mrs. Hill. Assistant Apothecary J. Thompson. Hospital Apprentice W. A. Emmor and wife. 82 Non-Commissioned Officers and men, 41 women, and 61 children. *84th Foot.* Lieutenant F. J. G. Saunders. 47 Non-Commissioned Officers and men. *1st K. M. Fusiliers.* 15 Non-Commissioned Officers and men. Lieutenant C. J. Glanville, 2nd E.B.F.	
			Tablet No. 3.		*2nd Light Cavalry.* Major E. Vibart, wife, and children. Captain E. C. Vibart. " E. G. Leppings, wife, and children. Captain R. U. and Mrs. Jenkins. Lieutenant R. O. Quin. " C. W. Quin. " J. H. Harrison. " W. J. Manderson. " P. S. M. Wren.	

List of Christian Tombs or Monuments in the Allahabad Division possessing historical or archæological interest.—(continued).

Name of cemetery, churchyard, or church.	Where situated (giving exact situation as far as possible).	District.	Tomb or Monument to the memory of—	Inscription on Tomb or Monument.	Inscription on slabs or pillars placed in churches or chapels.	Remarks. Tombs on road-sides, or battle-fields (furnishing information as in columns 3, 4, 5 and .)
2	3	4	5	6	7	8
All Souls' Memorial Church, Cawnpore.	East wall ...	Cawnpore,	Fourteen tablets in memory of persons murdered at Cawnpore between 6th June and 15th July 1857, erected by the Government of the North-Western Provinces.	...	Lieutenant M. G. Daniell. " M. Balfour. Cornet W. A. Stirling. Surgeon W. R. and Mrs. Boyes. Veterinary-Surgeon E. C. Chalwin and wife. Ridingmaster D. Walsh, wife, and children. Sergeant-Major H. Gladwell. Quartermaster-Sergeant F. and Mrs. Tress. Cornet C. Mainwaring, 6th L.C. Lieutenant A. J. Boulton, 7th L.C.	
					1st Native Infantry. Lieutenant-Colonel John Ewart, wife, and child. Lieutenant J. H. C. Ewart, 12th N.I. Captain A. Turner, wife, and child. " E. J. Elms. Lieutenant H. S. Smith. " R. M. Satchwell. " F. Redman. Ensign J. C. Supple. Surgeon A. W. R. Newenham, wife, and children. Sergeant-Major C. Hilling, wife, and child. Quartermaster-Sergeant T. Andrews and family. 18 Musicians. 5 women and 9 children.	
			Tablet No. 4.		*53rd Native Infantry.* Major W. R. Hillersdon. Captain J. H. Reynolds, wife, and child. " H., Mrs. and Miss Belson. Lieutenant F. G. Jellicoe, wife, and children. Lieutenant H. H. Armstrong. " G. A. Master. " O. S. Bridges. " W. G. Prole.	

			Tablet No. 5.		Lieutenant F. H. Tomkinson. Ensign A. Dawson. " T. W. Forman. Surgeon N. Collyer. Sergeant-Major T. McMahon, wife, and children. Quartermaster-Sergeant W. Gordon, wife, and children. 10 Musicians, women, and children. *56th Native Infantry.* Colonel S. Williams, wife, and daughters. Major W. R. and Mrs. Prout. Captain W. L. Halliday, wife and child. " G. Kempland, wife and children. Miss Kempland. Lieutenant T. A. Raikes. " G. R. Good. " W. A. Chalmers. " H. Fagan. " W. L. G. Morris. " H. J. G. Warde. " J. W. Henderson. " R. A. Stevens. Assistant Surgeon J. P. Bowling, wife, and children. Sergeant-Major T. Bell, wife, and children. Quartermaster-Sergeant T. and Mrs. Leak. 14 Musicians, 5 women and 5 children. Captain A. M. Turnbull, 13th N.I. Lieutenant C. and Mrs. Battine, 14th N.I. Lieutenant F. C. Angelo, 16th N.I. " C. J. Bax, 48th N. I. " P. H. and Mrs. Jackson, 67th N. I. Lieutenant R. W. Henderson, 72nd N. I. Surgeon C. Garbett. Assistant Surgeon H. P. Harris, wife, and child. Assistant Surgeon R. D. D., and Mrs. Allan. Assistant Commissary N. Reilly and family. Conductor W. Berrill, A.C.D., wife, and family. Officiating Sub-Conductor C. H. Manville and family. Assistant Apothecary A. Peters and family.	

All Souls' Memorial Church, Cawnpore.	East wall ...	Cawnpore,	Fourteen tablets, &c.		Sergeant-Major Heron and family.
					Schoolmaster Gill, wife and children.
					Sergeant Brooke, D. P. W., wife, and child.
					Sergeant Kelly, D. P. W., wife, and child.
					Sergeant Maclanders, D. P. W., wife, and infant.
					Sergeant Wheelan, D. P. W., wife, and children.
					Sergeant Parker, Overseer.
					Sergeant and Mrs. Carmoody.
			Tablet No. 6.		Bazar-Sergeant and Mrs. Reid.
					Cattle-Sergeant Ryan and family.
					Sergeant Swan.
					Drum-Major Murray.
					Sergeant Warren, pensioner.
					Pensioner Green and family.
					" Nixon Reid.
					" Price.
					" Maloney.
					Mr. C. G. Hillersdon, Magistrate and Collector.
					Mrs. Hillersdon and children.
					Mr. J. Mackillop, C.S.
					Revd. E. T. R. Moncrieff, wife, and child.
					Revd. J. Rooney, Roman Catholic Chaplain.
					Mr. Maxwell.
					" A. M. Miller, Resident Engineer, E. I. R.
					Revd. Haycock, S. P. G. and mother.
					" H. E. Cockey, S. P. G.
					Mrs. Blair and daughter.
					Mr. and Miss Campbell.
					Miss Brightman.
					" Isabella White.
					The two Misses Glasgow.
					Lieutenant Harris' child.

Tablet No. 7.

Tablet No. 8.

Mrs. F. L. Wade.
„ Fraser.
„ Evans and children.
„ Darby and infant.
Miss Bissett.
Mrs. Swinton and children.
Miss S. E. Cripps.
Captain Hollings.
Mr. E. F. Greenway and family.
„ T. Greenway and family.
„ S. Greenway and family.
„ H. H. Stacey, Deputy Collector.
„ Cox.
„ R. J. Collins, Inspector, P. O. and wife
Mr. R. B. Cook, Opium Department, wife, and family.
Mr. Alone, wife, and children.
„ J. C. Anderson, E.I.R., wife, and child
Mr. J. C. Baines, E. I. R. and wife.
„ Philip Baines.
„ Barlow.
Martha Batavia.
Miss Eliza Bennett.
Mrs. Beestal.
„ Bothwick.
Mr. E. Brierly, Telegraph Department.
Henry Brett.
The two Misses Burn.
Mr. Bunney.
Mrs. Carroll.
Two boys Caley.
Mr. and Mrs. Carter and infant.
Miss Emma Chandler.
Mary Cheeters.
Mr. and Mrs. Christie.
Three Misses Christie.
Miss Conway.
James Cousins.
Drummer Clooney.
Miss Colgan.
Mr. H. R. Cooper, E. I. R., wife, and family
Mrs. Copeman.
Master W. Copeland.
Mrs. Crabb.
Mr. Cummins, Surveyor, E. I. R.
Mrs. Dallas.
„ Darling and infant.
„ Dachey and infant.
„ Daly.
Mr. Davis and children.

List of Christian Tombs or Monuments in the Allahabad Division possessing historical or archæological interest.—(continued).

Serial number.	Name of cemetery, churchyard, or church.	Where situated (giving exact situation as far as possible).	District.	Tomb or Monument to the memory of—	Inscription on Tomb or Monument.	Inscription on Slabs or Pillars placed in churches or chapels.	Remarks. Tombs on road-sides, or battle-fields (furnishing information as in columns 3, 4, 5 and 6).
1	2	3	4	5	6	7	8
109	All Souls' Memorial Church, Cawnpore.	East wall ...	Cawnpore,	Fourteen tablets, &c. Tables No. 9.		„ J. K. DeGama. „ John Duncan. „ David Duncan and children. Miss DeCruz. Mr. DeRussett, wife, and children. Mrs. Dupton and sons. Master W. Dundas. Mr. Fagan, wife, and children. „ Farmer, Telegraph Department. Mrs. Fairburn. „ Fenn. Mr. John Fitzgerald and family. „ W. Forsyth, E. I. R. „ Freeman. Mrs. Mary Frost. „ Rebecca Frost. Miss Emelin Frost. „ Sophia Fulton. Master W. Fulton. Mr. Garret, Engineer, E. I. R. „ Galway, Telegraph Department. „ W. Gee and wife. Mrs. and Miss Gibson. Mr. Gilpin, wife, and children. „ Goodwin, Telegraph Department. „ Grinsey. „ Gun, E. I. R. „ and Miss Guthrie. „ Hogan. „ Harkness and child. „ Haycock and wife. „ J. D. Hay, wife, and children. „ Hanna, Assistant Engineer, E. I. R. Miss Hampton. Mr. M. C. Heberden. „ E. Henderson. Miss Elizabeth Holmes. Mr. W. James. „ F. Jacobi and wife.	

	Tablet No. 10.		Mr. H. Jacobi and wife.	
			Mrs. Jackford.	
			Mr. Jones and wife.	
			„ A. R. Johnston, E. I. R., wife, and family.	
			Mrs. Keeler.	
			„ Kinleside and children.	
			„ Knight and children.	
			„ Kirk, Senior.	
			Mr. J. Kirk, wife, and children.	
			„ J. Kirkpatrick, wife, and infant.	
			„ H. LaTouche, Assistant Engineer, E. I. R.	
			„ J. Lawrence, E. I. R., wife, and children.	
			„ Leary and sons.	
			Miss Leath.	
			James Lewis.	
			Mr. Little.	
			Miss Lucy Lyell.	
			Master McCullen.	
			Mrs. Mackinnon.	
			The two Misses Macmoran.	
			Miss N. Martindell.	
			„ Ellen Mark.	
			Mrs. Jane Morfett.	
			Mr. Murphy, E. I. R.	
			„ C. Mackintosh and family.	
			„ G. W. Maling.	
			„ John Maling.	
			Mrs. W. Marshall.	
			Mr. Nelson.	
	Tablet No. 11.		„ W. North.	
			Mrs. Norris.	
			Mr. James O'Brien and wife.	
			„ J. L. O'Brien and son.	
			Miss O'Connor.	
			Mr M. Ogle, Canal Department, wife, and family.	
			Mrs. Osborne.	
			Messrs. Fred. and Henry Palmer.	
			Mrs. and Georgie Peel.	
			Mr. C. H. Peake, Telegraph Department.	
			Harriett Pistol.	
			Mrs. Pogson.	
			Mr. Purcell, wife, and son.	
			„ Probett, wife, and children.	
			„ Ramsay, Telegraph Department.	
			„ Reilly.	
			„ George Reid, wife, and children.	

Cawnpore,	Fourteen tablets, &c.	...	Mr. Ricketts, E. I. R.
			,, Roach, Postmaster.
			,, Robinson, E. I. R.
			Mrs. Roberts.
			,, Russell.
			,, Eliza Russell.
			Mr. Saunders and son.
			,, Scott.
			,, John Schorn.
			,, Sherman.
	Tablet No. 12.		Mrs. Shore.
			Mr. Sinclair, E. I. R. and wife.
			Henry and William Simpson.
			Mr. Shaw.
			,, R. Sheridan, wife, and children.
			Daniel Shepherd.
			Mrs. Ellen Shepherd and children.
			Mr. Sliven.
			,, Smith, E. I. R.
			,, Stanley.
			Lucy and William Stoke.
			Miss Margaret Stowell.
			Mrs. Tibbets.
			,, Tomkins.
			Mr. Todd.
			Mrs. Tresham.
			Mr. Tritton.
			,, Vaughan.
			,, J. Virgin, E. I. R. and wife.
			,, Viscarde, E. I. R.
			Miss Wallett.
			Mr. C. Warden, E. I. R.
			,, Walsh, E. I. R., wife, and children.
			,, A. Walker and son.
			,, Wells, wife, and children.
			Mrs. Elizabeth West and children.
			Thomas, Katharine, and Jane Wideep.
			Mrs. Willis and child.
			Mr. Wilkinson, wife, and child.

			Tablet No. 13.		Mr. R. B. Wrixon, wife, and child. Miss Clara Wrixon. Mrs. Edward Williams. ,, Yates. *Futehgarh Fugitives, 10th Native Infantry.* Colonel G. A. Smith, wife, and child. Major R. Monro. ,, J. Phillott. Lieutenant C. W. Swetenham. ,, D. Henderson. Ensign R. S. Byrne. Surgeon T. G. and Mrs. Heathcote. Musician W. M. Wrixon. Colonel A. Goldie, wife, and daughters. Lieutenant J. R. Monkton, Bengal Engineers, wife, and child. Assistant Surgeon S. and Mrs. Maltby. Conductor M. Rohan, Ordnance Department, and family. Schoolmaster Shiels and family. Sergeant Hammond, Gun Carriage Department, and family. Pensioner Faulkner. Mr. M. B. Thornhill, Judge, wife, and children. Mrs. Tucker and children. Mr. Alexander. Mr. J. Brierly, wife, and children. Mr. R. Brierly, wife, and child. Miss E. and Miss F. Brierly. Mr. Billington. Revd. D. E. Campbell, wife, and children. Mr. Catania, wife, and child. Mr. Cawood, wife, and children. ,, Elliott, wife, and children. Revd. J. E. and Mrs. Freeman. Mr. Finlay, wife, and children. Miss Finlay. Mr. and Mrs. Guise.	
			Tablet No. 14.		Mr. J., Mrs. and Miss Ives. Revd. A. O. and Mrs. Johnson. Mr. J. Joyce, wife, and children. ,, J. B. Kew, wife, and children. Miss Kew. ,, Nancy Lang. Revd. J. and Mrs. MacMullen. Mr. and Miss Maclean. ,, Macklin, wife, and children. Mrs. Macdonald and children. Mr. J. R. Madden, wife, and children.	

List of Christian Tombs or Monuments in the Allahabad Division possessing historical or archæological interest—(continued).

Name of cemetery, churchyard or church.	Where situated (giving exact situation as far as possible).	District.	Tomb or Monument to the memory of—	Inscription on Tomb or Monument.	Inscription on slabs or pillars placed in churches or chapels.	Remarks. Tombs on road-sides or battle-fields (furnishing information as in columns 3, 4, 5 and 6).
2	3	4	5	6	7	8
All Souls' Memorial Church, Cawnpore.	East wall,	Cawnpore,	Fourteen tablets, &c.	...	Miss E. and Miss A. Madden. Mr. J. Palmer, wife, and children. Mr. R. and Miss E. Ray. Mr. and Mrs. Roach. Mrs. E. Shepherd and children. Miss Mary Shepherd. Mr. and Mrs. O. Hern. Head Tailor of Clothing Agency. Mrs. Robert Waresaw. Mrs. Woolear and children. Mr. R. Nisbet Lowis, wife, and two children. Our bones are scattered at the graves' mouth as when one cutteth and cleaveth wood upon the earth, but mine eyes are unto thee O God, the Lord.	
Ditto ...	North wall	Ditto ...	Tablet to the memory of Captain Whaley Nicol Hardy, Royal Artillery, killed 1857.	...	To the memory of Whaley Nicol Hardy, Captain, Royal Artillery, who was killed in battle at Lucknow, 17th November 1857, aged 30 years.	
Ditto ...	East wall ...	Ditto ...	Tablet to the memory of the officers and men of the 32nd Cornwall Regiment, Light Infantry, who were killed at Lucknow and Cawnpore in 1857.	...	In memory of the following officers of the Thirty-second Cornwall Regiment, Light Infantry, who with four hundred and forty-eight Non-Commissioned Officers and private soldiers were killed or died in the discharge of their duty during the defence of Lucknow and Cawnpore and the subsequent campaign against the mutineers in the year of Our Lord 1857 :— Colonel C. A. F. H. Berkeley, C.B. Lieutenant-Colonel W. Case. Captains C. Steevens, J. Moore, J. W. Mansfield, W. Power, B. M. Calie. Lieutenants E. DeL. Joly, J. D. Thompson, F. Wainwright, P. C. Webb, J. Brackenbury, E. C. Hill, W. H. Study, J. W. Charlton; also Mrs. Moore,	

						Mrs. Wainwright, Miss Wainwright, Mrs. Hill. Forty-three soldiers' wives and fifty-five children of the same Reigment, murdered at Cawnpore in June of the same fatal year. This monument is erected by friends and comrades in token of affection and sorrow. The sufferings of this present time are not worthy to be compared within the glory which shall be revealed in us.	
112	Ditto ...	West wall ..	Ditto ...	Tablet to the memory of the Officers of the 88th Connaught Rangers who were killed in 1857 or died between 1858 and 1870.	...	In memory of the under-mentioned Officers of the 88th Connaught Rangers :— Captain H. H. Day, killed in action at Pandu Nadi, 26th November 1857; aged 20 years. Ensign F. M. Mitchell, died at Cawnpore, 7th December 1857, of wounds received in action at Pandu Nadi, 26th November 1857, aged 36 years. Ensign W. King, died at Cawnpore, 20th June 1858, aged 24 years. Ensign J. R. Perrin, died at Lucknow, 11th October 1858, aged 23 years. Lieutenant R. Miller, died at Dehra Ghát, 5th November 1860, aged 23 years. Quartermaster M. Evans, died at Cawnpore, 20th June 1864, aged 23 years. Lieutenant F. M. M. Mapleton, died at Cawnpore, 17th August 1865, aged 21 years. Captain L. S. Watson, died at Galle, 12th September 1865, aged 33 years. Captain L. C. Scott, died at Jullunder, 1st April 1870, aged 31 years. Erected by their brother officers.	
113	Ditto ...	North wall...	Ditto ...	Tablet in memory of Captain Stuart Beatson, died 1857.	...	In memory of Stuart Beatson, Captain, 1st Regiment, Bengal Light Cavalry, who died at Cawnpore on the 18th of July 1857, in the discharge of his duty, as Assistant Adjutant-General with the force under the late Sir H. Havelock, aged 32 years.	NOTE.—There is a grave in the Experimental Farm, Cawnpore, with this name on it, which probably is the grave of this officer (see entry No. 148).

All Souls' Memorial Church, Cawnpore.	North wall..	Cawnpore,	Tablet in memory of Philip Hayes Jackson, Lieutenant, Jane Amelia, his wife, and her brother, Ralph Blythe Cooke, murdered in 1857.		Sacred to the memory of Philip Hayes Jackson, Lieutenant, late 67th Native Infantry, who with Jane Amelia, his wife, and her brother, Ralph Blythe Cooke, were massacred by the rebels at Cawnpore on the 27th June 1857. This tablet has been erected as a tribute of affection to them by their sorrowing relatives. Vengeance is mine, I will repay, saith the Lord.
Ditto ...	Ditto ...	Ditto ...	Tablet in memory of Lieutenant John Little, died 1858.	...	In memory of Lieutenant John Little, H. M.'s 20th Regiment, third son of John Little, Esq., of Stewartstown, Ireland, who died at the Field Hospital, Cawnpore, 9th April 1858, aged 22 years. This tablet is erected by his parents and family as a memorial of one deeply lamented. The dead shall be raised incorruptible.
Ditto ...	Ditto ..	Ditto ...	Tablet in memory of Lieutenant F. C. Angelo, killed 1857.	...	In memory of Lieutenant Frederick Cortland Angelo, 16th Grenadiers, B. N. I., Superintendent of the 4th Division, Ganges Canal. Who fell in the mutiny at Cawnpore on the 27th June 1857, in the 32nd year of his age. Jesus said: I am the resurrection and life, he that believeth in me, though he were dead, yet shall he live. This tablet is erected by his sorrowing widow.
Ditto ...	West wall,	Ditto ...	Tablet in memory of Anne Fawcett Fraser, killed in 1857.	...	In memory of Anne Fawcett, the beloved wife of Captain George William Fraser, 27th Bengal Native Infantry, who died at Cawnpore, July 1857, a victim of the great Indian Mutiny.

Ditto ...	Ditto ...	Ditto ...	Tablet in memory of Lieutenant John Nickleson Martin, killed 1857.		This tablet in memory of an excellent son is erected by his afflicted parents, Admiral and Mrs. Martin, to John Nickleson Martin, Lieutenant, Bengal Artillery, who whilst gallantly fulfilling his duties, was treacherously killed by the mutineers in the boats at Cawnpore on the 27th of June 1857, in his 18th year, respected and beloved by all that knew him. The Lord gave and the Lord hath taken away, blessed be the name of the Lord.	
Ditto ...	South wall,	Ditto ...	Tablet in memory of the Officers of H. M.'s 82nd Regiment, killed in 1857.		To the memory of Captain John Gordon, Lieutenant Arthur Platt Hensley, H. M.'s 82nd Regiment, who fell in the defence of Cawnpore in November 1857. Also of Ensign William Temple Thomson, H. M.'s 82nd Regiment, who was killed at the second relief of Lucknow on the 18th November 1857. This tablet is erected by their brother officers.	
Ditto ...	Ditto ...	Ditto ...	Tablet in memory of Veterinary-Surgeon E. C. Chalwin and his wife, killed in 1857.		To the memory of E. C. Chalwin, 2nd Light Cavalry, and his wife, Louisa, who both perished during the siege of Cawnpore in July 1857. These are they which came out of great tribulation.	
Ditto ...	Ditto ...	Ditto ...	Tablet in memory of the Officers and men of the Cumberland Regiment, killed at Cawnpore in 1857.		To the memory of Lieutenant Edward Jordon, Ensign Theophilus G. B. Applegate, died of wounds, Ensign Lyndon J. Grier, Colour-Sergeant Charles Feddon, Sergeant Patrick Jones, Corporal William Clarke, one drummer, and twenty-four privates, all of Her Majesty's 34th or Cumberland Regiment, who were killed in action or died of wounds received at Cawnpore on the 29th November 1857. This tablet is erected by the officers of the regiment to mark their esteem and regard for their late youthful and gallant brother officers, and to record the sincere sorrow expressed by all ranks at their early deaths; also as a tribute of respect and admiration to the bravery and devotion of their late comrades, the Non-Commissioned Officers, drummers, and private soldiers who fell upon the same occasion.	

To the memory of Engineers in the service of the East Indian Railway Company, who died and were killed in the great insurrection of 1857.

John Hodgson, Locomotive Superintendent, died at Allahabad, June 21st.

R. N. M. Mantell, District Engineer, died at Allahabad, June 30th.

A. M. M. Miller, Resident Engineer, killed at Cawnpore, June 27th.

A. C. Herberden, Resident Engineer, killed at Cawnpore, June 27th.

W. Digges LaTouche, Assistant Engineer, killed at Cawnpore, June 27th.

Robert Hanna, Assistant Engineer, killed at Cawnpore, June 27th.

J. C. Bayne, Assistant Engineer, killed at Cawnpore, June 27th.

Thomas Byrne, Assistant Engineer, died at Calcutta, July.

J. W. Allen, Assistant Engineer, died at Mirzapur, August 12th.

John Mackerness, Assistant Engineer, died at Agra, August.

W. Forsyth, Assistant Engineer, killed at Cawnpore, June 27th.

F. Cussen, Junior Engineer, died on board steamer.

C. B. Taylor, Junior Engineer, killed near Delhi, May 17th.

						A. Spencer, Junior Engineer, died at Agra, August. F. L. Mudge, Resident Engineer, died at Sitapahár, October. W. F. Thompson, Assistant Engineer, died near Buxar, July 19th. George Richardson, Foreman, died at Allahabad, August 11th. And to the following Foremen and Inspectors: W. S. Benn, Articled Inspector, killed near Dehli, May 17th. J. Holmes, Articled Inspector, killed at Cawnpore, June 27th. This monument is erected in affectionate remembrance by their brother Engineers in the North-Western Provinces, India.	
123	Ditto ...	East wall,	Ditto ...	Tablet in memory of Colonel A. Jack and A. W. Thomas Jack, killed in 1857.	...	To the memory of Colonel Alexander Jack, C.B., Brigadier Commanding at Cawnpore; Andrew William Thomas Jack, sons of the late Very Revd. William Jack, D.D., Principal of King's College, Aberdeen, who were killed in the entrenchment of Cawnpore during the investment of that place by the mutineers in June 1857.	
124	Ditto ...	South wall,	Ditto ...	Tablet in memory of John R. Mackillop, C.S., killed in 1857.	...	To the memory of John Robert Mackillop of the Bengal Civil Service, who was killed at Cawnpore, on or about the 25th June 1857, in his 31st year. He nobly lost his life when bringing water from the well for the distressed women and children. His death was deeply lamented.	
125	24 stone pillars near the Memorial Church, Cawnpore.	Round the boundary of Wheeler's Entrenchments near the Memorial Church.	Ditto ...	Wheeler's Entrenchment.	B. P. W. E. 1857.	...	NOTE.—The corner ones are substantial stone pillars built into brick bases, the intermediate ones are smaller fixed into the ground.
126	12 brick pillars near the Memorial Church, Cawnpore.	Marking spots of interest within Wheeler's Entrenchments.	Ditto ...	Ditto ...	(1) Main gate, (2) Hospital, (3) Married Quarters, (4) House, (5) Exford's Battery, (6) *Nil*, (7) Ashe's Battery, (8) Magazine, (9) Redan, 3 feet deep, (10) Dempster Battery, (11) Lieutenant C. M. W. Sotheby's Battery, (12) Provision Godown.	...	NOTE.—These pillars are 2' by 2' by 8' high, terminating in a projecting stone cap on which the names are cut out. The name printed on No. 11 is almost obliterated. These pillars were erected a few years ago.

List of Christian Tombs or Monuments in the Allahabad Division possessing historical or archæological interest—(continued).

Serial number.	Name of Cemetery, Churchyard or Church.	Where situated (giving exact situation as far as possible.	District.	Tomb or Monument to the memory of—	Inscription of Tomb or Monument.	Inscription on slabs or pillars placed in churches or chapels.	Remarks. Tombs on road-sides or battle-fields (furnishing information as in columns 3, 4, 5 and 6).
1	2	3	4	5	6	7	8
127	All Souls' Memorial Churchyard, Cawnpore.	At the south-west angle of Wheeler's Entrenchments at junction of Albert and Cambridge roads.	Cawnpore	Monument to the memory of the Garrison of Wheeler's entrenchment.	The garrison of the entrenchment consisted of about 950 souls, thus— 63 artillery men. | 55 women. 18 women. | 40 children. 20 children. | 100 non-military. 15 Madras Fusiliers. | 80 women. 84-32nd Regiment. | 100 children. 45 women. | 45 musicians, &c. 60 children. | 29 women. 48-84th Regiment. | 100 children. 100 officers.		
128	Ditto ...	At the south-east corner of the Church.	Ditto ...	Tombs to the memory of Major E. Vibart and 70 officers and men, who escaped from the massacre at Cawnpore in June 1857, but were captured and murdered at Shiurájpur.	In three graves within this enclosure lie the remains of Major Edward Vibart, 2nd Bengal Light Cavalry and about seventy officers and soldiers who, after escaping from the massacre at Cawnpore on the 27th June 1857, were captured by the rebels at Shiurájpur and murdered on the 1st July. These remains were originally deposited within the compound of Savada House and were removed to this place in April 1861. This memorial was erected by the Government, North-Western Provinces, in the month of October 1867. *In memoriam.* In the world ye shall have tribulation, but be of good cheer, I have overcome the world.	...	NOTE.—This monument is enclosed by a substantial cast iron railing fixed into a stone base. The first part of the inscription is on the slab. *In memoriam* is on the Minton tiled floor, and the rest of the inscription is on the coping of the enclosure wall.
129	Ditto ...	Ditto ...	Ditto ...	Tomb erected by the Memorial Church Committee over the remains of those who were the first to lose their lives in the entrenchments in June 1857.	This stone marks a spot which lay within Wheeler's Entrenchment; it covers the remains, and is sacred to the memory, of those who were the first to meet their death when beleaguered by the mutineers and rebels in June 1857.	...	NOTE.—This monument is enclosed by a substantial iron railing.

130	Ditto ...	To the south of the Church.	Ditto ...	Well which supplied the entrenchments with water in 1857.	...	...	NOTE.—The well is open and in use, and is still in good repairs. There is no doubt that a tablet, with a suitable inscription, should be affixed.
131	St. John's Churchyard, Cawnpore Cantonments.	To the south-west corner of the Church.	Ditto ...	Tomb erected to the memory of a number of soldiers killed during the Mutiny.		...	NOTE.—This is only a plot of ground about 70' by 80', enclosed by an iron railing which is said to contain the remains of a number of men killed during the Mutiny.
132	Koorsawan Muhammadan Cemetery.	About 100 yards to the back of Ilahi Bakhsh's shop, to the right of the road leading to Ram Narain Bazar.	Ditto ...	Tomb to the memory of Private John Reed, 2nd Battalion, Rifle Brigade, killed 1857.	In memory of No. 720, Private John Reed, 2nd Battalion, Rifle Brigade, who was killed at Cawnpore on the 7th December 1857.		NOTE.—The inscription is on a Maltese cross fixed into a stone slab, 2' by 2' by 4" which rests on a brick pillar, 2' by 2' by 12". There is no fence round the grave.
133	Memorial Gardens, Cawnpore.	Between the city and the Ganges river, in the 126th mile of the Loop Line Grand Trunk Road.	Ditto ...	Enclosure over the Memorial Well, with marble statue by Marochetti.	Sacred to the memory of a great number of Christian people, chiefly women and children, who near this spot were cruelly massacred by the followers of the Rebel, Nana Dhundu Pant of Bithur, and cast, the dying with the dead, into the well below, on the 15th day of July MDCCCLVII.	...	NOTE.—The monument consists of a marble statue of a palm-bearing angel standing on a stone base, at the foot of a cross; the inscription is incised on the base. The well is surrounded by a light Gothic screen of sandstone. Over the portal of the screen on the outside is inscribed:— "These are they which came out of great tribulation," and under the arch: "Designed by Colonel Henry Yule of the Bengal Engineers," and inside the portal is the following inscription:—"Erected by the British Government, MDCCCLVIII."
134	Memorial Garden Cemetery, Cawnpore.	Near the Memorial Well.	Ditto ...	Tomb to the memory of R. B. Thornhill, killed 1857.	In memory of Robert Bensley Thornhill, Judge of Fatehgarh, Mary, his wife, and their two children, killed July 15th, 1857. Though he slay me, yet will I trust in him.		
135	Ditto ...	Ditto ...	Ditto ...	Tomb to the memory of Lieutenant-Colonel C. J. Woodford, killed in 1857.	In memory of Lieutenant-Colonel C. J. Woodford, 2nd Battalion, Rifle Brigade, killed in action before Cawnpore, November 28th, 1857. This stone was erected to his memory by his brother officers.		

List of Christian Tombs or Monuments in the Allahabad Division possessing historical or archæological interest—(continued).

Serial number.	Name of cemetery, churchyard or church.	Where situated (giving exact situation as far as possible).	District.	Tomb or Monument to the memory of—	Inscription on Tomb or Monument.	Inscription on slabs or pillars placed in churches or chapels.	Remarks. Tombs on road-sides or battle-fields (furnishing information as in columns 3, 4, 5 and 6).
1	2	3	4	5	6	7	8
136	Memorial Garden Cemetery, Cawnpore.	Near the Memorial Well.	Cawnpore...	Tomb to the memory of Captain H. D. Campbell, died 1857.	In memory of Howard Douglas Campbell, Captain in the 78th Highlanders, who died at Cawnpore of cholera on the 16th August 1857, deeply regretted by his brother officers who have erected this tablet.		
137	Ditto ...	Ditto ...	Ditto ...	Tomb to the memory of Captain James Young, died 1857.	In memory of Captain James Young, 4th Bengal Native Infantry, born at Edinburgh, 27th November 1822, died at Cawnpore, 11th August 1857, of cholera, while serving under General Neill in the suppression of the great Mutiny.		
138	Ditto ...	Ditto ...	Ditto ...	Tomb erected to the memory of men of Her Majesty's 64th Regiment, who died or fell in 1857.	In memory of Sergeants J. Kelly, H. Donnaughey; Corporals J. Lankham, W. Smith, Private J. Gee of the Band, H. M.'s 64th Regiment, who died at Cawnpore between the months of September and November 1857, deeply regretted by their comrades, who have erected this stone. Also of B. Fitzpatrick and D. Muir, who fell at the action of Cawnpore on 28th November 1857.		
139	Ditto ...	Ditto ...	Ditto ...	Monument erected to the memory of the women and children of the 1st Company, 6th Battalion, Bengal Artillery, killed in 1857.	In memory of the women and children of the late ill-fated 1st Company, 6th Battalion, Bengal Artillery, who were slaughtered near this spot by mutineers on the 16th July 1857. This monument is erected by a non-commissioned officer who formerly belonged to the 1st Company, 6th Battalion. Spare thy people, O Lord, and give not thine heritage to reproach, that the heathen should rule over them, wherefore should they say among the people, where is their God? Fear not, O Lord, be glad and rejoice, for the Lord will do great things.		

140	Ditto ...	Ditto ...	Ditto ...	Monument to the women and children of Her Majesty's 32nd Regiment, who were killed in 1857.	In memory of the women and children of H. M.'s 32nd Regiment who were slaughtered near this spot, 16th July A.D. 1857. This memorial was raised by 20 men of the same Regiment who were passing through Cawnpore, November 21st, 1857. I believe in the resurrection of the body.		
141	Ditto ...	Ditto ...	Ditto ...	Memorial slab marking the spot where the women and children captured from the boats were massacred, in 1857.	*In memoriam.* On this spot stood the House of Massacre, July 15th, 1857.		
142	...	...	Ditto ...	Tomb of Colonel M. Wilson, killed 1857.	...	...	(3) In the north-west corner of the Government Harness Factory, on the river face, at Cawnpore, is a tomb with the following inscription:— (5) To the memory of Colonel M. Wilson, K. H., H. M.'s 6th Regiment, Brigadier Commanding at Cawnpore, who fell mortally wounded, while nobly leading his regiment to repel an attack made by the Gwalior rebels on Cawnpore, November 28th, 1857.
143	...	...	Ditto ...	Tomb of several officers of H. M.'s 34th Regiment, killed in 1857.	...	...	(3) In the Government Harness Factory grounds at Cawnpore, about 50 yards from the south wall in the low ground, there is a tomb bearing the following record:— (5) In memory of Lieutenant Edward Jordon, Ens. Thomas G. B. Applegate; Ens. Lyndon, J. Grier, H. M.'s 34th Regiment, who fell at Cawnpore on the 28th November 1857. This stone was erected by their brother officers.

List of Christian Tombs or Monuments in the Allahabad Division possessing historical or archæological interest.—(continued).

Where situated (giving exact situation as far as possible).	District.	Tomb or Monument to the memory of—	Inscription on Tomb or Monument.	Inscription on Slabs or Pillars placed in Churches or Chapels.	Remarks. Tombs on road-sides, or battle-fields (furnishing information as in columns 3, 4, 5 and 6).
3	4	5	6	7	8
...	Cawnpore...	Memorial cross, marking the scene of the massacre of the Cawnpore garrison in 1857.			At Chaura Sati Ghât, about a mile from the railway bridge, on the right bank of the Ganges, at Cawnpore, is a stone cross inscribed " *In memoriam*, 27th July 1857." This is the Ghât at which the people after leaving Wheeler's Entrenchment were embarked by the Nana who opened fire on them as soon as they got out on the river. It would add to the historical interest of the place if the Ghât and the temple were maintained by Government.
...	Ditto ...	Tomb of Captain E. Currie, killed 1857.	...	...	(3) In the Government Experimental Farm, at Cawnpore, between the Orphanage Road and the Director's Quarters, is a tomb, with the following inscription :— (5) Sacred to the memory of Captain Eugene Currie, 84th Regiment, who was mortally wounded at the action of Cawnpore, and died on the 19th July 1857, in the 32nd year of his age.
	Ditto ...	Tomb of Captain Stuart Beatson, killed 1857.	...	...	In a small brick enclosure, about a quarter of a mile to the east of the above, and at the same distance from the Orphanage Road, is a tomb enclosed by a brick wall without any inscription, only bearing the name "Stuart Beatson" (*see also entry No. 113.*)

147	...	...	Ditto ...	Memorial cross over the well outside Wheeler's Entrenchment marking the vast grave of about 250 victims killed in 1857.	...	...	(3) Close to the European Barracks No. 4, Cawnpore Cantonments, near General Wheeler's Entrenchment, stands a monument consisting of a large stone cross enclosed by an iron railing over the well, in which were buried in 1857 about 250 victims who lost their lives during the defence of the entrenchments. (5) In a well under this cross were laid by ye hands of their fellows in suffering, ye bodies of men, women, and children, who died hard by during ye heroic defence of Wheeler's Entrenchment when beleaguered by ye rebel Nana, June 6th to 27th. A.D. MDCCCLVII. Our bones are scattered at ye grave's mouth as when one cutteth and cleaveth wood upon ye earth. But our eyes are unto Thee, O God the Lord. At the four corners of the iron railing are stone crosses inscribed as under :— "In memory of Lieutenant Glanville, 2nd Battalion Fusiliers and Sergeant J. Magrath and 15 privates of No. 9 Company of the Madras Fusiliers who formed part of Sir H. Wheeler's Garrison and were killed during its investment by the Bengal Mutineers in June 1857. This stone is erected by the Madras Fusiliers in remembrance of the above brave men." "In memory of Captain Robert Urquhart Jenkins of the 2nd Light Cavalry, who died from wounds received shortly before the surrender of the Garrison of Cawnpore and was buried in this well with many others." Though he slay me, yet will I trust in him. "In memory of Captain Sir George Parker, Bart., 24th Regiment, Native Infantry, Cantonment Magistrate of this place. Died in Wheeler's Entrenchment, July 1857."

List of Christian Tombs or Monuments in the Allahabad Division possessing historical or archæological interest—(continued).

Serial number.	Name of cemetery, churchyard, or church.	Where situated (giving exact situation as far as possible).	District.	Tomb or Monument to the memory of—	Inscription on Tomb or Monument.	Inscription on Slabs or pillars placed in churches or chapels.	Remarks. Tombs on Road-sides, or Battle-fields (furnishing information as in columns 2, 4, 5 and 6).
1	2	3	4	5	6	7	8
147	...	...	Cawnpore,	Memorial cross over the well outside Wheeler's Entrenchment marking the vast grave of about 250 victims killed in 1857.	...	...	"In memory of Lieutenant E. Saunders, Sergeants Mulvehill, Gilder, and Grady; 3 Corporals and 45 privates of G. Company, H. M.'s 84th Regiment, who while serving in General Wheeler's Garrison fell fighting against the Nana and his followers; of this company one man, Private Murphy, escaped."
148	...		Ditto ...	Tomb of Lieutenant T. A. Chisholm, died 1857.		...	(3) Near the Magazine for European troops, Cawnpore, is a tomb with the following inscription:— (5) In memory of Lieutenant T. A. Chisholm of the Madras Fusiliers, who died at Cawnpore on the 19th August 1857. *R.I.P.*
149	Kacheri Cemetery to the north of the Collector's Office, Cawnpore.	A little to the left of the entrance gate.	Ditto ...	Tomb of Sir John Horsford, K.C.B., died 1817.	In memory of Sir John Horsford, Knight Commander of H. M.'s Most Honorable Order of the Bath, a Major-General on the Staff and Colonel Commandant of Artillery on the H. C's. Bengal Establishment, who after a long career of meritorious service distinguished by the most perfect integrity and honour, departed this life on the 20th of April A.D. 1817, aged 66. An exemplary victim to that spirited ardour and high sense of duty, which led him but a few weeks before under great bodily suffering and in very severe weather to manifest his professional skill and fortitude at the siege and capture of Hāthras.	...	Note.—The Kacheri graveyard is one of the oldest cemeteries in Cawnpore, and although it does not possess many tombs of much historical interest, judging from the epitaphs, it contains many very old graves with quaint inscriptions upon them. It is strange to observe that only the officers and well-to-do people seem to have been buried here, the men and poor people having been buried in the cemetery known as Hira Mankaporwa. Sir John Horsford served under Lord Cornwallis in the Karnatik and Maisur against Tipu Sultan; he also served during the whole of Lord Lake's campaigns, and under the Marquis of Hastings down to the siege and capture of the important fortress of Hāthras. After a service of 45 years in various parts of India, spent in constant and unwearied devotion to his duty, this eminent officer, whose sound constitution, hardened, by temperance, had long contended with an extraordinary complication of disease, ended a long life of useful services, on the 20th April 1817, ten days after his return from field-service at Hāthras. For military science extensive knowledge, systematic arrangement

						inward application, and spotless integrity, he stood unexcelled; his presence of mind and fortitude were great to the last: regular in the performance of his duties, military and domestic, till within less than 24 hours of his death. Sir John Horsford served nearly 39 years with his regiment as an officer, and was much employed on field-service during the eight years he commanded the Artillery, and his attention to its interests was exemplified in improving the situation of the soldier, both European and Native. He was one of the officers of the East Indian Company's service first selected for the honors of the Bath; and it may justly be added that the State in him lost a most upright servant; the Army one of its most distinguished officers: and the honorable Order of the Bath a member worthy of its distinction.
Ditto ...	In the enclosure wall to the right of the gate.	Ditto ...	Slab to the memory of Lieut.-Colonel Stainforth, died 1781.	To the memory of Lieutenant-Colonel Stainforth, who lived universally beloved and died equally lamented on October 27th, 1781.		
Mirpur Cemetery, Cawnpore, near Mirpur Bazar, in Old Cantonments.	Near the north-west corner.	Ditto ...	Tomb of Sir William Peel, R. N., K.C.B., died 1858.	To the memory of William Peel. His name will ever be dear to the British inhabitants of India, to whose succour he came in the hour of need and for whom he risked and gave his life. He was one of England's most devoted sons, and with all the talent of a brave and skilful sailor, he combined the virtues of a humble and sincere Christian. This stone is erected over his remains by his military friends in India and several of the inhabitants of Calcutta. Captain Sir William Peel, R. N., K.C.B., was born in Stanhope-street, Mayfair, on the 2nd November 1824, and died at Cawnpore on the 27th April 1858.	...	NOTE.—This cemetery is now closed; in the old portion of it, along the north wall, it contains many old tombs of military officers, amongst them that of Sir William Peel, R. N., K.C.B. This tomb is not in good order. The glass over the marble, on which the inscription is written, has fallen out, and the marble is cracked. Sir William Peel, Captain of the "Shannon" Brigade, was a man who would have made his mark in any age and under any circumstances. To an energy that nothing could daunt, a power that seemed never to tire, he added a freshness of intellect, a fund of resource, which made him, in the expressive language of one of his officers, "the main spring that worked the machinery." Starting from Calcutta on an expedition unprecedented in Indian warfare, he conquered every obstacle, he succeeded to the very utmost extent of the power to succeed. He showed eminently all the qualities of an organizer and a leader of men. Not one single speck of failure marred the brightness of his ermine. His remarkable success in a novel undertaking, on an untried field, was in itself a proof that had he survived, his great powers might have been usefully employed in larger and more difficult undertakings. There must have been something very much above the common in the man who, not exercising supreme command, was able to stereotype his name in the history of his native land. Yet William Peel accomplished this. The memory of his great name and his great deeds still survives. In the Eden Gardens, at Calcutta, a statue in white marble recalls the form and fashion of him who was indeed the noblest Volunteer of this or any age, who was successful because he was really great, and who, dying early, left a reputation without spot, the best inheritance he could bequeath to his countrymen.

List of Christian Tombs or Monuments in the Allahabad Division possessing historical or archæological interest.—(continued).

Serial.	Name of cemetery, churchyard, or church.	Where situated (giving exact situation as far as possible).	District.	Tomb or Monument to the memory of—	Inscription of Tomb or Monument.	Inscription on slabs or pillars placed in churches or chapels.	Remarks. Tombs on road-sides, or battle-fields (furnishing information as in columns 3, 4, 5 and 6.)
1	2	3	4	5	6	7	8
152	Christ Church, Civil Lines, Cawnpore.	In south wall.	Cawnpore,	Tablet in memory of Lieutenant G. M. W. Sotheby, killed in 1857.	...	In memory of George M. W. Sotheby, Lieutenant, Bengal Artillery, only son of G. H. Sotheby, Captain, 34th Regiment, Madras Infantry, who in the 19th year of his age met his untimely death amongst the victims of the massacre of Cawnpore, in June 1857. His orphan sister erects this memorial in token of her sorrow and devoted affection. And God shall wipe away all tears from their eyes.	
153	Ditto ...	Ditto ...	Ditto ...	Tablet in memory of officers and men of the 52nd and 64th Regiments, killed in 1857.	...	In memory of Major Sterling, Captain Murphy, Captain McCrea, Lieutenant Mackenna, Lieutenant Gibbins, 52nd Regiment, attached, and twelve Non-Commissioned Officers and men of the 64th Regiment, killed in action at Cawnpore, 27th November 1857.	
154	Ditto ...	In the east wall.	Ditto ...	Tablet in memory of Missionaries of the S. P. G., killed in 1857.		In memory of W. H. Haycock, Priest, and Henry Edwin Cockey, Deacon, of the S. P. G. Mission to Cawnpore; also of M. J. Jennings, Priest, Chaplain, and founder of the S. P. G. Mission to Delhi; also of Alfred Roots Hubbard, Priest, and Daniel Corrie Sandys, Catechist, and Louis Koch, Catechist of the S. P. G. Mission to Delhi. The Society for the Propagation of the Gospel in Foreign Parts dedicates this memorial of its brethren who glorified God by their deaths in the Mutiny of 1857. Here is the Patience and the Faith of the Saints.	

155	Ditto ...	In the north wall.	Ditto ...	Tablet in memory of certain members of the Mackintosh family, killed in 1857.	...	To record the melancholy fate of their parents and brother, and as a tribute of affection and esteem, this tablet is erected by Edwin and Isaac Mackintosh, in memory Mr. Charles Mackintosh, Mrs. Dorothy Charlotte Mackintosh, their son Joshua Alfred Mackintosh, and her mother, Mrs. Amelia Walker, Senior, who were for many years members of this Church and fell victims to the Mutiny at Cawnpore in June and July 1857. I called upon thy name, O Lord, out of the low dungeon. Thou drewest near in the day that I called upon Thee. Thou saidst, Fear not, I will ransom them from the power of the grave. I will redeem them from death.	
156	Ditto ...	Ditto ...	Ditto ...	Tablet in memory of Mr. William Gee, killed in 1857.		In memory of William Gee, who was killed in Sir Hugh Wheeler's Entrenchment during the Mutiny in 1857, aged 75 years. Erected by his children as a token of affection and respect.	
157	Christ Churchyard, Cawnpore.	South of the Church.	Ditto. ...	Tomb to the memory of F. M. Mitchell, 88th Connaught Rangers, died 1857.	...	In memory of Fitzgerald Massey Mitchell, 88th Connaught Rangers, who died in the Field Hospital at Cawnpore, 7th December, of wounds received in action on the 26th November 1857. This memorial is erected by his brother officers as a token of their esteem and regard.	
158	...		...	Tomb of Lieutenant Smith, killed about 1790.			(3) On the west of the Grand Trunk Road, opposite the 1st furlong post of 163rd mile from Allahabad, at Bilhaur, is a tomb with the following inscription :— (5) In memory of Lieutenant Smith of the Bengal European Regiment, who was killed in action on the Frontiers. It is believed that the tomb is nearly 100 years old.

List of Christian Tombs or Monuments in the Allahabad Division possessing historical or archæological interest.—(continued).

Serial number.	Name of cemetery, churchyard, or church.	Where situated (giving exact situation as far as possible).	District.	Tomb or Monument to the memory of—	Inscription on Tomb or Monument.	Inscription on slabs or pillars placed in churches or chapels.	Remarks. Tombs on road-sides, or battle-fields (furnishing information as in columns 3, 4, 5 and 6).
1	2	3	4	5	6	7	8
159	Fatehpur Cemetery.	...	Fatehpur	Tomb of Mr. Robert Tudor Tucker, Judge, killed on 9th June 1857.	R. T. Tucker fell at the post of duty 1857, looking unto Jesus.		NOTE.—Mr. R. T. Tucker, Judge of Fatehpur, was a devout Christian, earnestly and conscientiously treading the appointed path of official duty. His enthusiasm had been roused to a still higher pitch by the intensity of his religious convictions, which had been striking deeper and deeper root, in spite of all the discouragements and distractions of Eastern life. At the entrance to Fatehpur he had erected four stone pillars, on two of which were engraved the Ten Commandments in Urdu and Hindi, and on the others, in the same characters, scriptural texts containing the essence of the Christian Faith. When the storm of the great rebellion burst over Fatehpur on the 9th June 1857, and when the European community left the station by the light of burning bungalows, Mr. Tucker stood fast and could not be induced to quit his post, whatever might be the perils which environed him. Throughout the day he was most active in his endeavours to suppress crime and to restore order; single-handed he slew some rebels in the street, and fought desperately on the top of the kacheri, resolutely and fiercely he stood at bay, loading and firing, until he had shot down many of his assailants. It is said that he was not overcome at last until the insurgents had fired the kacheri. And so the quiet Christian Judge, so meek and merciful in time of peace, rose in the hour of war to the noblest heights of heroic daring, and died for the Government that he had served.
160	...	...	Ditto ...	Tomb of Colonel T. S. Powell, killed in 1857.	...	...	(5) Within a mango grove near the village of Karanpurá in tahsil Kora of the Fatehpur district, about 150 yards westwards from the middle of the 10th mile of the Fatehpur-Jahánabad Road, there is a tomb bearing, on a stone slab, the following inscription:—

							(8) Tomb erected by the Officers of the Regiment to the memory of Colonel Thomas Sidney Powell, 53rd Regiment, killed whilst in command of the force in a skirmish at Khajwa [Khajuha] during the Mutiny, 1st November 1857. This tomb is now in proper order and surrounded with an enclosure wall. The enclosure also contains two graves without tombstones. On a tree nailed to the trunk, greatly overgrown by the bark, is an inverted tin-plate on which the following words have been scratched:—"To the memory of Private Thomas Richards, Her Majesty's 5th Fusiliers, died 5th July 1858."
161		On the Bánda-Fatehpur Road, about 500 yards from St. George's Church, Bánda.	Bánda ...	Monument to the memory of British officers and men of General Whitlock's force, who fell in action or died during the Mutiny.	In memory of the British officers and men of the Madras column commanded by Major-General Whitlock, who fell in action or died during the campaign of 1858 and 1859, against the rebels and mutineers of the Bengal Army in Bundelkhand.		
162	St. George's Church, Bánda.	In the body of the Church.	Ditto ...	Memorial tablet in memory of Mr. H. E. Cockerell, of the Bengal Civil Service, murdered at Bánda during the Mutiny.	...	In memory of Henry Edmund Cockerell of the Bengal Civil Service, who perished in the insurrection in the town of Bánda on the 15th June 1857, in the twenty-seventh year of his age.	
163	Cemetery at Mánikpur in tahsil Karwi.	To the left of the road to the police station.	Ditto ...	Tomb in memory of William Evans, Chief Engineer and Charles Lamuel, Resident Engineer.	In memory of William Evans, Chief Engineer, and Charles Limuel, Resident Engineer, who were murdered by rebels at Entomah, near the 80th mile-stone from Allahabad, on the 20th February 1850.		

List of Christian Tombs or Monuments in the Allahabad Division possessing historical or archæological interest—(continued).

Serial number.	Name of cemetery, churchyard or church.	Where situated (giving exact situation as far as possible).	District.	Tomb or Monument to the memory of—	Inscription on Tomb or Monument.	Inscription on slabs or pillars placed in churches or chapels.	Remarks. Tombs on road-sides or battle-fields (furnishing information as in columns 3, 4, 5 and 6).
1	2	3	4	5	6	7	8
164	...	...	Bánda ...	Tomb of Mr. John Wauchope, Collector of Bundelkhand, died 1818.	...	...	(5) In the Fort of Kalinjar, tahsil Girwan, 33 miles south east of Bánda, is a tomb with the following epitaph :— (5) Age . . . In Bu . . . Alike. Emin . . . In his private and . . He was beloved of his kin . Amiable and affect . . Exclusive benevolence and . And as his . . . Was devoted to the exercise . His public conduct was . . By the zealous and cons . . Of the important duties with which . With distinguished ability and . And noble integrity and disinterest . He successfully exerted himself . To gain the affections and promote the happiness Of those over whom he was placed, And supported by his personal conduct and character. The honor and interests of Government, By whom his valuable services have been respectfully and most honorably acknowledged. John Wauchope was of the ancient family Of Niddrie near Edinburgh, And he departed this life, At Kalinjar on the 12th August 1818, In the 36th year of his age. Note.—The greater part of the beginning of this inscription has been damaged through exposure.

Ditto ...	Tomb of Lieutenant James McManus, died 1812.	. . . . .		(3) At Manipur, to the north-west of the Kalinjar Fort are twenty-one graves to the memory of James McManus, late of His Majesty's 8th or King's Royal Irish Dragoons, Captain Fraser, Lieutenant Nice and others, who died, 12th February 1812, of wounds received during the investment of the Fort Kalinjar. (5) Only one tomb bears the following inscription :— To the memory of James McManus, late of His Majesty's 8th or King's Royal Irish Light Dragoons, who died 12th February 1812, aged 29 years. NOTE.—The inscription slab on Lieutenant James McManus' tomb is broken; there are no inscriptions on the remaining graves.
Ditto ...	Tomb of Lieutenant W. Jameson, died 1809.			(3) At Siddhpur—Ragauli, in tahsil Girwan of the Bánda district, is a tomb to the memory of Lieutenant W. Jameson, died 1809. (5) In memory of Lieutenant W. Jameson, 1st Battalion, 19th N. B. V., who was mortally wounded at the assault of the heights of Ragauli, January 22nd, 1809, and died February 2nd.
Hamirpur,	Tomb of Sarah Caroline Carguist, died 1810.	Sacred to the memory of Sarah Caroline, infant daughter of Mr. Carguist, 1st Battalion, 17th Regiment. Born December 10th, A.D. 1809, and died June 8th, 1810.		
Ditto ...	Tomb of Lieutenant John Lawson Byers, died 1815.	Sacred to the memory of Lieutenant John Lawson Byers, Adjutant of the 6th Regiment, Native Cavalry, who departed this life on 27th August 1815, aged 28 years. He was esteemed by all that knew him and died sincerely lamented.		
Ditto ...	Tomb of Philip D'Auvergne Barnard, died 1817.	Sacred to the memory of Philip D'Auvergue Barnard. Born 14th March 1816, died 17th April 1817.		

List of Christian Tombs or Monuments in the Allahabad Division possessing historical or archæological interest—(continued).

Serial number.	Name of cemetery, churchyard or church.	Where situated (giving exact situation as far as possible).	District.	Tomb or Monument to the memory of—	Inscription on Tomb or Monument.	Inscription on slabs or pillars placed in churches or chapels.	Remarks. Tombs on road-sides or battle-fields (furnishing information as in columns 3, 4, 5 and 6).
1	2	3	4	5	6	7	8
170	Cemetery at Kaithi, tahsil Bath		Hamirpur,	Tomb of Mary Anne Sterling, died 1820.	Sacred to the memory of Mrs. Mary Anne Sterling, wife of Major R. G. Sterling, 7th Light Cavalry, who departed this life on the 18th day of March 1820.		
171	Ditto ...	...	Ditto ..	Tomb of Jane G. Harding, died 1820.	Sacred to the memory of Jane, the wife of Mr. G. Harding, Ridingmaster, 3rd Regiment, Light Cavalry, who departed this life on 20th November A.D. 1820. Aged 37 years. Most deeply regretted by her affectionate husband, parents, and friends.		
172	Ditto ..		Ditto ...	Tomb of Cornet John Pace, died 1822.	Sacred to the memory of Cornet John Pace, of the 2nd Regiment of Light Cavalry, who departed this life on the 11th of September 1822. Aged 19 years.		
173	Ditto ...		Ditto ...	Tomb of Mary Hawkins, died 1824.	Sacred to the memory of Mary, the wife of Lieutenant Hawkins, Adjutant, 38th Regiment, Bengal Native Infantry, who departed this life on July 15th, 1824. Aged 17 years. Most deeply mourned by her afflicted husband, parents, and friends.		
174	Ditto ...		Ditto ...	Tomb of Edward Thomas Lawrie, died 1825.	Sacred to the memory of Edward Thomas Lawrie * * * , a writer in the Department of Public Works, who departed this life on March 20th, 1825.		
175	Ditto ...		Ditto ...	Tomb of Catherine L. Urquhart, died 1826.	Sacred to the memory of Catherine Long, wife of G. T. Urquhart, Esq., M.D., who departed this life on the 20th January 1826, in the 22nd year of her age. This monument was erected by a disconsolate husband to record the virtues of an amiable and loving wife, a fond and tender mother, and a most generous and warm friend.		
176	Ditto ...	...	Ditto ...	Tomb of Sub-Conductor Almond, died 1820.	Sacred to the memory of Almond, Sub-Conductor of Public Works, who departed this life on 19th day of September 1820. Aged 29 years.		

177	Ditto ...	...	Ditto ...	Tomb of Lieutenant Charles Erskine, died 1827.	Sacred to the memory of Lieutenant Charles Erskine, 2nd Regiment, Native Infantry, who was unfortunately killed by a fall from his horse on the 29th September 1827. Aged 19 years 5 months and 5 days. This monument was erected by his brother-officers as a tribute of respect to his memory. He lived beloved and died deeply regretted.		
178	Ditto ...		Ditto ...	Tomb of Joseph William S. Loder, died 1828.	Sacred to the memory of Joseph William Sandly, only son of Major Joseph William and Harriet Mayor Loder, who departed this life on 10th January 1828. Aged 2 years 1 month and 26 days.		
179	Ditto ...		Ditto ...	Tomb of Surgeon James Hector Mackenzie, died 1828.	Sacred to the memory of James Hector Mackenzie, Surgeon to the 3rd Native Cavalry, H. C. S., who departed this life on the 23rd May 1828, aged 40 years and 5 months, in the full hope of the promise made to all who believe in our Saviour Jesus Christ. He was a dutiful son, an affectionate husband and brother. This small tribute is erected to his memory by his disconsolate widow.		
180	Ditto ...		Ditto ...	Tomb of Andrew Brookless Poole, died 1828.	Sacred to the memory of Andrew James Brookless Poole, son of Quartermaster-Sergeant Poole, 3rd Light Cavalry, and Sarah, his wife, who died on 26th June 1828, aged 3 months and 20 days.		
181	Ditto ...		Ditto ...	Tomb of John Stuart Miller, died 1829.	Sacred to the memory of John Stuart, infant son of Sergeant J. W. Miller, and Louisa, his wife, who departed this life on 26th April 1829, aged 4 months and 25 days.		
182	Ditto ...		Ditto ...	Tomb of Captain A. F. E. Macleod, died 1829.	Sacred to the memory of Captain A. F. E. Macleod, of the 22nd Regiment, Bengal Native Infantry, who departed this life on 4th June 1829, aged 43 years. This small token of esteem is erected by a well-wisher.		
183	Ditto ...		Ditto ...	Tomb of Patience Jordan, died 1829.	Sacred to the memory of Patience, infant daughter of Riding-Master M. Jordan, 7th Light Cavalry, and Annie, his wife, who departed this life on 7th June 1829, aged 11 months and 9 days.		

List of Christian Tombs or Monuments in the Allahabad Division possessing historical or archæological interest—(continued).

Serial number.	Name of cemetery, churchyard or church.	Where situated (giving exact situation as far as possible).	District.	Tomb or Monument to the memory of—	Inscription on Tomb or Monument.	Inscription on slabs or pillars placed in churches or chapels.	Remarks. Tombs on roadsides or battlefields (furnishing information as in columns 3, 4, 5 and 6).
1	2	3	4	5	6	7	8
184	Cemetery at Kaitha, in tahsil Kath.		Hamirpur,	Tomb of Sergeant S. Smith, died 1831.	Sacred to the memory of Quatermaster-Sergeant S. Smith * * * the 7th Light Cavalry, who departed this life on 19th * * 1831, aged 42 years. Beloved by his sincere friends S. Smith and Sergeant Buildings.		
185	Ditto ...	...	Ditto ...	Tomb of Frances LaTouche and Cecil LaTouche, died 1831.	Sacred to the memory of Frances, the beloved wife of Captain LaTouche, Major of Brigade in Bundelkhand, who departed this life upon the 22nd July A. D. 1831, aged 20 years 11 months and 20 days. Most deeply deplored by her disconsolate husband and relatives. Sacred to the memory of Cecil, the son of Captain LaTouche, who departed this life upon the 2nd July A.D. 1831, aged 1 year 6 months and 18 days. Most deeply lamented.		NOTE.—The masonry work of the tombs Nos. 167 to 185 is in a state of good preservation. Besides the tombs detailed above, there are some 38 graves more, the inscriptions on which are broken or pealed off through exposure to the weather.
186	Ditto ..	Fixed in the wall next to the right of the gate.	Ditto ...	Tombstone of Captain A. Tod, died 1817.	Here lie the mortal remains of Captain Alexander Tod, of the 26th Regiment of Native Infantry, whose soul left this world on the 31st January 1817. A memorial of friendship and esteem to departed worth.		
187	Ditto ..	Ditto ...	Ditto ...	Tombstone of J. F. Stedman, died 1829.	Sacred to the memory of John Frederick, eldest son of Captain R. A. and Anne Stedman, born 5th September 1822, died 10th August 1829. Of such is the kingdom of Heaven.		

188	Ditto ...	Fixed in the wall next to the left of the gate.	Ditto ...	Tombstone of Sergeant-Major Tanfield Elliot, died 1826.	James Tanfield Elliot, Sergeant-Major of the 32nd Regiment, Native Infantry, departed this life the 14th December A.D. 1826. Aged 36 years 4 months and 13 days.		
189	Cemetery at Hamirpur.	Ditto ...	Ditto ...	Tombstone of F. Herbert Gall, died 1825.	Sacred to the memory of Fortnam Herbert, eighth son of Lieutenant-Colonel Geo. Herbert Gall, B.L.C., died 15th December 1825, aged 2 months and 11 days. Ere sin could blight or sorrow fade, Death came with friendly care, The opening bud to heaven conveyed, And bade it blossom there.		
190	Ditto ...	Opposite the gate.	Ditto ...	Tomb of Robert Urquhart, Ordnance Conductor, died 1833.	Sacred to the memory of Robert Urquhart, Conductor of Ordnance, who died on the 25th September 1833. Aged 44 years 8 months. Sleep kindred dust till that last day, When earth and heaven shall flee away; Then shalt thou join thy soul above, And sing the chimes of heavenly love.		
191	Ditto ...	Near western wall.	Ditto ...	Tomb of Quartermaster-Sergeant Adam McGregor, N. I., died 1838.	Sacred to the memory of Adam McGregor, Quartermaster-Sergeant, 5th Native Infantry, who departed this life on the 17th April 1838. Aged 32 years.		
192	Ditto ...	Ditto ...	Ditto ...	Tomb of Mungo Fairlie Muir, B.C.S., died 1848.	Sacred to the memory of Mungo Fairlie Muir, Bengal Civil Service, died 30th May 1841. Aged 26 years.		
193			Allahabad.	Tomb of Quartermaster-Sergeant G. R. Watkins, killed 1857.			(3) In the Alfred Park, Allahabad, there is a tomb to the memory of Quartermaster-Sergeant G. R. Watkins, 6th Regiment, N. I., murdered in 1857 by the mutineers. The platform has slightly settled. (5) Sacred to the memory of George Richard Watkins, Quartermaster-Sergeant, of the 6th Regiment, who was killed on the 6th June 1857. Aged 30 years 1 month and 21 days.

List of Christian Tombs or Monuments in the Allahabad Division possessing historical or archæological interest—(continued).

Serial number.	Name of cemetery, churchyard or church.	Where situated (giving exact situation as far as possible).	District.	Tomb or Monument to the memory of—	Inscription on Tomb or Monument.	Inscription of slabs or pillars placed in churches or chapels.	Remarks. Tombs on road-sides or battle-fields (furnishing information as in columns 2, 4, 5 and 6).
1	2	3	4	5	6	7	8
194	Kydganj Cemetery, Allahabad.	...	Allahabad.	Tomb of seven officers of the 6th Native Infantry, who were murdered by their own men, on the 6th June 1857.	Beneath this stone were laid, June 18th 1857, the remains of seven officers of the 6th Regiment, N. I. who were the murdered by their own men at the mutiny of that regiment on the night of June 6th. Eight other officers of the same, or doing duty with it, were murdered at the same time; but their bodies were not recovered.		NOTE.—For details see entry No. 204.
195	Ditto ...		Ditto ...	Tomb of Lieutenant-Colonel Andrew Wilson Hearsey, died 1798.	To the memory of Lieutenant-Colonel A. W. Hearsey, who departed this life on 10th July 1798, aged 46 years. This monument is erected in token of regard by his affectionate widow Charlotte Hearsey.		NOTE.—Lieutenant-Colonel A. W. Hearsey, who rendered good services under Sir Eyre Coote, during the Karnatik and Mysore wars, was the first English Commandant of the important Fort of Allahabad.
196	Ditto ...	...	Ditto ...	Tomb of Lieutenant-Colonel Richard Humphray, died 1806.	Sacred to the memory of Lieutenant-Colonel Richard Humphray, Commandant of Allahabad, died April 14th 1806. Aged 49.		
197	Ditto ...	...	Ditto ...	Tomb of Lieutenant-Colonel R. Ralph, died 1804.	Leutenant- Colonel Richard Ralph, died on November 18th, 1804, aged 55 years.		
198	Ditto ...		Ditto ...	Tomb of R. Turner, Judge of Agra, died 1815.	Sacred to the memory of Richard Turner, Esq., late Judge and Magistrate of the zillah of Agra, died 21st September 1815.		
199	Ditto ...		Ditto ...	Tomb of Lieutenant Charles Bonning, died 1813.	Sacred to the memory of Lieutenant Charles Bonning of the 1st Battalion, 14th Regiment, N. I., who died at Allahabad on the 6th of April 1813, aged 28 years. Erected by the officers of his corps as a sincere mark of their esteem.		

200	Ditto ...	...	Ditto ...	Tomb of Anna Maria Baumgardt, died 1820.	In memory of Anna Maria, wife of Captain J. G. Baumgardt, 8th Light Dragoons, died 19th September 1820, in her twenty-eighth year.		
201	Ditto ...	On a slab let into the wall of the Cemetery.	Ditto ...	Tombstone of John Brannan, died 1798.	Here lieth the body of John Brannan of the L. Company, 78th Regiment, who departed this life October 8th, 1798. Born in the Parish of Boyle, Co. Roscommon, Ireland, aged 24 years. This stone is erected by Andrew Brannan, Cousin-german to the deceased.		
202	Ditto ...	Ditto ...	Ditto ...	Tombstone of Hobson Silchair, died 1798.	Here lies the body of Hobson Silchair, late of His Majesty's 78th Regiment, from Lincolnshire, who departed this life the 16th April 1798, aged 26 years.		
203	Allahabad Fort.	In a small enclosure on the glacis, south end of Fort.	Ditto ...	Tomb of Lieutenant A. H. Alexander, killed 1857.	In memory of Lieutenant A. H. Alexander, 68th N. I., 3rd Oudh Irregular Cavalry, killed by the mutineers at Allahabad on 6th June 1857.		
204	Holy Trinity Church, Allahabad.		Ditto ...	Tablet to the memory of persons, killed in June 1857.		IN MEMORY OF - John Plunket, Captain. Robert Stewart, Lieutenant and Adjutant. George H. Hawes, Lieutenant and Quartermaster. Thomas L. Balliff, Ensign. Philip S. Codd, Ensign. Marshall D. Smith, Ensign. Arthur M. H. Cheek, Ensign. George L. Munro, Ensign. George S. Pringle, Ensign. Thomas Foley, Sergeant-Major. George Watkins, Quartermaster Sergeant. Charles G. Way, Ensign. Edward S. Beaumont, Ensign. Arthur J. Scott, Ensign. Edward M. Smith, Ensign. DOING DUTY WITH 6TH REGIMENT, N. I. Thomas C. H. Birch, Captain, 31st Regiment, N. I., Fort Adjutant. Charles D. Innes, Lieutenant, Engineers, Executive Engineer, 6th Division. Augustus, H. Alexander, Lieutenant, 68th Regiment, N. I., Second in command, 3rd Oudh Irregular Cavalry.	

Allahabad...			Geoffry Coleman, Conductor, Ordnance Department. Anthony Fernando, pensioned Drummer. Julien Bollard, merchant. Henry Archer, merchant. Joseph Fulow, merchant. George D. Castro, pensioned clerk. David Thomas, inspector, E. I. R. William Lancaster, Assistant Contractor, E. I. R. Robert George, Platelayer, E. I. R. James Herrold, Toll Collector. Julia L., wife of Major Ryves, retired list, Madras Army. Mary wife of Sergeant Collins. Frederica, daughter of Mr. John Jones, W. R. R. Mary Thomas, widow. Susan Benson, widow. Ann, George and Catherine, wife, son, and daughter of Drummer Biddes. WHO WERE KILLED In the station and district of Allahabad, between the 6th and 10th days of June 1857, by sepoys of the 6th Regiment, Native Infantry, and other mutineers and rebels. This monument is erected by the surviving residents of Allahabad.
Ditto ...	Tablet to the memory of J. L. Ryves, died 1857.		Sacred to the memory of Julia Louisa, wife of Major Thomas James Ryves retired list, Madras Army, who departed this life on the 9th June, 1857, from exposure to the sun at Barwarie during the mutiny. Aged 45 years and 17 days.

206	Ditto ...	...	Ditto ...	Memorial tablet to H. Archer, merchant of Allahabad, killed in 1857.		Sacred to the memory of Henry Archer, who was killed by the mutineers at Allahabad on the 7th June 1857, aged 52 years. What though in lonely grief I sigh For husband loved, no longer nigh; Submissive still, I would reply:— "Thy will be done." This tablet is erected by his widow.	
207	Ditto ...		Ditto ...	Memorial tablet to the officers of Her Majesty's 3rd Regiment, killed in action or died of wounds in the State of Gwalior, 1843-44.		To the memory of the officers of Her Majesty's 3rd or Buffs Regiment, who were killed in action, or who died when on service in the State of Gwalior in 1843-44. Captain Donald Stewart, killed in action at Punniar, on the 29th December 1843. Aged 45. Captain Richard Nicholson Magrath, died of his wounds in camp at Gwalior on the 11th January 1844, Aged 33. Surgeon Alexander Macqueen, M. D., died in camp at Gwalior on the 24th January 1844. Aged 50. Captain Thomas Chatterton, died in camp at Seundah on the 27th January 1844, Aged 45. This tablet is inscribed by their brother-officers.	
208	Ditto ...		Ditto ...	Memorial tablet to the men of Her Majesty's 3rd Regiment, killed in action or mortally wounded in action in the Gwalior State, 1843.		This tablet is erected by the officers to the memory of the Non-Commissioned Officers and men of Her Majesty's 3rd Regiment or Buffs, who were killed or mortally wounded in action at Punniar on the 29th December 1843. Colour-Sergeants Jacob Wheeler, John Devory, Henry Ebonll, Sergeant Michael Mannion, Privates Thomas Allen, Francis Purton, James Thorne, Thomas Clarke, William Potworth, Andrew Travers, Joseph Britton, Thomas Baily, Thomas Watkins Wood, James Greig, Benjamin Lockwood, Edward Siommons.	
209			Ditto ...	Tomb of W. Griffin, died 1849.			(3) At mauza Usmanpur in pargana Kiwai of Tahsil Handia, within the indigo factory enclosure, is a tomb with the following inscription. (5) William Griffin, died on 13th April 1849.

List of Christian Tombs or Monuments in the Allahabad Division possessing historical or archæological interest—(continued).

Serial number.	Name of cemetery, churchyard or church.	Where situated (giving exact situation as far as possible).	District.	Tomb or Monument to the memory of—	Inscription on Tomb or Monument.	Inscription on slabs or pillars placed in churches or chapels.	Remarks. Tombs on road-sides or battle-fields (furnishing information as in columns 3, 4, 5 and 6).
1	2	3	4	5	6	7	8
210	...	...	Allahabad	Tomb of J. P. Barrett, murdered in 1857.	...	...	(3) At mauza Paharpur in pargana Jhusi of tahsil Phulpur is a tomb in memory of Mr. J. P. Barrett, murdered by the mutineers in 1857. (5) Sacred to the memory of James Philip Barrett, Collector of this toll-bar, Bairagi-ka-nala. Born November 1808, killed during the mutiny on the 7th June 1857. This tablet is erected by his son Mr. P. Barrett. I am killed here, leaving my beloved children and friends behind committed to the protection and guardianship of my Redeemer to the battle in pilgrimage of this dark world. Farewell children and brethren, the ransom of my sins has been paid. Shed no tears, but leave me here until my Redeemer Christ appears. The Grace of our Lord be with you all.
211	...	On a small hill near the Allahabad Bank, Civil Lines, Jhánsi.	Jhánsi ...	Memorial column to Major F. W. Pinkney, C. B., Commissioner of Jhánsi, died 1862.	In memory of Major F. W. Pinkney, C.B., Commissioner of Jhánsi, died 30th July 1862.		Note.—Major F. W. Pinkney, who did much to restore order after the mutiny, is buried in the old English Cemetery behind the Cavalry Lines.
212	...	On the Lalitpur road near the Polo-ground, Jhánsi.	Do. ...	Monument to the men of the 86th Regiment, who fell in the passage of the Betwa and the storming of Jhánsi Fort, 1858.	(a) Sacred to the memory of the soldiers of Her Majesty's 86th Royal Regiment, who fell gloriously at the battle of the Betwa and the storming of Jhánsi on the 1st and 3rd of April 1858. Erected to their memory by their comrades-in-arms. *R quiescant in pace.* (4) Sacred to the memory of Dr. Stack, Her Majesty's 86th Regiment, who was shot at the storming of Jhánsi on the 3rd of April 1858, whilst attending on a wounded soldier. Aged 39 years. Erected by his brother officers in testimony of their esteem.		

213	Old English Cemetery, Jhânsi.	On Barwa Sagar Road.	Do.	...	Monument erected to the memory of those, who fell during the Central India Campaign of 1857-58.	Erected by the Non-Commissioned Officers and Privates of the 3rd Bombay European Regiment to the memory of gallant comrades, who fell during the campaign of Central India under Major-General Sir Hugh Rose, K.C.B., 1857-59. *Sergeants.* Martin Hart. William Sharp. Thomas Cummings. John Anderson. James Wood Robert Stephens. Patrick O'Crady. *Corporals.* Michael Hennessy. Alexander Anderson. Luke O'Brien. Joseph Davis. William Tooth. William Taylor. James Evans. John Christie. George Nichols. *Privates.* Thomas Clivet. Cornelius McCormach. James Finlay. Thomas Robertson. William Smith. Thomas Jackson. Frederick Perry. Thomas Cannavan. Saunders Palmer. Charles Miller. John Osborne. Patrick Daly. Daniel Donovan. Hugh Cameron. Henry Eggington. John Hitchcock. Thomas Panton. James Madden. Peter Brown. Patrick Doyle. George West. John Hastings. John Reynolds. William Wilkinson. Robert Howard. Michael Congrave. John Paul. William Perry. James Harris. Thomas Craig. James Hyate. James Duane William Cannon. John Nye. William Dunn. John Bernan. Bernard Dempsey. William Amos. James Watson. John Harrison. James McLaren. John Crady. Thomas Burnham. John Kenna. Miles Brien. Patrick Mahan. William Wheeler. William Cox Charles Eston. George Baker. Patrick Moshan. Thomas Laird. George Toan. Stephen Darcy. Samuel Ford. James Sullivan. James Evans. Patrick Bryan. David Young. Richard Allen. Joseph Pitlon. William Healy. Charles Hudson. William Moore. Hugh Kennanlty. John Casty. John Flinn. John Hayes. George Booth. James Shields. Thomas Farrell. John Dunn. William Sturgeon. John Boyle. Ambrose Parfrey. Adam Falkner. John Smith. Josiah Woollaston. James Bleak.		

List of Christian Tombs or Monuments in the Allahabad Division possessing historical or archæological interest.—(continued).

Serial number.	Name of cemetery, churchyard, or church.	Where situated (giving exact situation as far as possible).	District.	Tomb or Monument to the memory of—	Inscription on Tomb or Monument.	Inscription on slabs or pillars placed in churches or chapels.	Remarks. Tombs on road-sides, or battle-fields (furnishing information as in columns 3, 4, 5 and 6.)
1	2	3	4	5	6	7	8
			Jhánsi ...		(6) In memory of the men, 1st Troop, Bombay Horse Artillery, killed and died from wounds received in action and otherwise during the Central India Campaign, A.D. 1857-59. R. Hiles. W. Bright. B. Berkley. T Paulding. J. Connors. M. Hennessy. E. Johnson. J. Cathcart. J. Saunders. D. Wardrop. T Dalton. W. Quinlan. F Hurst. O. Darley. D Burns. J. May. Raised by their officers and comrades as a memorial of their past worth and service.		
214		Under the City walls, close to the Sagar Gate, Jhánsi City.	Do. ...	Memorial Garden with the monument erected by Government to the memory of 66 persons, who were murdered at Jhánsi during the mutiny.	Erected by the British Government in memory of the persons who were murdered at Jhánsi in June 1857, and whose names are recorded within. A.D. 1862. Captain Alexander Skene, Superintendent. Mrs. Skene, and two children. Mrs. Browne, wife of Captain Browne, Native Infantry, Deputy Commissioner, Jalaun. Miss Browne. Captain F. D. Gordon, 10th Madras N. I., Deputy Commissioner, Jhánsi. Lieutenant Burgess, Revenue Surveyor, Bundelkhand. Lieutenant Turnbull, Assistant Revenue Surveyor, Bundelkhand. Lieutenant Powis, Irrigation.		

Mrs. Powis.
Mrs. Powis' child.
Dr. McEgan
Mrs. McEgan.
Mr. T. Andrews, Principal Sadar Amín, Jhánsi.
Mr. Robert Andrews, Deputy Collector.
Mrs. Andrews and three children.
Mr. W. S. Carshore, Collector of Customs.
Mrs. Carshore and four children.
Mr. D. C. Wilton, Patrol.
Mrs. Wilton and one child, and t·o sisters of Mrs. Wilton.
Mr. D. D. Blyth, Revenue Surveyor.
Mrs. Blyth, her mother and four children.
Sergeant Millard, Sub-Asst. Surveyor.
Mrs. Millard and three children.
Mr. Bennett, Sub-Assistant Revenue Surveyor.
Mr. J. Young, Ditto Ditto.
Mrs. Young.
Mr. G. Young, Apprentice.
Mr. Palfreyman, Ditto.
Mr. Munrow, Sub-Assistant Revenue Surveyor.
Mr A. Scott, Head Clerk, Deputy Commissioner's office.
Mr. G. Purcell, Head Clerk, Superintendent's office.
Mr. J. Purcell, Clerk, Deputy Commissioner's office.
Mr. Mutlow, Clerk, Superintendent's Office.
Mr. Mutlow, unemployed.
Mr.D.G. Elliott, Clerk, Deputy Commissioner's office.
Mr. Elliott, father of above.
Mrs. Elliott, mother of D. G. Elliott.
Mr. Flemming, unemployed.
Mr. Crawford, ditto.
Captain Dunlop, 12th Bengal Native Infantry, Commanding at Jhánsi.
Lieutenant Taylor, 12th Bengal Native Infant.y.
Lieutenant Campbell, Commanding Irregular Cavalry.
Quartermaster-Sergeant Newton.
Mrs. Newton and two children.

215			Jalaun ..	Tomb of Captain James Crawford, died 1770.	...		3) Standing out in the fields to the east of the village of Margayan in the Kalpi pargana and tahsil of the Jalaun district there is the tomb of Captain James Crawford, died A.D. 1770. 6 ماه برأے یادگاریست کہ بتاریخ سیوم جون سنہ ۱۷۷۰ع کپتان جیمس کرافرڈ صاحب بسنہ بست دو سال دریتجا وفات یافت NOTE.—The tomb is a large masonry structure, some 6 feet high, with a sandstone slab let into the upper block, on which the Urdu inscription is cut. The stone slab is, however, inserted upside down, and the inscription is getting worn away by the weather.
216	Kalpi Cemetery.	Near the Fort.	Do. ...	Various tombs of Privates of the 48th Regiment, 10th Company, who died at Kalpi in 1859.	(a) H. M. 48th Regiment— Edward Taffingham, aged 20 years. Matthew Beaumont, aged 30 years. Henry Clarke, aged 30 years. Samuel Montgomery, aged 27 years, died at Kalpi, on 2nd May, 3rd June and 5th July 1859. (b) 10th Company, H.M. 48th Regiment— Lawrence Russel, aged 33 years, died on 14th August 1859. (c) H. M. 48th Regiment— John Kearney, aged 33 years. James Glym, aged 26 years, died on 9th October 1859. (d) H. M. 48th Regiment— Robert Lugget, aged 34 years, died on 13th June 1859.		NOTE.—There are 20 graves without any inscriptions on them. Near the entrance gate, however, are lying four stone slabs, the inscriptions on which are given in column 6.

217	Kunch Cemetery.	Near the Kunch Tahsíli, on the north.	Do.	...	Memorial pillar to the officers and men who fell in action with Mir Khan, Pindari, in 1804.	Sacred to the memory of Captain Feade, Lieutenant Morris, Artillery; Lieutenant Gillespie, 1st Battalion, 18th Regiment; Assistant Surgeon Hooper, and other brave men, who fell in action with Mir Khan, Pindari, near Kunch, 22nd May 1804.		NOTE.—This inscription is on a stone-slab inserted in a masonry pillar in the middle of the cemetery. In it are a number of graves without epitaphs, apparently those of the men mentioned in the inscription. The Pindáris were freebooters, whose ravages were allowed, through the supineness of the British Government, to be the scourge of Central India and the Deccan from about 1804 to 1814. These banditti, who had their homes in Central India under the protection of Sindhia and Holkar, inherited the customs and traditions of the early Marathas under Sivaji. Mounted on hardy ponies, they used to sweep through the land in large bands, harrying the defenceless husbandmen at the spear's point, and carrying back stores of booty to their distant camps. Their audacity was so great that they paid no regard to the armies of the native powers, and were scarcely to be deterred by the presence of a British detachment.
218	Orai Cemetery	Near the Jail.	Do.	...	Tomb of Harriet Maria Thornton, died 1854.	Sacred to the memory of Harriet Maria, the beloved wife of Samuel Thornton, Asst. Superintendent of Jalaun, who departed this life at Garotha in Bundelkhand on the 28th June 1854, aged 24 years 8 months 13 days. In the midst of life we are in death.		
219	Ditto ...	Ditto ...	Do.	...	Tomb of Rita Passanah, killed in 1857.	Here lie the remains of Rita Passanah, widow of Urban Passanah, cruelly murdered by mutineers at Orai on the 15th of June 1857, aged 70 years. She sleeps in Jesus.		
220	Ditto ...	Ditto ...	Do.	...	Tomb of Joseph Rivett, Tahsíldár of Daboh, died 1859.	Sacred to the memory of Joseph Rivett, Tahsíldár of Daboh, who departed this life, 10th November 1859, aged 44 years and 2 days.		

Benares...	Monument to the memory of Mr. Cherry and his staff, who were murdered by Wazir Ali during the insurrection at Benares, 1799.	This obelisk was erected in memory of George Frederick Cherry, Esq., Governor-General's Agent, Captain Canway, Robert Graham, Esq., Richard Evans, Esq., who were murdered by Wazir Ali, 14th January 1799.		NOTE.- The monument consists of a large obelisk mounted on steps and surrounded by a stone railing. Wazir Ali Khan, the deposed Nawab of Oudh, who was living at Benares under the surveillance of Mr. Cherry, conceived a plot to murder all the English residents at the station. Mr. Cherry had invited Wazir Ali to breakfast, who drew his poignard and stabbed Mr. Cherry to the heart; and his followers began a general massacre of the Europeans. Mr. Samuel Davis, a Civil Servant of repute and a Sanskrit scholar, afterwards Director of the East India Company, retreated to the roof of his house, where he so gallantly saved the lives of his wife and children by his defence of a narrow winding staircase, armed only with a hogspear. The Hon'ble Mountstuart Elphinstone and his friend Houston mounted on horseback and rode for their lives.
Do. ...	Tomb of Lieutenant-Colonel Francis Wilford, died 1822.	Sacred to the memory of Francis Wilford, Lieutenant-Colonel in the Engineer Service of the East India Company, aged 71 years, deceased on the 4th of September 1822. Encouraged by the liberality of the Government of British India, he fixed his residence at Benares in the year 1788; and whilst yet in the vigour of his days, devoted his life to retirement and study, eminently qualified by previous education, extensive erudition, a true intellect and indefatigable zeal. He made himself master of the classical language and literature of the Hindus, and applied his knowledge to the eradiation of the dark periods of antiquity, with a success that perpetuates his own reputation and the honour of the British name in the East. In the social relations of life his merits were proportioned to his talents, and the abilities of the scholar were reflected by the virtues of the man.		NOTE.—Colonel Francis Wilford was a good classical and Sanskrit scholar, and his varied and extensive reading was successfully brought into use for the illustration of ancient Indian geography. But his judgment was not equal to his learning and his wild speculations on "Egypt" and on the "Sacred Isles of the West," in the 3rd and 9th volumes of the "Asiatic Researches," soon dragged him down to a lower position than he is justly entitled to both by his abilities and his attainments. His "Essay on the comparative geography of India," which was left unfinished at his death and which was published in 1851, is entirely free from the speculations of his earlier works, and is a living monument of the better judgment of his latter days.

223	...	At Chaitganj, north of Chaitganj police station, Benares City.	Do. ...	Enclosure surrounding the burial place of brave men who fell in the ómeute of 1781.	The enclosed ground was the burial place of brave men who died in the performance of their duty on the 16th August 1781 A.D. This wall has been built to protect the spot from desecration, A.D. 1862.		NOTE.—A slab over the gate has the inscription given in column 6. In 1781, the conduct of Raja' Chait Singh of Benares towards Warren Hastings, the Governor-General, was such as to require early punishment. On the 15th August 1781, the day after his arrival at Benares, Hastings sent the Raja a formal statement of the charges against him, with a demand for a full and categorical reply. Chait Singh's answer appeared so offensive in style and unsatisfactory in substance, that Hastings ordered Mr. W. Markham, the resident, to place him under arrest. Early on the morrow of the 16th August, Chait Singh was made a prisoner at large in his own palace at Shivala Ghat, with a Sepoy guard under Lieutenants Scott, Stalker, and Symes outside. He sent Hastings a submissive message; meanwhile his armed retainers from Ramnagar crossed the Ganges, and aided by the mob of the city, fell upon the Sepoy guard who, having only unloaded muskets and empty pouches were soon cut to pieces where they stood. Two more companies marching through the narrow streets were nearly destroyed; the whole number of killed and wounded amounting to about 205 men. Chait Singh himself dropped from the terrace by a rope of turbans into a boat, and was borne in safety to his castle-palace of Ramnagar.
224	...	In Muhalla Shivala, Benares City.	Do. ...	Three tombs to the memory of Lieutenants A. Scott, Jeremiah Symes, and J. Stalker, killed in 1781.	This tablet has been erected by the Government, North-Western Provinces, to preserve the last earthly resting place of— Lieutenants A. Scott, 1st Battalion, Sepoys; Jeremiah Symes, 2nd Battalion, Sepoys; J. Stalker, Resident's Bodyguard; who were killed, 17th August 1781, near this spot doing their duty.		
225	St. Mary's Church compound.	Benares Cantonment.	Do. ...	A memorial column to Lieutenants John Stalker, Archibald Scott, and Jeremiah Symes, killed in 1781.	This monument to the memory of Lieutenants John Stalker, Archilald Scott, and Jeremiah Symes, who were massacred at Shivala on the 17th day of August 1781, though erected by the hand of friendship, shall offer no praise which themselves might blush to read, yet be it remembered that the determined courage they showed was not an act of desperation, but a part of their characters as British officers that they fell not wholly useless to their country's cause in the sentiments of awe and respect they impressed on their enemies, in the tears of regret and emulation they drew from their fellow-soldiers.		NOTE.—Warren Hastings in his "Narrative" of the Benares insurrection writes:—"These officers were the first victims to the fury of the tumultuous assembly; but not until they had by astonishing efforts of bravery and undismayed amidst the imminent dangers which surrounded them, involved a much superior number of their enemies in their fate. In this general report of them, all accounts concur, though varying in circumstances. I yield to my own feelings in bestowing this just but unavailing tribute to these unhappy gentlemen."
226	Do. ...	Do. ...	Do. ...	Monument erected over the remains of all bodies removed from the old City burial-ground.	Erected over the remains of all bodies removed from the old City burial-ground to this spɔt, 10th January 1829, by James Prinsep.		

List of Christian Tombs or Monuments in the Benares Division possessing historical or archæological interest—(continued).

Serial number.	Name of Cemetery, Churchyard or Church.	Where situated (giving exact situation as far as possible.	District.	Tomb or Monument to the memory of—	Inscription on Tomb or Monument.	Inscription on slabs or pillars placed in churches or chapels.	Remarks. Tombs on roadsides or battlefields (furnishing information as in columns 3, 4, 5 and 6).
1	2	3	4	5	6	7	8
227	...	Old Artillery Lines, north-west of Oudh and Rohilkhand Railway Station, Benares.	Benares...	Tomb of Captain H. J. Guise, 13th Irregular Cavalry, killed 1857.	To the beloved memory of my husband, Captain Henry John Guise, 2nd son of General Sir D. W. Guise, Baronet, of Glocestershire, who fell when in command of the 13th Irregular Cavalry, and in the gallant discharge of his duty, by the hands of the mutineers, 4th June 1857.		
228	...	Old Artillery Lines, north-west of O. & R. Railway Station, Benares.	Do. ...	Tomb of Julian York Hayter, 25th Bengal Native Infantry, killed 1857.	Sacred to the memory of Julian York Hayter, 25th Bengal Native Infantry, who fell mortally wounded in the mutiny at Benares, June 4th, and died, June 16th, 1857, leaving a bright example of truly Christian fortitude and resignation under his sufferings.		
229	...	Cantonment, Benares, near boundary pillar No. 18.	Do. ...	Monument to the memory of Lieutenant-Colonel Pogson, 47th Native Infantry, died 1843.	Sacred to the memory of Lieutenant-Colonel Wredenhall Robert Pogson of the XLVII Regiment, Native Infantry. Born on the 1st July 1787, and died at Benares on the 6th of August 1843, aged 55 years, 1 month and 6 days. This monument is erected by the officers of the 47th and his friends and family as a token of respect to his memory.		
230	Rajghat Cemetery, Benares.	Near Dufferin bridge.	Do. ...	Tomb of Gunner Benjamin Biver, died 1858.	In memory of Benjamin Biver, Gunner of 8th Co., 2nd Battalion, Royal Artillery. Died May 23rd, 1858, aged 27 years. This stone was erected by his comrades.		
231	Ditto ...	Ditto ...	Do. ...	Tomb of Gunner William Taylor, died 1858.	In memory of William Taylor, Gunner of 8th Co., 2nd Battalion, Royal Artillery. Died May 23rd, 1858, aged 26 years. This stone was erected by his comrades.		

232	Ditto ...	Ditto ...	Do. ...	Tomb of Bombardier John Excell, died 1858.	In memory of John Excell Bombadier of 8th Company, 2nd Batallion, Royal Artillery. Died May 23rd, 1858, aged 27 years. This stone was erected by his comrades.		
233	Ditto ...	Ditto ...	Do. ...	Tomb of Private John Thornton, died 1858.	Sacred to the memory of Pt. John Thornton, H. M. 20th Regiment, who departed this life on the 8th of January 1858. Aged 38 years.		
234	Ditto ...	Ditto ...	Do. ...	Tomb of Henry Flanagan, died 1859.	Sacred to the memory of Henry Flanagan, of No. 2 Battery, 14th Brigade, Royal Artillery, who departed this life on the 27th day of May 1859. Aged 39 years. This stone is erected by the N.-C. officers of the company as a mark of respect.		
235	Ditto ...	Ditto ...	Do. ...	Tomb of Charles Henry Chamberlayne, died 1860.	Sacred to the memory of Charles Henry Chamberlayne, Bandman, H. M.'s 77th Regiment, who departed this life on the 6th July 1860, aged 28. Also to his daughter Mary, who died on the 20th July 1860, aged 4 hours. While I am on a pilgrimage here, Let thy love my spirit cheer, As my guide, my guard, my friend, Lead me to my journey's end. This stone is erected by his comrades of the Band.		
236	Ditto ...	Ditto ...	Do. ...	Tomb of Sergeant Henry Callaghan, died 1859.	In memory of the late Sergeant Henry Callaghan, H.M.'s 77th Regiment, who departed this life 14th October 1859, aged 34 years, leaving his beloved wife and child to lament his loss. Jesus receive me now as thine; In life and death O, be thou mine, And when before thy bar I stand, O, welcome me to thy right hand.		

List of Christian Tombs or Monuments in the Benares Division possessing historical or archæological interest—(continued).

Name of cemetery, churchyard, or church.	Where situated (giving exact situation as far as possible).	District.	Tomb or Monument to the memory of—	Inscription on Tomb or Monument.	Inscription on slabs or pillars placed in churches or chapels.	Remarks. Tombs on roadsides, or battlefields (furnishing information as in columns 3, 4, 5 and 6).
2	3	4	5	6	7	8
...	At Mauza Sitapur, in the compound of an old indigo factory garden.	Benares ...	Tomb of G. H. Hasted, died 1848.	Sacred to the memory of George Henry Hasted, the only son of G. Hasted, born on the 3rd February 1828, died on the 29th September 1848, leaving an unconsolable father to lament his untimely loss. "Oh my son, Absalom, my son, my son, Absalom, would to God I had died for thee, O Absalom, my son, my son! *Samuel* II, chapter XVIII, verse 33rd.		
...	Ditto ...	Do. ...	Tomb of George Hasted, died 1850.	Sacred to the memory of George Hasted, Esq., of the Dooleypur Indigo Concern, who departed this life on the 6th day of October 1850, born A.D. 1798, aged 51 years, 9 months, and 16 days. In this cold grave this frame must rest, And worms shall feed on this poor breast; These hands shall there be useless grown, And alas! no more be known. Then, my Lord, do thou be nigh, And bear and bring me to the sky. This is erected by his sincere friend M. B. T. William, Esquire.		
Mirzapur Cemetery.	Opposite Post-office.	Mirzapur.	Tomb of Margaret Lindsay, died 1833.	Sacred to the memory of Margaret, the beloved wife of C. Lindsay, Esq., C.S., who departed this life in childbed, aged 20 years, on the 7th October 1833.		
Do. ...	Ditto ...	Do. ...	Tomb of A. P. Currie, Judge of Mirzapur, died 1847.	Sacred to the memory of A. P. Currie, Esq., Judge of Mirzapur, who departed this life on the 3rd day of February 1847, Ætas 41. What I do thou knowest not now, but thou shalt know hereafter. *St. John*, chapter XIII, verse 7th. Erected as a last token of love by his afflicted widow.		

241	St. John's Church, Mirzapur.	Near the village of Fataha.	Do. ...	Tablet to the memory of A. P. Currie, Sessions Judge of Mirzapur, died 1847.		To the memory of Alfred Peter Currie, Civil and Sessions Judge of Mirzapur, one of the founders of this sacred edifice, who died on the 3rd day of February 1847. This tablet is dedicated by his friends as a testimonial of their esteem and regret. Take ye heed, watch and pray, for ye know not when the time is.	
242	Mirzapur Cemetry.	Opposite Post-office.	Do. ...	Tomb of Lieutenant Vere Lumby Ward, died 1801.	Here lies interred the body of Lieutenant Vere Lumby Ward, His Majesty's 27th Regiment, L. D., who departed this life 26th July 1801, aged 33 years.		
243	Ditto ...	Ditto ...	Do. ...	Tomb of Captain Andrew O'Shea, died 1817.	Sacred to the memory of Captain Andrew O'Shea. He was born at Cork in Ireland on the 21st March 1787, and he died at this place on the 18th November 1817. He was an honor to his friends, to his profession, and to society, and his loss will ever be deeply felt and lamented by his afflicted relations.		
244	Ditto ...	Ditto ..	Do. ...	Tomb of Ensign G. H. Venables, died 1834.	Ensign G. H. Venables, 29th Regiment, deceased 9th September 1834.		
245	Ditto ...	Ditto ...	Do. ..	Tomb of Lieutenant W. Platt, died 1830.	Sacred to the memory of Lieutenant W. Platt, of the 18th Regiment Native Infantry, who was drowned near Mirzapur on the 1st July 1830. This tomb was erected by his brother-officers as a token of their esteem.		
246	Ditto ...	Ditto ..	Do. .	Tomb of Lieutenant-Colonel Archibald MacDonald, died 1827.	Sacred to the memory of Lieutenant-Colonel Archibald MacDonald, K.C.B., late Adjutant General of His Majesty's Forces in India, who died on the 19th November 1827.		
247	Ditto ...	Ditto ...	Do. ...	Tomb of Lieutenant James Greenhill, died 1817.	Sacred to the memory of Lieutenant James Greenhill, of His Majesty's 77th Regiment of Foot, who departed this life near Mirzapur, 27th June 1817, aged 26 years. This monument is erected by his brother-officers as a testimony of the highest regard for a sincere friend and an honourable man.		

List of Christian Tombs or Monuments in the Benares Division possessing historical or archæological interest—(continued).

Serial number.	Name of cemetery, churchyard, or church.	Where situated (giving exact situation as far as possible).	District.	Tomb or Monument to the memory of—	Inscription on Tomb or Monument.	Inscription of slabs or pillars placed in churches or chapels.	Remarks. Tombs on Roadsides, or Battlefields (furnishing information as in columns 3, 4, 5 and 6).
1	2	3	4	5	6	7	8
848	Saint John's Church, Mirzapur.	Near the village of Fataha.	Mirzapur ...	Tablet to the memory of William Richard Moore, C. S., murdered by Jhuria Singh and his followers in 1857.	...	This tablet is erected to the memory of William Richard Moore, of the Bengal Civil Service, Joint Magistrate and Deputy Collector of Mirzapur, whose mortal remains rest in the burial-ground of this station. He was the second son of Major J. A. Moore and Sophia Stewart, his wife, and was among the early victims of the fearful mutiny which desolated India in 1857, having been barbarously and treacherously murdered while in the energetic performance of his duty on the 4th July in that year. The remembrance of his high qualities as a public servant, of his excellence in all the relations of life, of his unsullied purity and honor as a man, and of his warm and unaffected piety as a Christian, furnishes to surviving relatives and friends consolation under a loss of which, alas! it also tells the greatness. He was born on the 28th October 1832, and died on the 4th July 1857, in the 25th year of his age. He being made perfect in a short time, fulfilled a long time. *Wisdom*, chapter IV, verse 13.	NOTE.—See also entry No. 827. In July 1857, there were a number of townships on the left bank of the Ganges, which acknowledged as their chief Udwant Singh, a relative of Raja Chait Singh of Benares, who had been dispossessed by Warren Hastings, and were in open rebellion. Udwant Singh, taking the title of Raja of Bhadohi, appointed agents to collect the revenue, enrolled a force, plundered those of his neighbours who refused to acknowledge him, and closed the Grand Trunk Road for the English. Against this man and his followers Mr. Moore, who had charge of the estates of the Raja of Benares, was making head as good as he could. It happened that by a fortunate chance one of his agents managed to secure the person of the rebel chief and one of his accomplices. These, caught red-handed in the act of rebellion, were tried by court-martial, condemned and hanged. This act of summary justice, far from intimidating the rebels, incited them to defiance. The widow of Udwant Singh offered a reward of Rs. 300 to the man who would bring her the head of Mr. Moore. It happened that on the 4th July, Mr. Moore arrived at the Indigo Factory of Pali, bringing with him some rebels whom he had captured. Here he was suddenly attacked by Jhuria Singh and his followers. Moore defended himself vigorously, and, believing that a counter-attack would have its effect, sallied forth accompanied by the two managers of the factory, and some of his men, and charged the besiegers. These, however, were too numerous, and after a desperate fight, Moore and the two managers were captured. They were immediately put to death; Moore's head was severed from his body and carried to the widow of Udwant Singh, who paid for it the reward she had offered.
849	Mirzapur Cemetry.	Opposite Post-office.	Do. ...	Tomb of William Richard Moore, C. S., murdered 1857.	Sacred to the memory of William Richard Moore, Bengal Civil Service, Joint Magistrate and Deputy Collector of Mirzapur, who was murdered on duty at the Pali Factory in that district during the rebellion in India, on 4th July 1857, in the 25th year of his age. Blessed are they who die in the Lord.		

250	New Cemetery, Chunar.	To the north of the Roman Catholic Church.	Do. ...	Tomb of Fergusson Hoyer Hogg, C.S., died 1862.	To the memory of Fergusson Hoyer Hogg, Bengal Civil Service, who died at Chunar, 19th December, 1862, aged 35 years. *He rests in the Lord Jesus.*		
251	Mirzapur Cemetery.	Opposite Post-office.	Do. ...	Tomb of Elizabeth Helen Hogg, died 1862.	To the memory of Elizabeth Helen, wife of Fergusson Hoyer Hogg, who died at Mirzapur, 4th December 1862, aged 25 years. Blessed are the pure in heart, for they shall see God For ever with the Lord. I *Thessalonians*, chapter IV, verse 17.		
252	Ditto ...	Ditto ...	Do. ...	Tomb of Colonel C. S. Maling, died 1860.	To the much-loved memory of Colonel C. S. Maling, late Commandant of the 68th Regiment, Bengal Native Infantry, who departed this life at Mirzapur, March 18th, 1860, in perfect faith in his Redeemer. Most deeply deplored and lamented by his afflicted widow, family and friends, and sincerely regretted by his brother officers. The name of the Lord is a strong tower, the righteous runneth into it and is safe. *Proverbs*, chapter XVIII, verse 10. This sad monument is erected to the most fondly and most deeply-beloved memory of her beloved and very attached husband, by the sure and certain hope of being most gloriously re-united to him in heaven for ever. Not lost, but gone before.		
253	Ditto ...	Ditto ...	Do. ...	Tomb of Lieutenant Charles E. Handyside, died 1860.	Lieutenant Charles E. Handyside, 5th Bengal Europeans, son of H. Handyside, Edinburgh, died 28th September 1860. Erected by his sorrowing parents.		
254	Ditto ...	Ditto ...	Do. ...	Tomb of Lieutenant Henry Pitts-Forster, died 1850.	Lieutenant Henry Pitts-Forster, Adjutant, Shekhowattee Battalion, departed this life 26th May 1850, aged 27 years.		
255	Ditto ...	Ditto ...	Do. ...	Tomb of Ensign George Noble, died 1842.	Sacred to the memory of Ensign George Noble, 13th Native Infantry, who died here, November 10th, 1842, aged 18 years.		
256	Ditto ...	Ditto ...	Do. ...	Tomb of Alexander Francis Luid, C.S., died 1832.	Sacred to the memory of Alexander Francis Luid, C. S., born January 8th, 1798; died February 8th, 1832.		

257	Mirzapur Cemetery.	Opposite Post-office.	Mirzapur ...	Tomb of Nona Maling, died 1844.	Nona, the beloved wife of Captain C. S. Maling, 68th Native Infantry, died at Mirzapur, 28th March 1844, *ætas* 36 years. When from the dust of death I rise, To claim my mansion in the skies; E'en then shall this be all my plea, Jesus hath lived and died for me.
258	Ditto ...	Ditto ...	Do. ...	Tomb of H. Hope, C.S., died 1822.	Sacred to the memory of H. Hope, Esq., late of the Bengal Civil Service, second son by his second marriage of the late Sir Archibald Hope, Bart, of Craighall. Born A.D. 1783, died A.D. 1822, *ætas* 39.
259	Ditto ...	Ditto ...	Do. ...	Tomb of the Rev. M. W. Wollaston, died 1851.	Sacred to the memory of M. W. Wollaston, Missionary of Lens, at Mirzapur. He was born August 24th, 1802, joined the Mirzapur Mission, March 30th, 1844, and died June 10th, 1851. Them also which sleep in Jesus will God bring with Him. 1 *Thessalonians*, chapter IV, verse 14. This monument is erected as a last token of love on the part of his afflicted widow.
260	Ditto ...	Ditto ...	Do. ..	Tomb of Lieutenant-Colonel W. B. Salmon, died 1843.	To the memory of W. B. Salmon, Lieutenant-Colonel, 58th Regiment, Bengal Native Infantry, who departed this life on 5th February 1843, aged 56 years, after a service of 39 years. This monument is erected by his brother-officers as a tribute of their sincere esteem and respect.
261	Ditto ...	Ditto ...	Do. ...	Tomb of Major Henry Hinde, died 1837.	To the memory of Henry Hinde, Major, Brazilian Service, died 14th March 1531, aged 45 years.

262	Ditto ...	Ditto ...	Do. ...	Tomb of Lieutenant James Barber, died 1805	Sacred to the memory of James Barber, late a Lieutenant in the 1st Battalion, 19th Regiment, Native Infantry, who died on 5th May 1805, aged 25 years. To perpetuate the remembrance of an officer they esteemed and a friend they loved, this monument is erected by the 1st Battalion, 19th Regiment, Native Infantry.		
263	Ditto ...	Ditto ...	Do. ...	Tomb of Captain Chawil Barton, died 1816.	Sacred to the memory of Captain Chawil Barton, 8th Regiment, Native Infantry, a tender and beloved husband and father, who departed this life on the 30th of October 1816. This tomb is erected with affection and tributary tears by the bereaved wife.		
264	Ditto ...	Ditto ...	Do. ...	Tomb of Thomas John Dashwood, Civil and Sessions Judge, died 1836.	Sacred to the memory of Thomas John Dashwood, Esq., Civil and Sessions Judge of zillah Tirhoot, who died suddenly near Mirzapur on the 17th of June 1836, aged 44 years.		
265	Ditto ...	Ditto ...	Do. ...	Tomb of Charlotte Sarah Douglas, died 1827.	Sacred to the memory of Charlotte Sarah, wife of Lieutenant J. F. Douglas, who departed this life at Mirzapur on the 20th of April 1827, aged 25 years.		
266	Ditto ...	Ditto ...	Do. ...	Tomb of Catharine Sarah White, died 1801.	Sacred to the memory of Catharine Sarah White, daughter of Captain Samuel White, who departed this life, February the 19th, 1801. aged one year 9 months and 10 days.		
267	Ditto ...	Ditto ...	Do. ...	Tomb of James Ross, C.E., died 1863.	Sacred to the much-cherished memory of James Ross, Esq., Civil Engineer and Architect, born at Inverness, who departed this life on the 25th December 1863 at Mirzapur. This is erected by his much-pitied but sorrowing son, Duncan Ross.		
268	Ditto ...	Ditto ...	Do. ...	Tomb of Edward Fairlie, C.S., died 1862.	Sacred to the memory of Edward Fairlie, Esq., Bengal Civil Service, the fifth son of James Fairlie, Esq., who died here on the 30th September 1862, in the 25th year of his age, much regretted by all who knew him. Fear not, for I have redeemed thee; I have called thee by thy name; thou art mine.		

Opposite Post-office.	Mirzapur ...	Tomb of Captain Thomas Kirkpatrick, died 1864.	Sacred to the memory of Captain Thomas Kirkpatrick, Madras Staff Corps, who died June 12th, 1864, aged 31 years. This monument is erected by his attached brother J. Kirkpatrick, M.D.
Ditto ...	Do. ...	Tomb of John Demine, died 1864.	Sacred to the memory of John Demine, Commander of the Ganges Company Flat *Alpha*, who died of cholera at Mirzapur, June 3rd, 1864, aged 32 years. Verily, every man at his best state is altogether vanity. *Psalm* XXXIX, verse 5.
Ditto ...	Do. ...	Tomb of Captain Fryer Kowes Todd, died 1847.	Beneath this stone is interred all that was mortal of Fryer Kowes Todd, Captain in the Hon'ble Company's Military Service. He was born on the 25th Novembe 1800 and his spirit ascended to his God and Saviour on the 7th October 1847. Blessed are the dead which die in the Lord. *Revelation*, chapter XIV, verse 13. Erected as a last token of affection by his afflicted widow.
Ditto ...	Do. ...	Tomb of Hugh Rose, C.S., died 1847.	To the memory of Hugh Rose, of Kilravock in Scotland, a Civil Servant of the Hon'ble East India Company, who died at this place on the 29th January 1847, and is here interred.
Ditto ...	Do. ...	Tomb of Lorenza Hilaria Wollaston, died 1846.	Sacred to the memory of Lorenza Hilaria, the beloved wife of M. W. Wollaston, Missionary, who died 27th July 1846, aged 36 years. Also of Lorenza, their infant daughter, who died 30th July 1846, aged one year and one month.

Tomb of Emily Eliza Taylor, died 1840.	Sacred to the memory of Emily Eliza, the beloved child of R. J. Taylor, C.S., and Eliza, his wife, born on the 12th of May 1839, died on the 12th of August 1840. *Dolce nella memoria.*		
Tomb of Lieutenant John Campbell, died 1826.	Sacred to the memory of Lieutenant John Campbell, 4th Extra Regiment, who died 25th June 1826, much regretted by his brother.		
Tomb of Major Edward Humphreys, died 1783.	Sacred to the memory of Major Edward Humphreys, who died 6th May 1783, aged 46 years. This monument is erected by Captain Patrick McDougal, November 1783.		
Tomb of Lieutenant Andrew Black, died 1794.	To the memory of Lieutenant Andrew Black, of the 5th Battalion, who departed this life, October the 6th, 1794, aged 33 years.		
Tomb of Lieutenant C. Monteath, died 1789.	Sacred to the memory of Lieutenant C. Monteath, who died January 24th 1789, aged 38 years.		
Tomb of I. Wilkins, Assistant Surgeon, died 1792.	A tribute of friendship to the memory of I. Wilkins, Assistant Surgeon, who departed this life on the 27th March, A. D. 1792, aged 37 years.		
Tomb of infant child of Colonel Chare Whinyat, died 1796.	To the memory of the infant child of Colonel Chare Whinyat, who departed this life October the 29th, 1796, aged 22 months.		
Tomb of Captain Tof, died 1797.	Sacred to the memory of Captain Tof, of the 2nd Battalion, 8th Regiment, Native Infantry, who departed this life the 10th day of April 1797, aged 56 years.		
Tomb of Captain Mark White, died 1798.	Sacred to the memory of Captain Mark White, who died 9th August 1798.		
Tomb of Mrs. Ann Lloyd, died 1797.	Sacred to the memory of Mrs. Ann Lloyd, who departed this life, August 3rd, 1797, aged 24 years. This monument is erected by her affectionate husband Captain Edwin Lloyd.		

List of Christian Tombs or Monuments in the Benares Division possessing historical or archæological interest—(continued).

...rial ...mber.	Name of cemetery, churchyard, or church.	Where situated (giving exact situation as far as possible).	District.	Tomb or Monument to the memory of—	Inscription on Tomb or Monument.	Inscription of slabs or pillars placed in churches or chapels.	Remarks. Tombs on Roadsides, or Battlefields (furnishing information as in columns 3, 4, 5 and 6).
1	2	3	4	5	6	7	8
284	Old cemetery at Chunar.	At Shamapur,	Mirzapur ...	Tomb of Colonel Patrick McDougal, died 1797.	Sacred to the memory of Colonel Patrick McDougal, who died 9th September 1797, aged 40 years.		
285	Ditto ...	Ditto ...	Do. ...	Tomb of Lieutenant Reparry, died 1794.	This monument is erected to the memory of Lieutenant Reparry, of the 5th Battalion of Sepoys, who departed this life the 11th of October 1794, aged 33 years, by his disconsolate friend and schoolfellow, Elliot Vayle.		
286	Ditto ...	Ditto ...	Do. ...	Tomb of Lieutenant James Cheap, died 1794.	To the memory of Lieutenant James Cheap, of the 27th Battalion, who departed this life, September the 4th, 1794, aged 33 years.		
287	Ditto ...	Ditto ...	Do. ...	Tomb of Mary Bemusteuph, died 1800.	Sacred to the memory of Mary Bemusteuph, who departed this life the 10th of June 1800, aged 20 years. How loved, how valued, now avails thee not, To whom related or by whom begot, A heap of dust alone remains of thee; 'Tis all thou art and all the proud shall be. This monument was erected by her affectionate husband J. Bemusteuph, Master of 12th Native Regiment Band.		
288	Ditto ...	Ditto ...	Do. ...	Tomb of Mrs. Emma Maria Clayton, died 1793.	Sacred to the memory of Mrs. Emma Maria Clayton, who departed this life, June the 1st, 1793, aged 24 years. This humble tribute is erected in memory of her many exemplary virtues by her affectionate and disconsolate husband, Captain Thomas Clayton.		
289	Ditto ...	Near Dargah	Do. ...	Tomb of Captain Edward Dawson, died 1786.	Sacred to the memory of Edward Dawson, Esquire, Captain in the Hon'ble Company's Service, who died the 23rd of March 1786, aged 54 years.		

290	Ditto ...	Ditto ...	Do. ...	Tomb of Colonel Christian Kundson, died 1793.	Sacred to the memory of Christian Kundson, Colonel in the Hon'ble Company's Service, who died in command of of this station on the 31st of August 1793, aged 48 years.		
291	Ditto ...	Ditto ...	Do. ...	Tomb of Major Thomas Pennyne, died 1784.	To the memory of Major Thomas Pennyne, who died on the 22nd of July 1784, aged 54 years.		
292	Ditto ...	Bhaurahi ...	Do. ...	Tomb of Lieutenant Archibald Armstrong, died 1791.	A tribute of friendship to the memory of Lieutenant Archibald Armstrong, who departed this life on the 29th of August A.D. 1791, aged 27 years.		
293	Ditto ...	Near the Railway bridge, Shamspur, north of the railway line.	Do. ...	Tomb of Lieutenant Thomas Chawner, died 1794.	Sacred to the memory of Lieutenant Thomas Chawner, *obiit* October 10th, 1794, aged 20 years. Erected June 1795 by the officers of the 3rd Battalion, Sepoys.		
294	Ditto ...	Sultânpur...	Do. ...	Tomb of Brevet Captain Robert Trotter Knox, died 1841.	Sacred to the memory of Robert Trotter Knox, Lieutenant and Brevet Captain, 6th Regiment, Light Cavalry, who departed this life on the 20th November 1841, aged 33 years.		
295	Ditto ...	Ditto ...	Do. ..	Tomb of Cornet Frederic Elidor Whalley, died 1830.	Sacred to the memory of Cornet Frederic Elidor Whalley, 6th Regiment, Light Cavalry, who died on the 11th of October 1830, aged 19 years.		
296	Ditto ...	Ditto ...	Do. ...	Tomb of Miss Mary Glen Thomson, died 1830.	Sacred to the memory of Mary Glen Thomson, eldest daughter of Colonel Harry Thomson, died 11th September 1830, aged 17 years and 3 months.		
297	Ditto ...	Ditto ...	Do. ...	Tomb of Lieutenant Edmund Stuart, died 1833.	Sacred to the memory of Edmund Stuart, Lieutenant, His Majesty's 44th Regiment, who died near this spot, July 4th, 1833, in the 24th year of his age. This tomb is raised by his brother, Robert Stuart, Lieutenant, His Majesty's 44th Regiment, February 1839.		
298	Ditto ...	Ditto ...	Do. ..	Tomb of Walter Herbert Gall, died 1823.	To the memory of Walter Herbert, sixth son of Major G. H. Gall, 8th Light Cavalry, who departed this life, 5th of October 1823, aged 20 months & 9 days. Ere sin could blight or sorrow fade, Death came with friendly care; The opening bud to heaven conveyed, And bade it blossom there.		

Tomb of Lucius George Kempland, died 1816.	Sacred to the memory of a beloved child, Lucius George, son of Lieut. G. A. Kempland, 8th Native Cavalry, who departed this life on the 27th of August 1816, aged 15 months and 10 days; also of a second beloved child, who departed this life on the 27th of April 1817, 11 aged months.
Tomb of Major Francis John Spiller, died 1836.	To the memory of Francis John Spiller, Major, 8th Light Cavalry, *obiit* 5th October 1836, *ætas* 54 years. This monument is erected to his memory by the officers of the Corps.
Tomb of Lieutenant-Colonel Lucius R. O'Brien, died 1825.	Lieutenant-Colonel Lucius R. O'Brien, C. B., Colonel, Commandant, 8th Regiment, Bengal Light Cavalry, *obiit* July 10th, 1825, aged 51 years.
Tomb of Captain Alexander Maxwell Key, died 1832.	Sacred to the memory of Captain Alexander Maxwell Key, late of the 9th Regiment Light Cavalry, who departed this life on the 4th December 1832. This tomb is erected by his brother-officers as a mark of their respect and esteem.
Tomb of Charles Cusson, died 1799.	To the memory of Charles Cusson, infant son of Lieutenant Thomas Cusson, who departed this life, * * October 1799, aged seven months. Ere sense of sorrow, grief, or care, Therein from this rude world hastily I flew, Almighty God thro' his an * * Removed me hence to * *

304	Ditto ...	Ditto ...	Do. ...	Tomb of Ensign John Elisha Walsh, died 1789.	Sacred to the memory of John Elisha Walsh, Ensign in the Honorable Company's Service, who departed this life July 25th, 1789, aged 38 years.		
305	Ditto ...	Ditto ...	Do. ...	Monument to the British troops who fell in the engagement of the 24th October 1794, between the British and Rohillas near Fatehganj West in the Bareilly district.	Erected by order of the Governor-General in Council to the memory of Colonel George Burrington, Major Thomas Bolton, Captain Norman Macleod, Captain John Maubey, Captain James Mordaunt, Lieutenant Andrew Cummings, Lieutenant Edward Wells, Lieutenant William Hinksman, Lieutenant Joseph Richardson, Lieutenant John Plumer, Lieutenant Y. Z. M. Birch, Lieutenant William Odell, Lieutenant Edward Baker, Lieutenant Fireworker James Tilfer, and the European and Native Non-Commissioned Officers and Privates who fell near this spot in action against the Rohillas, October the 24th, A. D. 1794.		NOTE.—See entry No. 103.
306	New Cemetery at Chunar.	To the North of the Roman Catholic Church.	Do. ...	Tomb of the Rev. William Bowley, died 1843.	Sacred to the memory of the Rev. William Bowley, who departed this life 10th October 1843, aged 58 years. He was for 30 years an active, zealous and successful missionary of the Church Mission Society, by whom his loss is deeply lamented. They that be wise shall shine as the brightness of the firmament; and they that turn many to righteousness as the stars for ever and ever.		
307	Holy Trinity Church, Chunar.	Lower Lines.	Do. ...	Tablet to the memory of the Rev. W. Bowley, died 1843.		Sacred to the memory of the Reverend William Bowley, who died October 10th 1843, aged 58 years. He was for thirty years an active, zealous, and successful missionary of the Church Missionary Society. To the erring Natives of India he was the unwearied evangelist, ever proclaiming: "Behold the Lamb of God!" To the converts (and God give him many), and every Christian within the sphere of his ministrations, he was the faithful and tender shepherd, feeding them with food "convenient for them." They that be wise shall shine as the brightness of the firmament; and they that turn many to righteousness as the stars for ever and ever. *Daniel, chapter XII, verse 3.*	

List of Christian Tombs or Monuments in the Benares Division possessing historical or archæological interest—(continued).

Serial number.	Name of cemetery, churchyard, or church.	Where situated (giving exact situation as far as possible)	District.	Tomb or Monument to the memory of—	Inscription on Tomb or Monument.	Inscription on slabs or pillars placed in churches or chapels.	Remarks. Tombs on road-sides, or battle-fields (furnishing information as in columns 3, 4, 5 and 6).
1	2	3	4	5	6	7	8
308	New Cemetery, Chunar.	Lower Lines,	Mirzapur...	Tomb of Lieutenant-Colonel Charles Heath Lloyd, died 1849.	To the memory of Charles Heath Lloyd, Lieutenant-Colonel, Commandant of the Garrison, Chunar, who died on the 20th August 1849, aged 65 years.		
309	Ditto ...	Ditto ...	Do. ...	Tomb of Lieutenant-Colonel James Auriol, died 1833.	Sacred to the memory of Lieutenant-Colonel James Auriol, Commanding the European Invalids and Garrison of Chunar, died 18th September 1833.		
310	Ditto ...	Ditto ...	Do. ...	Tomb of Lieutenant E. W. Ravenscroft, died 1856.	Sacred to the memory of Lieutenant E. W. Ravenscroft of the 72nd Bengal Native Infantry, who departed this life on the 22nd December 1856, aged 43 years This tablet is raised by his, affectionate widow. Many are the afflictions of the righteous, but the Lord delivereth him out of all.		
311	Ditto ...	Ditto ...	Do. ...	Tomb of the Revd. Robert Richard, died 1855.	Sacred to the memory of the Revd. Robert Richard, an old servant of the Church Missionary Society, who departed this life on the 17th February 1855, aged 66 years.		
312	Ditto ...	Ditto ...	Do. ...	Tomb of Major Hamilton Maxwell, died 1829.	Sacred to the memory of Major Hamilton Maxwell, who died 17th June 1829, aged 42 years.		
313	Old cemetery at Chunar.	Below the Fort.	Do. ...	Tomb of Ensign Hugh Stranack Cameron, died 1782.	Here lies the body of Ensign Hugh Stranack Cameron, of Forbaluss, county of Ross in North Britain, who departed this life the 21st of October 1782, aged about eighty.		
314	Ditto ...	Ditto ...	Do. ...	Tomb of Lieutenant-Colonel Lewis Grant, died 1822.	Sacred to the memory of Lieutenant-Colonel Lewis Grant, who died 10th November, A. D. 1822, aged 70 years.		

315	Ditto ...	Ditto ...	Do. ...	Tomb of Harriott Marley, died 1797.	In memory of Harriott Marley, infant daughter of Major B. Marley, who died 18th April 1797.		
316	Ditto ...	Ditto ...	Do. ...	Tomb of Captain George Nugent, died 1819.	Sacred to the memory of Captain George Nugent, late Fort Adjutant & Barrack-Master, who departed this life on the 14th of June 1819, aged 39 years He was a man of most honorable and upright principles, a tender, kind and indulgent husband, a fond and affectionate father, a warm and sincere friend, possessing an elegant mind, an energy and wit blended with the most affable manner; he was a charming companion and an excellent member of society.		
317	Ditto ...	Ditto ...	Do. ...	Tomb of Lieutenant H.N. Lionell Berkelly, died 1809.	Sacred to the memory of Lieutenant H. N. Lionell Berkelly, a sincere Christian. How loved, how valued, now avails thee not; To whom related or by whom begot. A heap of dust alone remains of thee; 'Tis all thou art and all the proud shall be. He departed this life on the 25th October 1809, aged 52 years 10 months 13 days.		
318	Ditto ...	Ditto ...	Do. ...	Tomb of Lieutenant John L. Lewellyn, died 1808.	This monument, sacred to the memory of Lieutenant John L. Lewellyn, who died October 16th, 1808, aged 54 years, was erected by his faithful friend Flora.		
319	Ditto ...	Ditto ...	Do. ...	Tomb of Captain Christopher Gale, died 1808.	Sacred to the memory of Captain Christopher Gale, Commissary of Ordnance, who departed this life on the * * December 1808, aged * * years.		
320	Ditto ...	Ditto ...	Do. ...	Tomb of William Henry Grant, died 1807.	Sacred to the memory of William Henry, the adopted son of Lieutenant-Colonel Lewis Grant, who departed this life the 2nd of August 1807, aged 4 years and 1 month.		
321	Ditto ...	Ditto ...	Do: ...	Tomb of Mary Grant, died 1810.	Sacred to the memory of Mary, the daughter of Lieutenant-Colonel and Mrs. Grant, who died at Chunar, the 15th August 1810, aged 7 months and 20 days.		

List of Christian Tombs or Monuments in the Benares Division possessing historical or archæological interest—(continued).

Name of Cemetery, Churchyard or Church.	Where situated (giving exact situation as far as possible).	District.	Tomb or Monument to the memory of—	Inscription on Tomb or Monument.	Inscription on slabs or pillars placed in churches or chapels.	Remarks. Tombs on roadsides or battlefields (furnishing information as in columns 3, 4, 5 and 6).
2	3	4	5	6	7	8
Old Cemetery at Chunar.	Below the Fort.	Mirzapur...	Tomb of Charlotte Jane Grant, died 1810.	Sacred to the memory of Charlotte Jane, the daughter of Lieutenant-Colonel and Mrs. Grant, who departed this life on the 1st of February 1810, aged 6 months and 12 days.		
Ditto ...	Ditto ...	Do. ...	Tomb of Captain W. Butler, died 1798.	To the memory of Captain W. Butler, Fort Adjutant and Barrack-Master, who departed this life August the 2nd, 1798.		
Ditto ...	Ditto ...	Do. ...	Tomb of Lieutenant-Colonel Harth, died 1797.	Sacred to the memory of Lieutenant-Colonel Harth, who died 24th October 1797.		
Ditto ...	Ditto ...	Do. ...	Tomb of Colonel John White, died 1794.	Sacred to the memory of Colonel John White, who departed this life on the 6th day of October, MDCCXCIV, aged 64. To all acquainted with him he was known to be a kind and tender husband, an affectionate father, a zealous officer during the 38 years which he served in the country, and a sincere friend. This monument is erected by his affectionate and disconsolate widow.		
Ditto ...	Ditto ...	Do. ...	Tomb of Ensign S. McGower, died 1798.	To the memory of Ensign S. McGower, Engineer, who departed this life, May the 27th, 1798.		
Ditto ...	Ditto ...	Do. ...	Tomb of Sergeant-Major Charles Edwards, died 1809.	Sacred to the memory of Charles Edwards, Sergeant-Major of the 2nd Battalion, Native Invalids, who departed this life at Chunar on the 19th of February 1809, aged 56 years. He was a man useful to his country and an old servant. He served with credit on the Coromandel Coast in the war		

					with Tippu Sultán and a number of years first writer in the Adjutant General's office with the Army against that tyrant. Erected by his disconsolate housekeeper Rosa, who lived with him many years.		
328	Ditto ...	Ditto ...	Do. ...	Tomb of Captain W. T. Wilson, died 1821.	Sacred to the memory of Captain W. T. Wilson of the corps of European Invalids, who departed this life 2nd July 1821, aged 36 years.		
329	Ditto ...	Ditto ...	Do. ...	Tomb of Ensign David Campbell, died 1822.	Sacred to the memory of Ensign David Campbell of the 19th Regiment, Native Infantry, who died at Chunar on the 25th of November 1822, in the 19th year of his age: erected by the officers of his corps, the old XIX Volunteers, in testimony of their extreme regret.		
330	Ditto ...	Ditto ...	Do. ...	Tomb of Surgeon Adam Mitchell, died 1809.	Sacred to the memory of Adam Mitchell, Esq., Surgeon, who died at Chunar, January 23rd, 1809.		
331	Ditto ...	Ditto ...	Do. ...	Tomb of Robert Motherall, died 1824.	Sacred to the memory of Robert Motherall, Esq., Deputy Commissary of Ordnance, who departed this life on the 7th October 1824, aged 41 years 11 months and 7 days.		
332	Ditto ...	Ditto ...	Do. ...	Tomb of Mrs. Sophia Plumer, died 1803.	Sacred to the memory of Mrs. Sophia Plumer, who departed this life on the 31st of October A. D. 1803, in the 34th year of her age.		
333	Ditto ...	Ditto ...	Do. ...	Tomb of Ensign J. Cates, died 1822.	Sacred to the memory of Ensign J. Cates, 2nd Battalion, 19th Regiment N. I., who died 13th September 1822, aged 20 years.		
334	Trinity Church, Chunar.	Lower Lines,	Do. ...	Tablet to the memory of Major William Murray Stewart, died 1850.		Sacred to the memory of William Murray Stewart, Major in the 22nd Regiment of Native Infantry, Agent to the Governor-General, &c., formerly for nearly twenty years resident in this station. In commemoration not of his virtues and good deeds, for those do follow him and will outlast this cenotaph, but of the respect and gratitude they inspired, this tablet is erected by a few of the inhabitants of Chunar, and the soldiers of the Invalid Battalion, MDCCCL.	

List of Christian Tombs or Monuments in the Benares Division possessing historical or archæological interest—(continued).

Where situated (giving exact situation as far as possible).	District.	Tomb or Monument to the memory of—	Inscription of Tomb or Monument.	Inscription on slabs or pillars placed in churches or chapels.	Remarks. Tombs on roadsides, or battlefields (furnishing information as in columns 3, 4, 5 and 6).
3	4	5	6	7	8
Lower Lines,	Mirzapur ...	Tablet to the memory of Lieutenant-Colonel George Blake, died 1860.		In memory of Lieutenant-Colonel Geo. Blake, of the European Invalid Battalion, Commanding at Chunar, who died near Ghâzipur on his way to Darjeeling, on the 6th day of November 1860, after a lingering illness borne with Christian meekness and resignation, aged 67 years 10 months and 6 days. This tablet is erected as a last token of affection and regard by his disconsolate relatives and friends.	
	Ditto ...	Monument to the memory of the men who fell in storming the Fort of Bhopari, 1811.			(3) Opposite the police station at Halia, in pargana Kantit of the Mirzapur district, on the right bank of the Adhwa river stands a monument to the memory of those who fell during the capture of the Fort of Bhopari on the Son river on the 18th April 1811. The following inscription is roughly cut on a large flat slab, about 7 feet 8 inches high by 4 feet 2 inches broad. (5) Under the auspices of Lord Minto, Governor-General of India, and General Hewett, Commander-in-Chief and Vice-President, a passage was made through the Kirahe Pass of vast height, two miles in extent, into Burdee for 18-pounders, &c., by Lieutenant-Colonel James Tetley, Commanding the 2nd Battalion, 21st Regiment, Native Infantry, aided by the great exertions of his gallant and willing corps, the following of whom fell courageously assaulting Boharrah Churry in Burdee, 18th April A. D. 1811, which is now destroyed and levelled with the ground.

				Golaub Singh, Naik, Sepoys Cassic Deen, Pheroo Singh, Jyeookh Deenah, Boodie, Incha, Byjenant, Gooranjee Singh, Pooran Bahádder Cauri; Golandauze Punchoo, Gun Laskar; Soane, Head Bullock man. · Tillooek Singh of the same corps killed at Bisore Gaut. Feby. IIIII Jem 2 Havol IIIII Naik IIIIII 30 sepoys defending the post against 800 bandits beating them off. NOTE.—The reverse bears a Hindi inscription in the Kaithi character to the same effect. The stone has been considerably injured, apparently by having been used as a target. The last two lines are much defaced. This monument was erected to commemorate a little expedition undertaken at the instance of Lalla Naik, a well-known merchant of Mirzapur, to punish the marauders of Rewah who used to plunder the rich convoys of merchandise which passed between Mirzapur and the Dekkan. In March 1893 a cupola, or pakka masonry dome, was placed over the stone to preserve it.
Ditto ...	Tombs of E. Short Jones and C. M. Kemp, killed in 1857.			(3) At Gopiganj in pargana Bhadohi of tahsil Family Domains, near the junction of the Gopiganj-Mirzapur and Grand Trunk Road, are two tombs in a small enclosure which mark the burial place of two European managers of the Pali Indigo Factory who were murdered on the 4th July 1857, together with Mr. Moore (see Nos. 248 and 249), by Jhuria Singh and his followers in revenge for the execution of Udwant Singh, the *soi-disant* Rája of Bhadohi. (5) (*a*) In memory of Edmond Short Jones, killed at Pallee, July 4th, 1857, aged 27 years. (*b*) In memory of Clinton Melville Kemp, killed at Pallee, July 4th, 1857, aged 15 years.
Ditto ...	Tomb of Charlotte Andrews, died 1828.			(3) Close to the thána of Ujh in pargana Bhadohi, in the first furlong of 467 mile of the Grand Trunk Road, stands an isolated grave in a field with the following inscription :—

				(5) To the memory of Charlotte, daughter of Captain Chas. Andrews. She departed this life the 6th November 1828, aged 13 months and 20 days.
Mirzapur,	Tomb of J. E. Vandeoil Mowviobu, died 1805.			(5) In the garden of the Gurguri Kothi (now in the possession of the Rája of Benares), on the left bank of the Ganges and opposite Mirzapur, stands a huge masonry tomb with the following French inscription :— (5) Ci-git Joseph E. Vaudeoil Mowviobu, né à Rennes le 15 Aout 1749, mort le 10 Novembre 1805.
Ditto ...	Tomb of E. Elliott, died 1809.			(5) At Bikhna, to the south of the Tanda road, are two isolated tombs in a masonry enclosure with the following inscriptions :— (5) (a) In memory of Mrs. Elizabeth Elliot, wife of Sergeant-Major Thos. Elliot, 1st Battalion, 1st Regiment, Native Infantry, who died on the 17th day of March 1809. The unaffected simplicity of her heart joined to a life of virtue must ever make her husband and her children feel and friends lament her loss.
	Tomb of Captain W. D. Turner, died 1813.			(b) Sacred to the memory of William D. Turner, late a Captain-Lieutenant in the 1st Battalion, 15th Regiment, Native Infantry, who departed this life on the 24th June A.D. 1813. This monument was erected by his brother-officers, in token of the high respect they entertained for his conduct as a soldier, and affection as a friend.

341			Ditto ...	Tomb of Eliza Dodd, died 1833.			(3) At mauza Teleyani in thána Bindhachal stands an isolated tomb with the following inscription:— (5) Sacred to the memory of Eliza Dodd, who departed this life on the 2nd November 1833. This monument was erected by the affection of a disconsolate husband.
342	Old Cemetery at Kakurgahna, Jaunpur.	Three miles north of Jaunpur city.	Jaunpur...	Tomb of Lieutenant James Hamilton, died 1814.	Sacred to the memory of Lieutenant James Hamilton, 2nd Battalion, 12th Native Infantry Regiment, native of Galway in Ireland, who died near this place on the 9th November 1814 A.D., *æt* 33. The officers of his Battalion, deeply lamenting the untimely fall of their friend, have erected this monument in testimony of their respect for his professional character and for his private virtues.		
343	Ditto ...	Ditto ...	Ditto ...	Tomb of the infant sons of Richard Owen and Sarah Wynne, died 1812 and 1813.	(a) To the memory of the infant son of Richard Owen and Sarah Wynne, died September 28th, 1812. (b) To the memory of the infant son of Richard Owen and Sarah Wynne, born the 24th August 1813, died the 6th October 1813.		
344	Ditto ...	Ditto ...	Ditto ...	Tomb of Lewis Cupola, died 1825.	To the memory of Lewis Cupola, who departed this life the 28th April 1825, aged 28 years and four months. This monument a hapless widow rears To prove her love, and to record her tears. 'Tis here on lasting marble to attest How good her husband was, herself how blest, Yet for those virtues mercy will be shown. What caused her happiness, will cause his own. Erected by his disconsolate widow, Catherine Cupola.		
345	Ditto ...	Ditto ...	Ditto ...	Tomb of Lieut. Henry Ingle, died 1824.	Sacred to the memory of Henry Ingle, late Lieutenant, 31st Regiment N.I., who departed this life 15th September 1824, aged 32 years. Grant, Lord, when he from death shall wake, He may of endless joys partake. This monument is erected by his disconsolate widow, Helen Ingle.		

List of Christian Tombs or Monuments in the Benares Division possessing historical or archæological interest—(continued).

Serial Number.	Name of Cemetery, Churchyard or Church.	Where situated (giving exact situation as far as possible).	District.	Tomb or Monument to the memory of—	Inscription on Tomb or Monument.	Inscription of Slabs or Pillars placed in Churches or Chapels.	Remarks. Tombs on road-sides or battle-fields (furnishing information as in columns 3, 4, 5 and 6).
1	2	3	4	5	6	7	8
346	Old Cemetery at Kakurgahna, Jaunpur.	Three miles north of Jaunpur City.	Jaunpur ...	Tomb of Catherine Olivia Lowther, died 1811.	Sacred to the memory of Catherine Olivia Lowther, who departed this life the 6th of August 1811, aged 9 months and 29 days, youngest daughter of William Lowther, Esq., of Jaunpur. The parent's heart that nestled fond in thee, That heart now sunk a prey to grief and care, So deck'd the woodbine sweet yon aged tree; So from it ravish'd leaves it bleak and bare.		
347	Ditto ...	Ditto ...	Ditto ...	Tomb of Robert Glass Davies, died 1819.	Sacred to the memory of Robert Glass, son of Robert and Sarah Davies, died on the 2nd July 1819, aged 7 years, 11 months and 10 days.		
348	Ditto ...	Ditto ...	Ditto ...	Tomb of James Watt, died 1803.	Sacred to the memory of James Watt, born in London the 8th October 1768, died at Baksha on the 18th day of August 1803.		
349	Ditto ...	Ditto ...	Ditto ...	Tomb of Mrs. Harriet Showers, died 1826	Sacred to the memory of Harriet Showers, wife of Major H. D. Showers of the Hon'ble Company's Service, who departed this life on the 17th October in the year of our Lord one thousand eight hundred and twenty-six, aged 37 years.		
350	Ditto ...	Ditto ...	Ditto ...	Tomb of Robert Owen Lowther, died 1813.	This sacred spot contains the earthly remains of Robert Owen Lowther, only son to William Lowther, Esq., of Jaunpur, removed from this to a better world in the tender age of infancy, being only 10 months and 17 days old. May 24th, 1813.		
351	Ditto ...	Ditto ...	Ditto ...	Tomb of S Northam, died 1828.	Sacred to the memory of Samuel Northam, who departed this life on the 2nd June 1828, aged 33 years and 7 months, leaving a wife and three helpless children to bemoan his loss.		

352	Ditto ...	Ditto ...	Ditto ...	Tomb of Valentine Cook, died 1796.	To the memory of Valentine Cook, Esq., who departed this life the 20th of April 1796, aged 32 years.		
353	Trinity Church, Jaunpur.	Near the village of Kharka, near Line Bazár.	Ditto ...	Tablet to the memory of M. Collingwood Ommanney, B. C. S., died 1857.		In memory of Manaton Collingwood Ommanney, B.C.S., Judicial Commissioner in Oudh, who rebuilt this church in the year 1852. He died at Lucknow during the siege, July 8th, 1857, aged 44 years.	
354	Ditto ...	Ditto ...	Ditto ..	Tablet to the memory of Mary Anne Threipland, died 1840.		Sacred to the memory of Mary Anne, beloved wife of Thomas Threipland, Esq., Deputy Collector of Jaunpur, who departed this life on the 4th August 1840, aged 29 years 9 months. Also of Maria, their only daughter, who died on the 7th i em, six days old.	
355			Ditto ..	Tomb of Mary Hollier, died 1808			(3) In Ramdayalganj, in the 3rd furlong of mile 5th of the Jaunpur-Mirzapur r.ad stands a tomb with the following inscription :— (5) Sacred to the memory of Mrs. Mary Hollier, who departed this life the 6th of September A.D1808, aged 35 years. This tribute of affection and regard is erected by her disconsolate husband, John Hollier.
356	Cemetery near Police Lines, Jaunpur.	North-east of mauza Bharmra.	Ditto ...	Tomb of Robert Taylor, died 1850.	Sacred to the memory of Robert Taylor, Esq., who departed this life on the 3rd May 1850, aged 37 years. *Spes mea Christus.*		
357	Ditto ...	Ditto ...	Ditto ...	Tomb of Elizabeth Smith, died 1829.	Sacred to the memory of Elizabeth Smith, widow of the late Fife-Major James Smith, 16th Regiment, Native Infantry, who departed this life on the 22nd February 1829, aged 14 years 9 months and 21 days. This tomb is erected in memory of esteem by her affectionate father.		
358	Ditto ...	Ditto ...	Ditto ...	Tomb of G. J. Doveton Burney, died 1835.	Sacred to the memory of George John Doveton, beloved son of Captain George Burney, born at Barrackpore, 13th April 1833, died at Jaunpur, 11th May 1835.		
359	Ditto ...	Ditto ...	Ditto ...	Tomb of Mary Anne Threipland, died 1840.	Sacred to the memory of Mary Anne, beloved wife of Thomas Threipland, Esq., Deputy Collector of Jaunpur, who departed this life on the 4th August 1840, aged 29 years 9 months. Also of Maria, their only daughter, who died on the 7th *idem*, six days old.		

List of Christian Tombs or Monuments in the Benares Division possessing historical or archæological interest—(concluded).

Serial number.	Name of cemetery, churchyard or church.	Where situated (giving exact situation as far as possible).	District.	Tomb or Monument to the memory of—	Inscription on Tomb or Monument.	Inscription of slabs or pillars placed in churches or chapels.	Remarks. Tombs on road-sides or battle-fields (furnishing information as in columns 3, 4, 5 and 6).
1	2	3	4	5	6	7	8
360	Cemetery near Police Lines, Jaunpur.	North-east of mauza Bharsara.	Jaunpur...	Tomb of Lieutenant Charles Wemys Havelock, killed 1858.	Sacred to the memory of Charles Wemys Havelock, Lieutenant, 66th Goorkhas, and Second in Command, 12th Irregular Cavalry, the beloved and only son of Lieutenant-Colonel Charles Frederick Havelock, H.M.'s Service, and of Mary his wife, aged 24 years. He was killed in action at Tighra with Sir E. Lugard's force, whilst gallantly leading his men of the 12th Irregular Cavalry in a charge against the rebels. Born February 16th, 1834, died 11th April 1858.		*Note*.—This gallant officer who had rendered excellent service during the Mutiny, was a nephew of the renowned general.
361	Ditto ...	Ditto ...	Ditto ...	Tomb of Isabella Jane Turnbull, died 1834.	Sacred to the memory of Isabella Jane, the beloved wife of Gavin Turnbull, Esq., Civil Surgeon, died 11th September 1834, aged 32 years.		
362	Ditto ...	Ditto ...	Ditto ...	Tomb of James South Barwise, murdered 1844.	Sacred to the memory of James South Barwise, Esq., late of Faridabad in the zillah of Jaunpur, *obiit* December 15th, 1844, *ætas* 54 years.		NOTE.—Mr. James South Barwise settled down as Indigo Planter at Faridabad in the Jaunpur district in 1827, and became soon possessed of considerable property in indigo factories and landed estates. Owing to the enmity incurred by a long course of successful litigation with Mahesh Narayan Singh, a zamindár of the Jaunpur district, for the possession of a large estate, the property of the ancestors of Mahesh Narayan, he was attacked in his house at Faridabad on the night of the 15th December 1844, and cruelly murdered by, it is generally supposed a band of dakaits employed by that person, who was arrested and tried for the crime, but, in absence of any direct evidence, acquitted. As the founder of a school at Faridabad in connection with the Church Mission Society, and many other acts of beneficence and kindness towards the natives, amongst whom he was deservedly popular, Mr. Barwise is justly entitled to be ranked among the benefactors of India.
363	Ditto ...	Ditto ...	Ditto ...	Tomb of Captain George Cracklow, died 1832.	This monument was erected by the officers of the 6th Regt. N. I. to the memory of their brother-officer Captain George Cracklow, who departed this life 5th October 1832.		

364	[illegible]	...	Ditto ...	Tomb of Lucy Howe, died 1807.			(3) In the Jaunpur Free School compound is a tomb with the following inscription :— (5) Sacred to the memory of Lucy Howe, who departed this transitory life on Friday, the 13th of November in the year of our Lord MDCCCVII, in the 28th year of her age.
365			Ditto ...	Tomb of the infant daughter of W. Matthews, died 1825.			(3) In the compound of the Blattowish Indigo Factory, about seven miles north of Jaunpur, are two tombs with the following inscriptions :— (5) (a) Sacred to the memory of the infant daughter of William Matthews, Esq., who departed this life on the 20th January 1825, aged six months and five days.
				Tomb of the infant son of Mr. and Mrs. Murray, died 1809.			(b) The infant son of Mr. and Mrs. Murray, who departed this life on the 18th June 1809, aged nine months and 22 days.
366			Ditto ...				(3) In the compound of Kolingush Indigo Factory, about 10 miles from Jaunpur, are two tombs with the following inscriptions :—
				Tomb of James Ferrier, died 1827.			(5) (a) Sacred to the memory of James Ferrier, Esquire, who died on the 19th June 1827, aged 40 years, deeply lamented by his surviving brothers, who have erected this tomb. What I say unto you, I say unto all, watch.—*St. Mark, XIII, 37.*
				Tomb of Terence Maguire, died 1811.			(b) Sacred to the memory of Terence Maguire, who departed this life on the 5th day of June in the year of our Lord one thousand eight hundred and eleven, aged 39 years.

List of Christian Tombs or Monuments in the Benares Division possessing historical or archæological interest—(concluded).

Serial number.	Name of cemetery, churchyard or church.	Where situated (giving exact situation as far as possible).	District.	Tomb or Monument to the memory of—	Inscription on Tomb or Monument.	Inscription on slabs or pillars placed in churches or chapels.	Remarks. Tombs on roadsides or battlefields (furnishing information as in columns 3, 4, 5 and 6).
1	2	3	4	5	6	7	8
367		Gházipur Cantonments.	Gházipur,	Monument to the memory of Lord Cornwallis, Governor-General and Commander-in-Chief in India, died 1805.	Sacred to the memory of Charles, Marquess Cornwallis, Knight of the Most Noble Order of the Garter, General in His Majesty's Army, Governor-General and Commander-in-Chief in India, &c., &c. His first administration, commencing in September 1786, and terminating in October 1793, was not less distinguished by the successful operations of war, and by the forbearance and moderation with which he dictated the terms of peace, than by the just and liberal principles which marked his internal Government. He regulated the remuneration of the servants of the State on a scale calculated to ensure the purity of their conduct. He laid the foundation of a system of revenue which, while it limited and defined the claims of Government, was intended to confirm hereditary rights to the proprietors, and to give security to the cultivators of the soil. He framed a system of Judicature which restrained within strict bounds the power of public functionaries, and extended to the population of India the effective protection of laws adapted to usages and promulgated in their own languages. Invited in December 1804 to resume the same important station, he did not hesitate, though in advanced age, to obey the call of his country. During the short term of his last administration he was occupied in forming a plan for the pacification of India which, having the sanction of his high authority, was carried into effect by his successor. He died near this spot,		NOTE.—The monument is a heavy structure with a domed roof supported by Doric columns. The floor is raised some 12 feet from the ground, and is of handsome grey marble. In the centre stands a cenotaph of white marble, bearing on the south side a medallion bust of Lord Cornwallis between the figures of a Bráhman and a Musalman, and on the north side the figures of a European and native soldier in attitudes of sorrow. The cenotaph is from the chisel of Flaxman. There is a statue of Cornwallis by Bacon, junior, in the Town Hall at Calcutta, and an excellent full length portrait hangs on the walls of the Council Chamber at Government House in the same city.

					where his remains are deposited, on the 5th day of October 1805, in the 67th year of his age. This monument, erected by the British inhabitants of Calcutta, attests their sense of those virtues which will live in the remembrance of grateful millions long after it shall have mouldered in the dust		
368	Ghazipur Cemetery...		Gházipur,	Tomb of M. E. M. F. Wharton, died 1827.	Beneath this column are deposited the mortal remains of Madelina Elizabeth Maria Frances Wharton, eldest daughter of the late J. J. LeMarchand, Esq., of Muddiford House, Christ's Church, in the county of Hants wife of Thos. Ramsay Wharton, Esq., late of the 8th or K. R. I. Hussars, who departed this life on the 2nd December A. D. 1827, aged 36 years.		
369	Ditto ...		Ditto	Tomb of C. LaTouche, B. C. S., died 1837.	Sacred to the memory of Cornwallis LaTouche, Esq., Bengal Civil Service, who died 17th April 1837, aged 29 years. The tribute of attached friends.		
370	Ditto ...		Ditto	Tomb of Lieutenant-Colonel W. Frith, died 1831.	To the memory of William Frith, Esq., Companion of the Most Honorable Military Order of the Bath, Lieutenant-Colonel, H. M. 39th Regiment, born July 1780, died 27th May 1831. This column has been raised as a tribute of their sincere esteem and respect by the Officers, Non-Commissioned Officers and Privates of the Corps.		
371	Christ Church, Gházipur ...		Ditto	Tablets in memory of Lieutenant Eugène De L'Etang, died 1829, and Chevalier Antoine De L'Etang, died 1840.		(a) Lieutenant Eugène De L'Etang, 1st European Regiment, born 5th May 1803, died 15th November 1829. (b) Chevalier Antoine De L'Etang, Knight of St. Louis born 20th July 1757, died 1840. *Requiescant in pace.*	

List of Christian Tombs or Monuments in the Gorakhpur Division possessing historical or archæological interest.

Serial number.	Name of Cemetery, Churchyard or Church.	Where situated (giving exact situation as far as possible.	District.	Tomb or Monument to the memory of—	Inscription on Tomb or Monument.	Inscription on slabs or pillars placed in churches or chapels.	Remarks. Tombs on roadsides or battlefields (furnishing information as in columns 3, 4, 5 and 6).
1	2	3	4	5	6	7	8
372	Gorakhpur Cemetery.	South-east corner of Gorakhpur Cantonment.	Gorakhpur	Tomb of F. M. Bird, B.C.S., died 1867.	Sacred to the memory of Frederick Martins Bird, B.C.S., son of Robert Martins Bird, Esq., late of the Bengal Civil Service, who departed this life on the 7th September 1867, aged 41 years.		Note.—The name of Mr. Bird, who distinguished himself in Gorakhpur during the Mutiny, lives in the Gorakhpur district and is cherished by the old residents and is familiar to the young. He has contributed to the history of English rule in this part of India.
373	Ditto ...	Ditto ...	Ditto ...	Tomb of Joshua Augustin, killed in 1858.	In memory of Joshua Augustin, who fell a victim during the Mutiny on 21st April 1858.		
374	Ditto .	Ditto ...	Ditto ..	Tomb of G. Clermont Armstrong, died 1827.	Sacred to the memory of George Clermont, infant son of James Armstrong, C. S., and Susan his wife, who departed this life on the 15th day of November 1829, aged 9 months and 8 days. Jesus said:—Suffer little children to come unto me and forbid them not, for of such is the kingdom of Heaven.		
375	Ditto ...	Ditto ..	Ditto ..	Tomb of Charles Barker Crommelin, died 1827.	Sacred to the memory of Charles Barker Crommelin, born 13th December 1790, died 27th February 1827. He was a dutiful son, an affectionate husband and brother, a tender parent and a sincere friend; his conduct was marked by integrity, disinterestedness and liberality in all his transactions. He was the benefactor of the poor and the cheerful contributor to every charitable purpose during a residence of fourteen years at Gorakhpur, where his numerous acts of kindness and benevolence ensured to him while living the affection of his friends, and to his memory the regret of his survivors.		

...	Ditto ...	Do. ...	Tomb of James Armstrong, C.S., died 1835.	To the memory of James Armstrong, Magistrate and Collector of Gorakhpur, who departed this life on the 10th September 1835, aged 37 years. This tablet is erected by the residents of the station in token of their esteem for the many virtues which adorned his character.		
...	Ditto ...	Do. ...	Tablet in memory of Eliza Stainforth, died 1835.	This tablet is placed here in sorrowful and affectionate remembrance of Eliza, wife of Frederick Stainforth, Esq., C. S., and daughter of John Thornton, Esq., who, after a residence of 3 years at this place, died at Allahabad on the 30th December 1835 in the 27th year of her age. The following words are inscribed in willing compliance with her dying request :— Them which sleep in Jesus will God bring with him.		
...	Ditto ..	Gorakhpur	Tomb of George Sym, died 1833.	This tablet is erected to the memory of George Sym, Esq., sixth son of James Sym, Esq., of Glasgow: whose uprightness, gentleness and meekness gained him the respect and affection of his friends and associates, while his even and kind temper and high principles conciliated the regard of the natives; his early and sudden death was deeply regretted by all who knew him. He died at Gorakhpur on the 10th December 1833 in the 21st year of his age. All flesh is as grass, and the goodliness thereof is as the flower of the field; but the mercy of the Lord is from everlasting to everlasting upon them that fear him.—*Psalm CIII*, 17.		
...	Ditto ..	Do. ...	Tomb of Agabel Clark, died 1826.	This tablet is erected in memory of Agabel Clark, sister to the Civil Surgeon of Gorakhpur, who closed her short and exemplary life in humble dependence on the blood and righteousness of the Redeemer for acceptance before God, July 25th, 1826, aged 19 years 5 months. In the Lord put I my trust, for we which have believed do enter into rest. Happy the soul who loves the Lord, And makes His grace their only trust.		
...	Ditto ...	Do. ...	Tomb of J. W. Grant, died 1815.	Sacred to the memory of J. W. Grant, Esq., late Collector of Gorakhpur, who departed this life on the 1st November 1815, aged 34 years.		

List of Christian Tombs or Monuments in the Gorakhpur Division possessing historical or archæological interest.—(continued).

Serial number.	Name of cemetery, churchyard, or church.	Where situated (giving exact situation as far as possible).	District.	Tomb or Monument to the memory of—	Inscription on Tomb or Monument.	Inscription on slabs or pillars placed in churches or chapels.	Remarks. Tombs on road-sides, or battle-fields (furnishing information as in columns 3, 4, 5 and 6.)
1	2	3	4	5	6	7	8
881	Gorakhpur Cemetery.	South-east corner of Gorakhpur cantonment.	Gorakhpur	Tomb of Mrs. Jane Grant Bird, died 1821.	Here reposeth all that is perishable of Jane Grant, daughter of the Rev. D. Brown, and wife of Robert G. Bird, Esq., C. S., who fell asleep in Christ on the 6th September 1821. *Neta* 22nd August 1792; *Nupta* 21st September 1810.		
882	Ditto ...	Ditto ...	Do. ...	Tomb of Captain A. M. Rowland, died 1817.	To the memory of Captain A. M. Rowland, 17th N. I., died 9th August 1817, aged 34 years.		
883	Ditto ...	Ditto ...	Do. ...	Tomb of Philip Monckton, died 1820.	Sacred to the memory of Philip Mounckton, Judge and Magistrate of Gorakhpur, died on 6th January A. D. 1820, aged 33 years.		
884	Pitto ...	Ditto ...	Do. ...	Tomb of the Rev. F. Wybrow, died 1840.	Sacred to the memory of the Rev. Frederick Wybrow, of the C. M. S., who died after 10 days of severe suffering on the 19th of December 1840, aged 36 years. This tablet is erected by his sorrowing widow in remembrance of the most affectionate of husbands and most faithful of ministers.		
885	Ditto ...	Ditto ...	Do. ...	Tomb of Mrs. Susannah Currie, died 1832.	This tablet is inscribed in memory of Susannah, eldest daughter of J. P. Larkins, C. S., wife of Fred. Currie, Judge of Gorakhpur, born 10th November 1802, married 7th August 1820, who departed this life on the 14th January 1832. In sure faith in the atonement of Jesus and humble dependence for pardon and acceptance on His merits, resigned her spirit into the hands of God her Father. Them which sleep in Jesus will God bring with Him.		

386	Ditto ...	Ditto ...	Do. ...	Tomb of Mrs. L. E. Currie, died 1835.	In memory of Lucy Elizabeth, daughter of R. M. Bird, Esq., C. S., and Jane Grant, his wife, and wife of F. Currie, Esq., C. S., born 19th September 1811, died 25th July 1835. She walked with God and God took her.		
387	Ditto ...	Ditto ...	Do. ...	Tomb of Lieutenant J. Nunn, died 1832.	Sacred to the memory of Lieutenant J. Nunn, 7th N. I., died 8th October 1832, aged 29 years.		
388	St. Thomas' Church, south of Collector's Court, Gorakhpur.	On Church wall.	Do. ...	Tablet to the memory of William Peppe, died 1889.	...	In memory of William Peppe, son of George Peppe, died 19th July 1859. He rendered valuable services during the troubled times of the Indian Mutiny, which Government rewarded by a grant of land in this district.	Note.—Mr. Peppe died on his passage to (or from) England in the Red Sea, where he was buried.
389			Basti ...	Tomb of Captain W. A. F. Thompson, died 1858.			(3) Near a mango grove on the north side of Mr. Churcher's house between the Civil Station and Old Basti stands a masonry tomb of Captain W. A. F. Thompson, who died 1858. (5) Sacred to the memory of Captain W. A. F. Thompson, 5th Native Infantry, died at Basti, 1858.
390	...	...	Do. ...	Tomb of Captain A. Gifford, and Trooper Adrian Curran, killed 1858.			(3) In a mango grove at mauza Mali Maniha, near the road bungalow at Domariaganj, stands a masonry tomb of Captain Arthur Gifford and Trooper Adrian Curran, Bombay Army, killed in 1858. (5) Sacred to the memory of Captain Arthur Gifford, Bombay Army, Second in Command, B.Y.C., and Trooper Adrian Curran, B.Y.C., who were killed in action with the mutineers near Domariaganj, 27th November 1858.

List of Christian Tombs or Monuments in the Gorakhpur Division possessing historical or archæological interest—(continued).

Where situated (giving exact situation as far as possible).	District.	Tomb or Monument to the memory of—	Inscription on Tomb or Monument.	Inscription on slabs or pillars placed in churches or chapels.	Remarks. Tombs on Roadsides, or Battlefields (furnishing information as in columns 3, 4, 5 and 6).
3	4	5	6	7	8
...	Basti ...	Tomb of Lieutenant H.B. Troup, died 1858.			(3) At mauza Jatipur in pargana Amorha of tahsil Harraiya, situated on the north side of the Gorakhpur-Basti-Fyzabad road, opposite the 4th furlong of mile 65, stands a masonry tomb of Lieutenant Hugh Bedford Troup, who died 1858. (5) To the memory of Hugh Bedford Troup, Lieutenant, Bengal Army, son of Colonel R. Troup, who died of wounds received in action with the rebels on the 17th April 1858. Born 5th February 1836.
	Azamgarh.	Monument to the memory of Captain W. H. Jones, and 11 men of the 13th Regiment who fell at the relief of Azamgarh, 1858.			(3) At the south-east corner of the Public Gardens, Azamgarh, stands a monument erected to the memory of Captain W. H. Jones and 11 men of the 1st Battalion, 13th Light Infantry, who were killed or died of wounds in 1858, with the following inscription :— (5) In memory of Captain Wilson H. Jones and Privates William Brown, William Claybyn, Thomas Collins, Patrick Connell, George Staywell, John Stewart, Thomas Wilson, Edward Crawford, Robert Smith, John Sutton, George Amos, 1st Battalion, 13th Light Infantry. All were killed or died of wounds received in action at the relief of Azamgarh on the 6th April 1858.

393	...		Do. ...	Tomb of Captain W. H. Jones, killed 1858.			(3) In the same enclosure stands the tomb of Captain Wilson Henry Jones, bearing the following inscription :— (5) Sacred to the memory of Wilson Henry Jones, Captain, H. M.'s 13th Light Infantry, third son of Wilson Jones, Esq., of Hartsheath, Flintshire, North Wales. Killed in action at Azamgarh, the 6th April 1858, aged 27 years.
394	...		Do. ...	Tomb of Edward Bury, died 1824.			(3) On the same spot stands the tomb of Edward Bury, Esq., died 1824. (5) Sacred to the memory of Edward Bury, Esq., of the Bengal Civil Establishment, born at Nazing in Essex, and died at Azamgarh on the 11th November 1824, aged 27 years.
395	...	...	Do. ...	Tomb of Thomas Newal, died 1858.	-		(3) The same enclosure contains a tomb of Thomas Newal, Royal Artillery, died 1858. (5) To the memory of Thomas Newal, Royal Artillery, died April 21st, 1858, aged 23 years.
396	Trinity Church, Azamgarh.	South-west corner of the nave.	Ditto ...	Tablet to the memory of Edward Frederick Venables, killed in 1858.		Sacred to the memory of Edward Frederick Venables, Esq., of Deoriaghat near Azamgarh, who, though not in the service of Government, upheld its authority in this district during a time of trial and difficulty, with equal valour, ability and prudence, and after attaining the highest personal distinction, fell in the gallant discharge of his duty, leaving a name dear both to his own countrymen and to the loyal portion of the native community, by whose joint subscriptions this monument is erected.	NOTE.—Mr. Venables, an indigo planter, had by his unflinching daring saved the district of Azamgarh in June 1857, when its natural guardians had withdrawn from it. Subsequently he had struggled bravely against the invaders from Oudh, and had ridden with Brigadier-General Franks as a volunteer in his glorious march from the eastern frontier of Oudh to Lucknow. Withdrawing thence to Allahabad, "broken in health and spirits, anxious for rest, looking forward eagerly to his return to England," he was persuaded by Lord Canning to return to Azamgarh, once again seriously threatened. It was in the performance of the great services he then rendered to the gallant Lord Mark Kerr and to Sir E. Lugard, inspired by the highest sense of duty that, on the 15th April, he was struck down. The wound was mortal. A few days afterwards death, resulting from the wound, cut short the sufferings and belied the hopes of this brave, self-denying gentleman, one among many such who in those days of sharp trial proved their right to be held in equal honor with the best rewarded officers of the East India Company and the Crown.
397	Old Cemetery, Azamgarh.	In the middle of the cemetery.	Ditto ...	Tomb of Edward Frederick Venables, Esq., killed 1858.	Sacred to the memory of Edward Frederick Venables, Esq., of Deoriaghat, near Azamgarh, who, though not in the service of Government, upheld its authority in this district during a time of trial and difficulty, with equal valour, ability and prudence, and after		

List of Christian Tombs or Monuments in the Gorakhpur Division possessing historical or archæological interest—(concluded).

[Ser]ial [N]umber.	Name of Cemetery, Churchyard or Church.	Where situated (giving exact situation as far as possible).	District.	Tomb or Monument to the memory of—	Inscription on Tomb or Monument.	Inscription on slabs or pillars placed in churches or chapels.	Remarks. Tombs on road-sides or battle fields (furnishing information as in columns 3, 4, 5 and 6).
1	2	3	4	5	6	7	8
397	Old Cemetery, Azamgarh.	In the middle of the Cemetery.	Azamgarh.	Tomb of Edward Frederick Venable, Esq., died 1858.	attaining the highest personal distinction, fell in the gallant discharge of his duty, leaving a name dear both to his own countrymen and to the loyal portion of the native community, by whose joint subscriptions this monument is erected.		
398	Ditto ...		Ditto ...	Tomb of Captain Adoniah Smith, died 1829.	Sacred to the memory of Captain Adoniah Smith, late 50th Regiment N. I., who departed this life on the 10th January 1829, aged 38 years. This tomb is erected by the brother-officers of the deceased as a small token of their high esteem and regard which, during his life, he so deservedly merited.		
399	Ditto ...		Ditto ...	Tomb of Gerras Leigh, died 1830.	Sacred to the memory of Gerras Leigh, Esq., who departed this life on the 24th March 1838, aged 40 years.		
400	Ditto ...		Ditto ...	Tomb of Jane Clarke, died 1821.	Sacred to the memory of Jane, eldest daughter of J. H. Clarke, Esq., who departed this life the 13th May 1831, in her 31st year.		
401	Ditto ...		Ditto ...	Tomb of A. Gordon, died 1841.	In remembrance of Alexander Gordon, who died at Azamgarh on the 5th December 1841, aged 22 years. Erected by a small circle of friends, amongst whom he was most sincerely esteemed, and his early death deeply regretted. Better is the memory engraved on warm hearts, Than what the steel can plough on cold earth.		

402	In a mango grove, near the old Cantonments, Azamgarh.		Ditto ...	Tomb of Mrs. Sarah Ammaun.	Sacred to the memory of Mrs. Sarah Ammaun and her stillborn son, who departed this life on the 29th June 1820. Just fifteen years she was a maid, And scarce eleven months a wife ; Four days and nights in labour laid, Brought forth, and then gave up her life. Ah! loveliest of beauties! Whither art thou flown ? Thy soul which knew no guile, Is sure to heaven gone, Leaving thy friends and thy kindred, Thy sad exit to mourn.		

List of Christian Tombs or Monuments in the Kumaun Division possessing historical or archæological interest.

Serial number.	Name of cemetery, churchyard or church.	Where situated (giving exact situation as far as possible).	District.	Tomb or Monument to the memory of—	Inscription on Tomb or Monument.	Inscription on slabs or pillars placed in churches or chapels.	Remarks. Tombs on road-sides or battle-fields (furnishing information as in columns 3, 4, 5 and 6).
1	2	3	4	5	6	7	8
403	Church of St. John in the Wilderness, Naini Tal.	Above the altar. On east wall, south side of altar.	Naini Tal	Brass tablets in memory of the persons who perished in the great landslip at Naini Tal, 18th September 1880.		To the glory of God and those who perished in the great landslip, 18th September 1880. They died according to the word of the Lord and he buried them in this valley. Lester, Lance Corporal, 1st Battalion, 25th Regiment. McEwan, Sergeant Instructor, 92nd Regiment and Naini Tal Volunteer Corps. C. Morgan, Clerk, Government Secretariat, North-Western Provinces and Oudh. E. Morgan, Municipal Road Overseer, late 89th Regiment. Martin Murphy, Major, 40th Regiment. Isabell Murphy, wife of last-named. E. Moss, Assistant to W. Bell. G. H. Carden Noad, Esq., North-Western Provinces and Oudh Police. Revd. A. Robinson, M.A., Senior Chaplain, Bengal Establishment. R. S. P. Robinson, Second-Lieutenant, 33rd Regiment. R. I. Rogers, Sergeant-Major, 1st Battalion, 25th Regiment. A. Shiels. C. Shiels. I. W. Shiels, Plate-layer, East Indian Railway. T. W. Shiels J. E. H. Sullivan, Lieutenant, 73rd Regiment. F. S. Taylor, Brevet. Colonel, Royal Engineers. Leonard Taylor, Esq., Bengal Civil Service. W. F. Tucker, Clerk, Government Secretariat, North-Western Provinces and Oudh. Sarah Kate, wife of H. F. Turnbull, Captain, 40th Regiment.	

	On east wall, north side of altar.				Turner, Private, 73rd Regiment. Archibald Balderston, Captain, 34th Regiment. W. Bell, Merchant, and Captain, Naini Tal Volunteer Rifle Corps. Brown, Private, 73rd Regiment. J. B. H. Carmichael, Second-Lieutenant, 33rd Regiment. Chisholme, Private, 73rd Regiment. James Drew, Assistant to W. Bell. Farrance, Private, 13th Hussars. Infant son of Mr. Francis. Flood, Sergeant, 33rd Regiment. Talbot Goodridge, Captain, Bengal Staff Corps. W. S. Gray, Assistant to W. Bell. Grover, Sergeant, 33rd Regiment. C. J. L. Halket, Second-Lieutenant, 73rd Regiment. J. B. Hannah, M.B., Surgeon-Major, Army Medical Department. Hayes, Private, 33rd Regiment. H. S. F. Haynes, Captain, Royal Engineers. Helmuth, Private, 2nd Battalion, 6th Regiment. Kennedy, Private, 73rd Regiment. G. A. Knight, Assistant to W. Bell. Infant daughter of G. A. Knight.	
Ditto ...	In south transept on west wall.	Ditto ...	Tablet in memory of the officers and men of the Naini Tal Volunteer Rifle Corps, killed by the landslip of 1880.		In memory of— Captain W. Bell, Sergeant G. A. Knight. Volunteer G. H. C. Noad. " J Drew. " E. T. Mors. " C. Morgan. " A. Shiels, " T. Shiels, " C. Shiels, Sergeant-Instructor A. McEwan of the Naini Tal Volunteer Rifle Corps, who were killed by the landslip on the 18th September 1880. This is erected by their comrades.	
	Ditto ...	Ditto ..	Tablet in memory of Dr. J. Barlow Hannah, killed in the great landslip of 1880.		Sacred to the memory of John Barlow Hannah, A. M. D, Staff Surgeon, Allahabad, who was killed in the great landslip at Naini Tal, while nobly endeavouring to save life, 18th September 1880. This tablet is erected as a token of love and respect by his widow.	

List of Christian Tombs or Monuments in the Kumaun Division possessing historical or archæological interest—(concluded).

Serial Number.	Name of Cemetery, Churchyard, or Church.	Where situated (giving exact situation as far as possible).	District.	Tomb or Monument to the memory of—	Inscription on Tomb or Monument.	Inscription on slabs or pillars placed in churches or chapels.	Remarks. Tombs on roadsides, or battlefields (furnishing information as in columns 3, 4, 5 and 6).
1	2	3	4	5	6	7	8
406	Church of St. John in the Wilderness, Naini Tal.	In north transept on north wall.	Naini Tal	Tablet in memory of Thomas Maiston Francis, killed by the landslip of 1880.		In loving remembrance of Edward Maiston Francis, the dearly loved son of Thomas Maiston and Maria Eyre Francis, killed by a landslip at Naini Tal on the 18th September 1880. Aged 1 year and 11 months. Also in memory of Martha, A faithful native Christian servant, who perished with the child in her arms.	
407	Ditto ...	On a brass let in to the windowsill, north side of chancel.	Do. ...	Tablet in memory of Colonel F. S. Taylor, R. E., killed by the landslip of 1880.		In memory of Frederick Sherwood Taylor, Colonel, R. E., Consulting Engineer for Railways to the Government of India. Born, November 10th, 1828, over whelm- ed by the landslip in this place, September 18th, 1880.	
408			Do. ...	Enclosure surrounding the burial-place of six or eight privates of the 42nd Highlanders, killed in action at Melaghat, 1858.			(S) At Melaghat on the banks of the western branch of the Sarda in the Naini Tal district is an enclosure containing the graves of six or eight privates (believed to have belonged to the 42nd Highlanders), who were killed in action in November or December 1858. There is no inscription on any of the graves nor over the enclosure.
409		On the top of Sitoli hill near Almora.	Almora	Monument to the memory of Lieutenants Kirk and Tapley, killed in the Gurkha War of 1815.		Sacred to the memory of Lieutenants Kirk and Tapley, of the 2nd Battalion, 27th Regiment, Native Infantry. The latter was killed on the evening of the 26th April 1815 on duty at an advanced post in the town of Almora. The former died on the 16th of May following, a victim to zealous and continued exertion in the final operations of the campaign.	NOTE.—In 1815, Lord Hastings, the Governor-General of India, determined to carry the Gurkha War into the Nepalese province of Kumaun, which was untouched by the former hostilities and was almost unoccupied by the enemy. Being short of troops, he raised levies among the Rohillas and selected two officers to command them, Colonel W. L. Gardiner (see entry No. 94) and Major Hyder Young Hearsey, who, previous to 1802, had served in the Maratha forces. These irregular bodies of troops

Tomb of Mrs. M. Lushington, died 1839.	Sacred to the memory of Marianne, the beloved wife of George Lushington, B.C. S., who departed this life on the 16th day of February 1839, after giving birth to a son stillborn, aged 30 years. He that loveth not knoweth not God, for God is love. Blessed are the dead which die in the Lord.

List of Christian Tombs or Monuments in the Lucknow Division possessing historical or archæological interest.

…	Where situated (giving exact situation as far as possible).	District.	Tomb or Monument to the memory of—	Inscription on Tomb or Monument.	Inscription on slabs or pillars placed in churches or chapels.	Remarks. Tombs on road-sides, or battle-fields (furnishing information as in columns 3, 4, 5 and 6).
	3	4	5	6	7	8
…es- …no- …ck-	Near Aminabad, in mohalla "Fakir Muhammad Khan-ka-Hata," also known as "Kalan-ki-lat."	Lucknow,	Tomb of Colonel John Collins, died 1807.	In memory of Colonel John Collins, Resident at the Court of Lucknow, 1806-7, died 11th June 1807.		NOTE.—Colonel Collins was a distinguished and popular officer, who had previously been Resident with Daulat Rao Sindhia; and it was to this officer that Vazir Ali, of Benares notoriety, surrendered on the 1st December 1799 at Jaypur, at which place he had taken refuge after the murder of Mr. Cherry (see entry No. 221). On his death the following Gazette Extraordinary was issued by the Governor-General on the 18th June 1807: "* * * The public and private virtues which distinguished the character of the late Colonel Collins and his long and eminent public services have rendered his decease a subject of deep regret and concern to the Governor-General in Council; and have placed the late Colonel Collins among the number of those esteemed and lamented officers whose abilities and exertions have contributed to the honor and prosperity of the British Government in India; and whose memory is endeared to it by the obligations of public respect, public gratitude and public applause * * *".
…	Ditto …	Ditto …	Tomb of F. F. Ricketts, died 1827.	Frederick Fitzgerald, son of Mordaunt and Charlotte Ricketts, born 10th October 1827, died 8th March 1828. I shall go to him, but he shall not return to me.		
…	Ditto …	Ditto …	Tomb of Lieutenant Charles V. Wylde, died 1828.	Sacred to the memory of Charles Vincent Wylde, Lieutenant and Adjutant, 14th Regiment, Bengal Native Infantry, born 14th February 1798, died 19th October 1828. This tomb was erected by the officers of his regiment to commemorate their esteem for him whilst alive, and their regret at his early death.		
…	Ditto …	Ditto …	Tomb of Mrs. Sophia Patton, died 1831.	Sacred to the memory of Mrs. Sophia Patton, who departed this life on the 3rd of November 1831, deeply regretted.		

415	Ditto ...	Ditto ...	Ditto ...	Tomb of Mrs. Sarah Moore, died 1835.	Sacred to the memory of Sarah, the beloved wife of Lieutenant-Colonel George Moore, 59th Regiment, Native Infantry, who departed this life the 23rd December 1835, aged 31 years.		
416	Ditto ...	Ditto ...	Ditto ...	Tomb of Mrs. L. F. Monteith, died 1837.	Sacred to the memory of Lucinda Florence, the lady of Lieutenant-Colonel Monteith, 35th Regiment, who died at Lucknow on the 2nd of September 1837.		
417	Ditto ...	Ditto ...	Ditto ...	Tomb of Mrs. M. E. Mercer, died 1845.	To the memory of Maria Caroline, the beloved wife of T. W. Mercer, Esq., 46th Regiment, Bengal Native Infantry. She was born on the 7th November 1826, married 7th November 1841, and departed this life 7th November 1845, aged 19 years. To thee, dear Lord, my flesh and soul I joyfully resign; Blessed Jesus, take me for thine own, for I am doubly thine; "For our light affliction which is but for a moment, worketh for us a far more exceeding and eternal weight of glory."		
418	Ditto ..	Ditto ...	Ditto ...	Tomb of Colonel J. Wilcox, astronomer to the Court of Oudh, died 1847.			NOTE.—The inscription tablet was despoiled in the Mutiny.
419	Residency Cemetery, Lucknow.	Inside the Residency enclosure.	Ditto ...	Tomb of Sir Henry Montgomery Lawrence, died 1857.	Here lies Henry Lawrence, who tried to do his duty. May the Lord have mercy on his soul. Born 28th June 1806, died 4th July 1857.		NOTE.—In one of the upper rooms of the Residency building there is a small stone tablet bearing the following inscription:— "In this room Sir H. Lawrence was wounded by a piece of shell on the 2nd July 1857." And in a room in Dr. Fayrer's house in the Residency enclosure there is another small tablet with the following inscription— "Here Sir H. Lawrence died, 4th July 1857." Sir Henry Lawrence was one of those rare characters which it is difficult to overpraise. The adjective "noble" expresses most nearly what he was. His thoughts and his deeds were alike noble. The nobleness of his nature, the honesty of his mind, his unqualified love of justice, displayed themselves in his every act. He was just to others because he was true to himself. Than his, it is difficult to imagine a purer, a more unselfish, a more blameless, and at the same time a more useful life. Great as were his services to his country, those he rendered to mankind were still greater. The establishment of the Lawrence Military Asylum

List of Christian Tombs or Monuments in the Lucknow Division possessing historical or archæological interest—(continued).

Serial number.	Name of Cemetery, Churchyard or Church.	Where situated (giving exact situation as far as possible.	District.	Tomb or Monument to the memory of—	Inscription on Tomb or Monument.	Inscription on slabs or pillars placed in churches or chapels.	Remarks. Tombs on roadsides or battlefields (furnishing information as in columns 3, 4, 5 and 6).
1	2	3	4	5	6	7	8
419	Residency Cemetery Lucknow.	Inside the Residency enclosure.	Lucknow,				at Sanawar, an institution which provides, in the healthy mountainous ranges of the Himalayas, food, lodging and instruction for the children of our European soldiers, was not the least important of those services. To it Sir Henry gave his time, his savings, the energies he could spare from his duties. The credit of the successful defence of the Lucknow Residency is due in the first place to Sir Henry Lawrence. He alone made it possible to successfully defend it. In a word, he devoted all his energies without reserve to the country he served so well. That Sir Henry felt to the last the inner conviction that he had so given himself wholly and without stint, is evidenced by the expression of his dying wish that, if any epitaph were placed on his tomb it should be simply this: "Here lies Henry Lawrence, who tried to do his duty." See entry No. 521.
420	Ditto ...	Ditto ...	Ditto ...	Monument to the memory of Brigadier-General J.G.S. Neill, C.B., and several officers and men of the First Madras Fusiliers, who fell during 1857-58.	Sacred to the memory of Brigadier-General J. G. S. Neill, C.B., and A.-D.-C. to the Queen. Lieutenant-Colonel J. L. Stephenson, C. B., Major G. C. S. Renaud. Lieutenant W. J. Groom. " W. B. Arnold. " J. A. Richardson. " F. Dobbs. 352 non-commissioned officers, drummers and rank and file of the First Madras Fusiliers, who fell during the suppression of the Rebellion in Bengal, 1857-58. This monument is erected over the remains of the late Brigadier-General Neill by the surviving officers of the regiment, as a mark of esteem for their late comrades, and in remembrance of their noble example and glorious deeds.		NOTE.—Near the Government Telegraph Office there is an old Nawábi Gateway which has been preserved, and is known as Neill's Gate. About 60 yards north of this gate stands a pillar bearing the following inscription:—"*Dulce et decorum est pro patria mori.* This tablet marks the spot where, towards the evening of the 25th September 1857 A. D., General Neill fell mortally wounded by a shot fired from the top of the adjacent gateway." Neill was a very remarkable man. He stands in the very front rank of those to whom the Indian Mutiny gave an opportunity of distinction. Not only did he succeed in everything he undertook, but he succeeded when the cases were all but desperate. He succeeded because he dared; because he threw into all he attempted the energy of one of the most determined characters ever bestowed on man. Such a man could not fail and live. His whole soul was in his profession. He made his regiment, the Madras Fusiliers, equal to any regiment in the world. He was a born warrior, very cool, very keen-sighted and very determined.

481	Ditto ...	Ditto ...	Ditto ...	Monument to the memory of the officers, non-commissioned officers and privates of Her Majesty's 90th Light Infantry, who fell during the Indian Rebellion of 1857-58.	This monument is erected by the officers of Her Majesty's 90th Light Infantry in memory of their comrades who fell during the Indian Rebellion of 1857 and 1858, and as a tribute to their gallantry:—Colonel Robert P. Campbell, C.B., died of his wounds at Lucknow, 12th November 1857, Major Roger Barnster, died of his wounds at Cawnpore, 23rd December 1857, Brevet Major James Perrin, died of his wounds at Alum Bagh, 30th September 1857, Captain Harry Denison, died of his wounds at Lucknow, 29th October 1857, Lieutenant Nicol Graham, killed in action at Alum Bagh, 23rd September 1857, Lieutenant John Joshua Nunn, killed in action at Alum Bagh, 24th September 1857, Lieutenant Arthur Moultrie, killed in action at Lucknow, 26th September 1857, Lieutenant W. H. L. Carleton, died of small-pox at Lucknow, 19th April 1858, Lieutenant R. D. Synge, died of consumption at Lucknow, 8th September 1858, Lieutenant N. Preston, died of his wounds at Alum Bagh, 27th September 1857, Ensign Arthur Chute, died of dysentery at Calcutta, 23rd February 1858, Ensign Hugh Gordon, died of *coup de soleil* at Lucknow, 26th May 1858, Assistant Surgeon R. Nelson, died of fever, 18th August 1857. Also to the memory of 271 non-commissioned officers and privates of the regiment, who fell in the gallant performance of their duty at the Relief, the Defence and the Capture of Lucknow and during the subsequent campaign in Oudh.		
482	Ditto ...	Ditto ...	Ditto ...	Monument to the memory of the officers, non-commissioned officers and privates of the 84th York and Lancaster Regi-	To the memory of Lieutenant-Colonel C. Seymour, Captain E. Currie, Captain R. Pakenham, Lieutenant B. Sandwith, Lieutenant F. Saunders, Lieutenant H. Ayton, Lieutenant P. Chute, Lieutenant A. Gibaut, Lieutenant W. Poole, Lieutenant		

List of Christian Tombs or Monuments in the Lucknow Division possessing historical or archæological interest—(continued).

Serial number	Name of cemetery, churchyard or church.	Where situated (giving exact situation as far as possible).	District.	Tomb or Monument to the memory of—	Inscription on Tomb or Monument.	Inscription of slabs or pillars placed in churches or chapels.	Remarks. Tombs on roadsides or battlefields (furnishing information as in columns 3, 4, 5, and 6).
1	2	3	4	5	6	7	8
482	Residency cemetery Lucknow.	Inside the Residency enclosure.	Lucknow ...	ment, who fell during the Indian Mutiny campaign of 1857-58.	R. Maybury, Ensign H. Kenny, Paymaster G. Eddy, Quartermaster H. Donelan, and 360 non-commissioned officers and privates of the 84th York and Lancaster Regiment, who were killed, died of their wounds or of disease, during the Indian Mutiny campaign, nobly performing their duty. To record the devotion, gallantry and true discipline displayed by the above at all times and on all occasions, this monument is erected by the officers of the regiment.		
483	Ditto ...	Ditto ...	Ditto ...	Monument to the memory of the officers, non-commissioned officers and privates of Her Majesty's 5th Fusiliers, who lost their lives during the Mutiny campaign of 1857 58.	Sacred to the memory of Major J. E. Simmons, Captain J. W. L'Estrange, Captain A. E. Johnson, Captain W. M. Carter, Lieutenant E. J. Haig, Lieutenant J. C Brown, 5 Sergeants, 2 Corporals, and 77 privates of Her Majesty's 5th Fusiliers, who lost their lives in the advance upon Lucknow under General Havelock, during the defence of the Residency under Sir J. Outram, G.C.B, during the subsequent operations at the Alum Bagh and at the final capture of Lucknow. This monument is erectd by the officers of the regiment, now in India, December 1st, 1858.		
484	Ditto ...	Ditto ...	Ditto ...	Monument to the memory of the officers of the 13th Regiment, Native Infantry, who fell during the defence of Lucknow in 1857.	Sacred to the memory of Major C. F. Bruere, Captain R. B. Francis, Lieutenant G. W. Green, Ensign R. L. Inglis of the Hon'ble East India Company's 13th Regiment Native Infantry, who fell whilst serving with their Regiment in the defence of Lucknow in 1857.		

			Also of Captain A. M. Turnbull, who died in the Cawnpore entrenchment and Lieutenant E. W. Barwell, killed at Hissar. This monument is erected by their brother-officers as a testimony of the respect and affection with which they cherish their memory.		
...	Ditto ...	Tomb of Major J. Banks, died 1857.	Near this spot is interred the remains of John Sherbrooke Banks, Major of the 33rd Regiment N. I., who fell at Lucknow on the 21st July 1857. I shall go to ; but he will not return to him.		
...	Ditto ...	Tomb of M. C. Ommaney, C.S., died 1857.	Sacred to the memory of Manaton Collingwood Ommaney, Esq., for 26 years in the Bengal Civil Service, the sixth son of Sir F. M. Ommaney, Kt., and Georgiana Frances, his wife. He was born March 19th, 1813, and died July 8th, 1857, from the effects of a round shot during the memorable defence of Lucknow in the Province of Oudh, of which he was Judicial Commissioner, leaving a widow and six children to sorrow, not without hope, for the one thus suddenly cut off in his career of Christian integrity, benevolence and usefulness, beloved by themselves and esteemed by all who knew him. The righteous are taken away from the evil to come.—*Isaiah, LVII—1.*		*Note.*—See entry No. 353.
...	Ditto ...	Tomb of Captain G. W. W. Fulton, killed 1857.	Sacred to the memory of Captain G. W. W. Fulton, Bengal Engineers, who was killed in the Residency during the siege of Lucknow on the 14th September 1857, aged 32 years.		
...	Ditto ...	Monument to the memory of the officers of the Bengal Artillery, who died during the defence of the Lucknow Residency, 1857.	To the memory of Captain A. P. Simons, Lieutenant D. C. Alexander, Lieutenant E. P. Lewin, Lieutenant J. H. Bryce, Lieutenant F. J. Cunliffe, officers of the Bengal Artillery, who died of wounds, disease and exposure while defending the Residency, Lucknow, during the memorable months of July, August and September 1857. Erected by their brother-officers who survived the siege.		

Tomb of Colonel W. H. Kalford, died 1857.	In memory of William Hamilton Halford, Colonel Commanding 71st Regiment, Bengal Native Infantry, who died at Lucknow, 27th July 1857, from the effects of the siege. This monument is erected by his bereaved widow.
Tomb of Captain J. S. Shepherd, killed 1857.	Sacred to the memory of Captain James S. Shepherd, 7th Bengal Light Cavalry, who was killed during the defence of the Lucknow Residency on 26th July 1857.
Tomb of Captain C. W. Radcliffe, died 1857.	Sacred to the memory of Captain Charles Wilbraham Radcliffe, 7th Light Cavalry, who died from the effects of his wounds on the 25th September 1857, aged 35 years. Erected by his only son, Captain A. W. T. Radcliffe, 14th Sikhs.
Tomb of Captain J. F. Cosserat, died 1858.	Here lie the remains of Captain J. F. Cosserat, 34th Madras Light Infantry, who died of his wounds, 10th April 1858, aged 32. A tribute of affection from the officers of his regiment to the memory of a brave and beloved comrade.
Tomb of Captain A. Becher, died 1857.	In memory of Andrew Becher, Captain, 40th Native Infantry, who died in the Residency of wounds received in Havelock's advance, whilst serving with Her Majesty's 90th Regiment.

434	Ditto ...	Ditto ...	Ditto ...	Tomb of Captain F. D. Lucas, killed 1857.	In memory of Fitzherbert Dacre Lucas, formerly Captain in the Tipperary Militia Artillery, third son of the Right Hon'ble Edward Lucas of Castle Sha[n]e Monaghan, born in August 1823. Travelling in India when the Mutiny broke out, his services were accepted of as a Volunteer by Sir Henry Lawrence. He fell mortally wounded in the last sortee of the Garrison of Lucknow on the 29th September 1857.		
435	Ditto ...	Ditto ...	Ditto ...	Tomb of Lieutenant A. J. Dashwood, died 1857.	In memory of Alexander John Dashwood, Lieutenant, 48th Regiment, Bengal Native Infantry, who died at Lucknow, July 9th, 1857, aged 27 years. Also of his second on, Herbert John Garrett, who died at eLucknow, August 19th, 1857, aged on year.		
436	Ditto ...	Ditto ...	Ditto ...	Tomb of Lieutenant L. A. Arthur, killed 1857.	In memory of Leonard Augustus Arthur, Lieutenant, 7th Bengal Light Cavalry, who fell while commanding the Cawnpore Battery, 19th July MDCCCLVII.		
437	Ditto ...	Ditto ...	Ditto ...	Tomb of Lieut. E. P. Lewin, killed 1857.	In memory of Lieutenant Edward Powney Lewin, Bengal Artillery, who was killed at his post, the Cawnpore Battery, in the defence of this position, on the 26th of July 1857, aged 24 years 11 months. Also of his daughter, Edith Scot, who died within the Residency entrenchment on the 20th of August 1857, aged one year seven months. Father, I will that they also, whom thou hast given me, be with me.—*St. John*, XVII, 24.		
438	Ditto ...	Ditto ...	Ditto ...	Tomb of Lieut. W. R. Moorson, killed 1858.	In memory of Lieutenant W. R. Moorson, Her Majesty's 52nd Regiment, killed in action near the Iron Bridge, March 11th, 1858. *Fervent in spirit serving the Lord.*		
439	Ditto ...	Ditto ...	Ditto ...	Tomb of Second-Lieut. F. J. Cunliffe, died 1857.	Sacred to the memory of Foster John Cunliffe, 2nd Lieutenant in the Bengal Artillery. Born October 14th, 1834, died September 22nd, 1857.		

List of Christian Tombs or Monuments in the Lucknow Division possessing historical or archæological interest—(continued).

Serial number.	Name of cemetery, churchyard, or church.	Where situated (giving exact situation as far as possible).	District.	Tomb or Monument to the memory of—	Inscription on Tomb or Monument.	Inscription on slabs or pillars placed in churches or chapels.	Remarks. Tombs on Roadsides, or Battlefields (furnishing information as in columns 3, 4, 5 and 6).
1	2	3	4	5	6	7	8
440	Residency Cemetery, Lucknow.	Inside the Residency enclosure.	Lucknow.	Tomb of J. Graham, died 1857.	Sacred to the dear and beloved memory of James Graham, 4th Battalion Light Cavalry, who departed this life during the siege of Lucknow on the 5th September 1857. Also of his two children, Fanny Jane, who died on the 2nd September 1857, aged one year and seven months, and Georgina Mary Louisa, who died on the 27th September 1857, aged one month and four days. And they shall be mine, saith the Lord of hosts, in that day when I make up my jewels.—*Malachi*, iii, 17. This monument is erected by his widow.		
441	Ditto ...	Ditto ...	Ditto ...	Tomb of Colou-Sergeant R. Springate, died 1858.	Sacred to the memory of Colour-Sergeant Richard Springate of Her Majesty's XCth Light Infantry, who departed this life on the 19th of April 1858, aged 36 years and 5 months. Deeply regretted by all who knew him.		
442	Ditto ...	Ditto ...	Ditto ...	Tomb of A. P. Grant, killed 1857.	To the memory of Aldourie Patrick Grant, 71st Native Infantry, killed on duty at Murison in the Mutiny of 1857.		
443	Ditto ...	Ditto ...	Ditto ...	Tomb of J. B. Thornhill, B.C.S., died 1857.	Sacred to the memory of John Bensley Thornhill, Bengal Civil Service, born May 7th, 1832, died from wounds received during the siege of Lucknow, October 12th, 1857. Also of Mary Charlotte Bensley Thornhill, infant daughter of John Bensley and Mary Thornhill, died September 1st, 1857, aged six days.		

					The Lord gave and the Lord hath taken away; blessed be the name of the Lord.		
444	Ditto ...	Ditto ...	Ditto ...	Tomb of Rev. H. S. Polehampton, died 1857.	In memory of Henry Stedman Polehampton, Chaplain of this station, born February 1st, 1824, died July 20th, 1857. Also of Henry Allnutt, his only child, born December 30th, 1856, died January 3rd, 1857. Enter thou into the joy of thy Lord.—*Matthew* xxv, 21.		*Note.*—See also entry No. 530.
445	Ditto ...	Ditto ...	Ditto ...	Tomb of Rev. H. Kirwan, died 1858.	*In Christ.* Revd. Hyacinth Kirwan, Chaplain of the 2nd Division of the Besieging Army, who died at Lucknow, 3rd April 1858. This stone is erected by his friend, Revd. H. Smith, D.D., Chaplain of the Field Hospital.		
446	Ditto ...	Ditto ...	Ditto ...	Tomb of Rev. P. Fairhurst, died 1858.	Pray for the soul of the Revd. Patrick Fairhurst, who, to assist his Catholic Brethren amid the perils of the great Indian Rebellion, left his home and fell a martyr to charity, a victim to hardship and privations on the 16th of June A. D. 1858. The Catholic soldiers of Her Majesty's 53rd Regiment here testify their admiration and gratitude.		
447	Ditto ...	Ditto ...	Ditto ...	Tomb of James Fullerton, died 1857.	In memory of James Fullerton, born in Argyleshire, August 30th, 1833, died in the Residency at Lucknow during the defence, September 15th, 1857, and of his child, Elphinstone Fullerton, born November 28th, 1856, died August 7th, 1857. Looking for that blessed hope, and the glorious appearing of the Great God and our Saviour Jesus Christ.—*Titus*, ii, 13. Erected by his widow and mother.		
448	Ditto ...	Ditto ...	Ditto ...	Tomb of W. Marshall, died 1857.	Sacred to the memory of William Marshall, who died 13th July, 1857, of a wound received while defending Sago's Garrison. Also of his mother-in-law, Anna Sanson, who died within		

List of Christian Tombs or Monuments in the Lucknow Division possessing historical or archæological interest—(continued).

Serial Number.	Name of Cemetery, Churchyard or Church.	Where situated (giving exact situation as far as possible).	District.	Tomb or Monument to the memory of—	Inscription on Tomb or Monument.	Inscription on slabs or pillars placed in churches or chapels.	Remarks. Tombs on road-sides or battle-fields (furnishing information as in columns 3, 4, 5 and 6).
1	2	3	4	5	6	7	8
449	Residency Cemetery, Lucknow.	Inside the Residency enclosure.	Lucknow...		the Residency entrenchment on the 24th October 1857. Enter thou into the joy of thy Lord. This monument is erected by his disconsolate widow and daughter.		
450	Ditto ...	Ditto ...	Ditto ...	Tomb of J. Clancey, killed 1857.	Near this spot are interred the remains of Thomas John Clancey of the Chief Commissioner's office, Lucknow, who was killed during the siege of Lucknow on the 1st of July 1857, aged 28 years and 5 months. I shall go to him, but he will never return to me. This tomb has been erected by his beloved wife, Elizabeth Clancey; and subsequently renewed by his sons John, Charles and Dominic James. *Requiescat in pace.*		
451	Ditto ...	Ditto ...	Ditto ...	Tomb of T. W. Ereth, died 1857.	Sacred to the memory of T. W. Ereth, who died on the 2nd July 1857 from wounds received during the siege, aged 32 years 3 months and 13 days.		
452	Ditto ...	Ditto ...	Ditto ...	Tomb of Mrs. F. E. Hale, died 1857.	Sacred to the memory of Frances Ellen Hale, the beloved wife of George Herbert Hale, Lieutenant-Adjutant, 2nd Oudh Light Infantry, who died in Lucknow Garrison on the morning of the Battle of Chinhut, 1857, aged 20 years. Sacred also to the memory of Kate Caroline Sophia, eldest child of the above, who died in Lucknow Garrison		

					on the 23rd of September 1857. Sacred also to the memory of Henrietta Georgina Frances, her infant child, who died at Seerora, Oudh, on the 16th of April 1857. The Lord is good, a stronghold in the day of trouble; and he knoweth them that trust in him.—*Nahum*, I, 7.		
453	Ditto ...	Ditto ...	Ditto ...	Tomb of Mrs. C. E. Thomas, died 1857.	Sacred to the memory of Cordelia Ellen, the beloved wife of Captain Lancelot F. C. Thomas, Madras Artillery, who died during the siege of Lucknow, 13th July 1857, aged 22 years. Those that seek me early shall find me. *Proverbs*, VIII, 17.		
454	Ditto ...	Ditto ...	Ditto ...	Tomb of Mrs. E. A. Ouseley, died 1857.	Sacred to the memory of Elizabeth Anne, the beloved wife of Ralph Ouseley, Esq., who died at Lucknow on the 14th of November 1857, aged 24 years and 6 months, and of their two children Ralph and Gore, who left them on the 20th of September, 1857. The Lord gave and the Lord hath taken away; blessed be the name of the Lord.		
455	Ditto ...	Ditto ...	Ditto ...	Tomb of Mrs. R. E. Arnow, killed 1857.	Sacred to the memory of Mrs. Rebecca Elizabeth Arnow, who departed this life on the 7th of October A.D. 1857, burnt with a shell ball during the siege, aged 37 years. My great Physician, Thy will be done. Sorrow not, even as others which have no hope. *I. Thess*, IV, 13.		
456	Ditto ...	Ditto ...	Ditto ...	Tomb of Mrs. A. Allnutt, died 1857.	In memory of Ann, wife of Mr. C. D. Allnutt, late Accountant, Delhi Bank, Lucknow, who died during the siege on the 17th August 1857, aged 37 years and 8 months. Also of their infant daughter, Louisa Ellen, died 28th August 1857, aged one month.		
457	Ditto ...	Ditto ...	Ditto ...	Tomb of J. Connell, died 1857.	Sacred to the memory of John Connell, the beloved child of Overseer Andrew Connell and his wife Mary. He died		

List of Christian Tombs or Monuments in the Lucknow Division possessing historical or archæological interest—(continued.

Serial number.	Name of cemetery, churchyard or church.	Where situated (giving exact situation as far as possible).	District.	Tomb or Monument to the memory of—	Inscription on Tomb or Monument.	Inscription on slabs or pillars placed in churches or chapels.	Remarks. Tombs on road-sides or battle-fields (furnishing information as in columns 3, 4, 5 and 6).
1	2	3	4	5	6	7	8
457	Residency Cemetery, Lucknow.	Inside the Residency enclosure.	Lucknow		at Lucknow during the siege on the 4th of November 1857, aged 13 months. God himself will come and will save you. *Isaiah*, XXXV, 4.		
458	Ditto ...	Ditto ...	Ditto ...	Tomb of E. F. Huxham, died 1857.	Sacred to the memory of Ellen Frances, the beloved child of Lieutenant and Mrs. G. C. Huxham, 48th Native Infantry, who died on the 9th August 1857, aged 11½ months, in the Residency during the siege of Lucknow. Of such is the kingdom of heaven.		
459	Ditto ...	Ditto ...	Ditto ...	Tomb of G. E. Boileau, died 1857.	Sacred to the memory of Georgina Emma, child of Major and Mrs. G. W. Boileau, who died on the 18th September 1857 in the Garrison of Lucknow, aged two years and six days.		
460	Ditto ...	Ditto ...	Ditto ...	Tomb of J. R. B. Martin and H. B. Martin, died 1857.	Sacred to the beloved memory of James Ronald Burnard and Henry Burnard, the children of Simon and Mary Martin, who died during the siege of Lucknow, August 1857. Of such is the kingdom of heaven.		
461	Ditto ...	Ditto ...	Ditto ...	Tomb of J. F. Fitzgerald, died 1857.	Sacred to the memory of Justitia Florence, the beloved child of Mr. and Mrs. W. Fitzgerald, died at Lucknow during the siege on the 18th of August 1857, aged 18 months. Of such is the kingdom of God.		

462	Ditto ...	Ditto ...	Ditto ...	Tomb of C. R. J. Morgan, died 1857.	Sacred to the memory of Charles Robert John, the beloved son of Mr. J. J. Morgan, Barrack-Master, Cawnpore, who died at Lucknow during the siege on the 19th July 1857, aged 13 months and 17 days. Of such is the kingdom of heaven.		
463	Ditto ...	Ditto ...	Ditto ...	Tomb of M. H. D. Strangways, died 1857.	Sacred to the memory of Mary Hamilton Dunbar, the beloved child of Captain and Mrs. George Strangways, who died in the Residency during the siege of Lucknow on the 17th July 1857, aged two years and two months. Of such is the kingdom of heaven.		
464	...	In the Residency enclosure, south of the cemetery.	Ditto ...	Monument to the memory of the officers, non-commissioned officers and men of the 78th Highland Regiment, who fell in 1857 and 1858.	Sacred to the memory of the officers, non-commissioned officers and private soldiers of the 78th Highland Regiment, who fell in the suppression of the Mutiny of the Native Army in India in the years 1857 and 1858. This monument is erected as a tribute of respect by their surviving brother-officers and comrades, and by many officers who formerly belonged to the regiment, A. D. 1883.		
465	...	In the Residency enclosure, near the Baillie Guard Gate.	Ditto ...	Monument to the memory of Colonel R. H. M. Aitken, V.C., died 1887.	This monument is erected to the memory of Colonel Robert Hope Moncrieff Aitken, V.C., Bengal Staff Corps, and formerly of the 13th Regiment, Bengal Infantry, by some of his surviving comrades and other friends in token of their appreciation of his sterling worth as a man, and of the splendid gallantry and chivalrous devotion, which he displayed as a soldier in command of this post, which he held with the faithful and loyal remnant of the regiment to which he belonged throughout the defence of the Residency of Lucknow. Born 8th February 1828, died 18th September 1887.		

List of Christian Tombs or Monuments in the Lucknow Division possessing historical or archæological interest.

Serial number.	Name of Cemetery, Churchyard, or Church.	Where situated (giving exact situation as far as possible).	District.	Tomb or Monument to the memory of—	Inscription on Tomb or Monument.	Inscription on slabs or pillars placed in churches or chapels.	Remarks. Tombs on road-sides, or battle-fields (furnishing information as in columns 3, 4, 5 and 6).
1	2	3	4	5	6	7	8
466	...	Lucknow Residency, inside Baillie Guard building (Aitken's Post)	Lucknow,	Tablet to the memory of the Native Officers and men of the 13th Bengal N. I., who fell in 1857.	Erected in memory of the devoted gallantry and fidelity of the Native Officers and Sepoys of the Hon'ble Company's 13th Bengal Native Infantry (*Garud ka Pultan*), who fell during the defence of Lucknow. This monument is erected by the surviving European officers of the regiment in the Baillie Guard Post, which was held by the regiment throughout the defence. Subadar Doondayal Pandey. " Ram Pershad. " Sheo Charan Singh. Jamadar Bhowani Bux, Chawbe. Kalka Tewari. 9 Havildárs. 8 Naiks. 5 Drummers, 24 Sepoys.		
467	...	Residency enclosure, north of Baillie Guard Gate.	Ditto ...	Monument to the memory of the Native Officers and Sepoys who fell in the defence of the Residency, 1857.	To the memory of the Native Officers and Sepoys of the 13th Native Infantry, 41st Native Infantry, the Oudh Irregular Force, Native Pensioners, New Native Levies, Artillery, and Lucknow Magazine, who died near this spot, nobly performing their duty, this column is erected by Lord Northbrook, Viceroy and Governor-General of India, 1875.		*Note.*—On the north, west and south sides are inscriptions in Persian, Urdu and Hindi to the same effect.
468		Inside the Residency enclosure, on a high mound between the Residency building and Banqueting Hall.	Ditto ...	Memorial Cross in memory of Sir H. Lawrence and the men who fell in defence of the Residency.	In memory of Major-General Sir Henry Lawrence, K.C.B., and the brave men who fell in the defence of the Residency, A. D. 1857.		

Inside Residency enclosure, to the south-east of the Residency building.	Ditto ...	Monument to the memory of Major-General Sir John Inglis, K.C.B., died 1862.	*On the north face.*—Sacred to the memory of Major-General Sir John Inglis, K.C.B., Colonel, Her Majesty's 32nd Regiment, who with a handful of devoted men defended the Residency of Lucknow for 87 days, from 3rd July 1857 to 27th September, against an overwhelming force of the enemy. *On the west face.*—Born November 15th, 1814, died at Homberg, Germany, September 27th, 1862. *On the south face.*—This memorial is erected by his surviving comrades and friends, A. D. 1894.	NOTE.—To command a small party defending a weak entrenchment against an overwhelming force, certain sterling qualities are necessary. A man need not be a strategist, or a tactician. But whilst confident in bearing, unyielding in temper, he must be bold, determined and resolute in action. He must likewise possess the valuable quality, the existence of which displays itself in the capacity to weigh correctly the professional opinions of the officers about him. By the testimony of all, Brigadier Inglis fulfilled all these conditions. His daring obstinacy in resisting, his confident mien, his cool courage, gained him the respect and affection of officers and men. For the defence of a weak post with a small force few men were better qualified than Brigadier Inglis, and certainly no one more merited than he the honours and promotion by the bestowal of which a grateful country showed its sense of the eminent service he had rendered.
Inside the Residency enclosure, on the east verandah wall of the Women's Quarters.	Ditto ...	Tablet in memory of S. Palmer, killed 1857.	Susanna Palmer, killed in this room by a cannon ball on the 1st July 1857, in her nineteenth year.	
Ditto, on the south verandah wall of the Women's Quarters.	Ditto ...	Memorial tablet recording the events of the siege and the defence of the Lucknow Residency in 1857	The Right Hon'ble the Earl of Canning, G.C.B., G. C.S.I., Viceroy and Governor-General of India, expressed his admiration of the defence of the Residency of Lucknow in the following words:— "There does not stand recorded in the annals of war an achievement more truly heroic than the defence of the Residency at Lucknow." On 30th June 1857 A.D., the day after the battle of Chinhut, the siege began. On the 2nd July, Sir Henry Lawrence was mortally wounded by a shell which burst within the Residency building. The command then devolved on Brigadier J. E. W. Inglis, Her Majesty's 32nd Regiment. The force within the defences then consisted of 130 officers, British and Native, 740 British and 700 native troops, and 150 Civilian Volunteers. There were 237 women, 260 children, 50 boys of La Martiniere College, 27 non-combatant Europeans, and 700 non-combatant Natives, being a total of 2,994 souls.	

List of Christian Tombs or Monuments in the Lucknow Division possessing historical or archæological interest—(continued).

Serial number.	Name of cemetery, churchyard, or church.	Where situated (giving exact situation as far as possible).	District.	Tomb or Monument to the memory of—	Inscription on Tomb or Monument.	Inscription on slabs or pillars placed in churches or chapels.	Remarks. Tombs on roadsides, or battlefields (furnishing information as in columns 3, 4, 5 and 6).
1	2	3	4	5	6	7	8
471	...	Inside the Residency enclosure, on the south-verandah wall of the Women's Quarters.	Lucknow,		From the 30th June until the 25th September, for 86 days, they were closely invested, subjected to a heavy artillery fire day and night from all sides, and had to sustain several general attacks on the position. On the 25th September 1857 A.D., Generals Outram and Havelock with a large force endeavoured to release the garrison; after having with great loss effected a junction with them, they were however unable to withdraw, and the whole combined force was besieged for a period of 53 days, until finally relieved by Sir Colin Campbell on the 17th November 1857 A. D. There remained of the original garrison when reinforced on the 25th September a total of 979 souls, including sick and wounded, of whom 577 were Europeans and 402 natives.		
472	...	Inside the enclosure of the tomb of Saadat Ali Khan, King of Oudh, and his wife Mahal Janab Alia, to the north of the Kaisar Bagh.	Ditto ...	Monument to the memory of Captain J. Clarke, Lieutenant Brownlow and several Sappers of the Royal Engineers, killed in 1858.	To the memory of Captain J. Clarke, Royal Engineers. Lieutenant E. P. Brownlow, Bengal Engineers. Corporal Frederick Morgan. Lance-Corporal James Davis. Sapper James Bunting. " George Beer. " Michael Daly. " John Ford. " Andrew Fairservice " David Northwood. " William Outerson. " William Robinson. " James Slade. " Alfred Smith. " Charles Tucker. " John Yeo. } Of the 23rd Company of the Royal Engineers.		

					Who were killed by the explosion of a quantity of gunpowder, abandoned by the mutineers in their retreat from Lucknow, on the 17th March 1858.		
473	...	On Neill's Road, near China Bazár, opposite the Police Post.	Ditto ...	Monument to the memory of Sir Mountstuart Jackson, Bart., and the other fugitives from Sitapur, killed in 1857.	*On south face.*—Sacred to the memory of 1. Sir Mountstuart Jackson, Bart. 2. Captain Patrick Orr. 3. Lieutenant C. J. H. Burnes, 1st Bombay European Fusiliers. 4. Sergeant-Major Mortan, Victims of 1857. *On north face.*—Sacred to the memory of 1. G. P. Carew, Esq. 2. Mrs. Greene. 3. Miss Jackson and others, European and Natives, faithful servants of Government. Victims of 1857.		
474	Vilaiti Bagh Cemetery, Lucknow.	On the south bank of the river Gumti, near the village of Bibiapur.	Ditto ...	Tomb of Mate H. P. Garvey, of H. M.'s "Shannon" killed, 1858.	Here lies Mr. Henry P. Garvey, Acting Mate, Her Majesty's Ship "Shannon," killed before Lucknow, March XIth, MDCCCLVIII. Blessed are the dead which die in the Lord.		
475	Ditto ...	Ditto ...	Ditto ...	Tomb of Captain W. H. Hutchinson, died 1858.	Sacred to the memory of Captain W. Helly Hutchinson, 9th Royal Lancers. Born 5th March 1833, mortally wounded in an attack on the rebels near the Moosa Bagh, 9th March 1858, died 22nd March 1858. This monument is erected by his brother-officers.		
476	Ditto ...	Ditto ...	Ditto ...	Tomb of Sergeant S. Newman, 9th Lancers, died 1858.	In memory of Sergeant S. Newman, 9th Queen's Royal Lancers, who fell mortally wounded in pursuit of the rebels near the Moosa Bagh, 19th March 1858.		

List of Christian Tombs or Monuments in the Lucknow Division possessing historical or archæological interest—(continued).

Serial number.	Name of cemetery, churchyard or church.	Where situated (giving exact situation as far as possible).	District.	Tomb or Monument to the memory of—	Inscription on Tomb or Monument.	Inscription on slabs or pillars placed in churches or chapels.	Remarks. Tombs on roadsides or battlefields (furnishing information as in columns 3, 4, 5, and 6).
1	2	3	4	5	6	7	8
477	...	In the vault of La Martiniere College building, Lucknow.	Ditto ...	Tomb of Major-General Claude Martin, died 1800.	Here lies Claude Martin, born at Lyons, the 5th day of January 1735. Arrived in India as a common soldier and died at Lucknow, the 13th September 1800, a Major-General. Pray for his soul.		NOTE.—Claude Martin was the son of a silk manufacturer at Lyons, and at an early age enlisted in the French army. For his good conduct he was removed from the infantry to the cavalry and appointed a trooper in Count de Lally's bodyguard, a small corps of select men formed for the purpose of accompanying that officer to Pondicherry, of which place he had then been appointed Governor. Soon after Lally's arrival at Pondicherry, he exercised his power with such oppressive severity and enforced the discipline of the army with such rigid minuteness, that his conduct excited dissatisfaction throughout the settlement. Several remonstrances on his conduct were transmitted to France, and many officers of distinction resigned the service. He, nevertheless, persevered in his injudicious system of discipline and the troops became so dissatisfied and driven to despair by the misery and famine which desolated Pondicherry in 1760, that when the English army laid siege to it, great numbers deserted from the garrison, and at last Lally's own bodyguard went over in a body to the English, carrying their horses, arms, &c., along with them. This corps was well received, and Martin was soon noticed for his spirit and ability which he displayed on many occasions. On the return of the British army to Madras, after the surrender of Pondicherry, Martin obtained permission to raise a company of Chasseurs from among the French prisoners, of which he got the command, with the rank of Ensign in the Company's service. A few weeks after he received this appointment, he was ordered to proceed with his Chasseurs to Bengal. On their passage the ship in which they were embarked sprung a leak, and Martin, by great fortitude and perseverance, but with much difficulty, saved himself and some of his men in one of the ship's boats. On his arrival in Calcutta he was appointed a Cornet of Cavalry, in which service he continued until he had risen by regular succession to the rank of Captain in the line, when he obtained a company of Infantry. Shortly after this promotion he was—being an able draftsman,—employed to survey the north-eastern districts of Bengal, and on

completing that task he was sent to Oudh, in order to assist in surveying that province. While employed in this service he resided chiefly at Lucknow, where he amused himself in showing his ingenuity in several branches of mechanics and his skill in gunnery, which gave the Nawâb, Asaf-ud-daulah, so high a notion of the value of his services, that he solicited and obtained permission from the Governor and Council of Calcutta to appoint him Superintendent of his artillery park and arsenal. Captain Martin was so well satisfied with this appointment and with his prospects in the service of the Nawab, that he proposed to the Governor and Council to relinquish his pay and allowances in the Company's service, on condition of his being permitted to retain his rank and to continue in the service of the Nawâb Vazir. His proposal being acceded to, he was admitted into the confidence of the Vazir, and in the different changes which took place in the Councils of the Nawâb as well as in the various negotiations with the English Government, Captain Martin was his secret adviser. He seldom, however, appeared at the Darbár, and he never held any ostensible situation in the administration of the Vazir's Government; but few measures of importance were adopted without his advice being previously taken. Hence his influence at the Court of Lucknow became very considerable, not only with the Vazir but with his ministers, and that influence enabled him to amass an immense fortune. After having lived 25 years at Lucknow, he had attained, by regular succession, the rank of Lieutenant-Colonel in the Company's service. At the commencement of the war with Tipu Sultân in 1790, Lieutenant-Colonel Martin presented the Company at his private expense with a number of fine horses sufficient to mount a troop of cavalry. He was soon afterwards promoted to the rank of Colonel in their service, and in 1796, when the Company's officers received brevet rank from His Majesty, Colonel Martin obtained that of Major-General. By his will, after providing for his dependents, and leaving large sums of money to be given away in charity, he founded schools at Lucknow, Calcutta, and Lyons. He left directions that his house "Constantia," at Lucknow, the present La Martinière, should never be sold, but serve as a mausoleum for his remains; and he committed it to the care of the ruling power in the country for the time being. The will concludes with a curious exposition of the principles by which he regulated his conduct through life. He avows that self-interest was his sole motive of action, and that the sins of which he had been guilty were very great and manifold; and he concludes by asking forgiveness of God, which he hopes his sincere confession of wickedness will avail to obtain.

List of Christian Tombs or Monuments in the Lucknow Division possessing historical or archæological interest—(continued).

Serial number.	Name of Cemetery, Churchyard or Church.	Where situated (giving exact situation as far as possible).	District.	Tomb or Monument to the memory of—	Inscription on Tomb or Monument.	Inscription on slabs or pillars placed in churches or chapels.	Remarks. Tombs on roadsides or battlefields (furnishing information as in columns 3, 4, 5 and 6).
1	2	3	4	5	6	7	8
478	...	La Martinière Park, Lucknow, north of the road leading to the College building and near the College hospital.	Ditto ...	Tomb of Major Hodson of Hodson's Horse, killed 1858.	Here lieth all that could die of William Stephen Raikes Hodson, Captain and Brevet-Major, 1st E. B. Fusiliers, and Commandant of Hodson's Horse, son of the Ven'ble George Hodson, Archdeacon of Stafford. Born March 19th, 1821, fell in the final assault at Lucknow, March 11th, 1858. A little while, II Cor. IV, 12.		NOTE.—Hodson was a man of rare energy of character, daring, always courting danger, and reckless. He had been, some years before the Mutiny, one of that noble band of pioneers who, under Henry Lawrence, had cleared the way for the civilisation of the Panjâb, and he had afterwards risen to the command of that famous Guide Corps, the institution of which had been one of the most cherished and the most successful projects of his accomplished chief. But, amidst a career of the brightest promise, a heavy cloud had gathered over him, and shortly before 1857 he had rejoined his old regiment, the 1st (Company's) Fusiliers, as a subaltern, chafing under a sense of wrong, and eager to clear himself from what he declared to be unmerited imputations upon his character. This gloom was upon him when, in May 1857, General Anson, discovering his many fine qualities, offered him a place in the department of the Quartermaster-General, and especially charged him with the intelligence branch of its duties, in prosecution of which he was to raise an entire new regiment of Irregular Horse. His fearlessness, his contempt of danger, his joy in the battle, his ever cool brain, made him invaluable to a commander. The only stain upon his character is the shooting of the three unresisting Dehli princes on the 21st September 1857, one of the most painful episodes connected with the Mutiny.
479	...	Ditto ...	Ditto ...	Tomb of Captain L. Dacosta, killed 1858.	Sacred to the memory of Captain L. Dacosta, 56th N. I., attached to Ferozepore Regiment of Sikhs, who fell in the final assault on the Kaisar Bagh, the 13th March 1858, aged 32 years.		
480	...	La Martinière Park, south of the metalled road passing through the Park.	Ditto ...	Tomb of Lieutenant A. O. Mayne, killed 1857.	Here lies the body of Lieutenant Augustus Otway Mayne, Bengal Artillery, killed in action at the relief of Lucknow on the 14th of November 1857, in the 28th year of his age. Waiting the coming of the Lord Jesus Christ.		

481		Near the Sikander Bagh Gate, north of Clyde Road, Lucknow.	Ditto ...	Tomb of Lieutenant F. Dobbs and some men, killed in 1857.	Sacred to the memory of Lieutenant Francis Dobbs, who was killed in action at the storm of the Shah Najaf on the 16th November 1857 and buried here; also of Privates Edward Donaghey, Hugh Gray, Alexander Comb, Patrick Collins, Thomas Kenny, who were killed in action on the same day and interred in the same grave.		NOTE.—The name of Lieutenant F. Dobbs also appears in the inscription on the monument of Brigadier-General Neill in the Residency Cemetery.—(*See No. 420.*)
482	Alam Bagh Cemetery.	In the Alam Bagh, about 5 miles out of Lucknow on the Cawnpore road.	Ditto ...	Tomb of Major-General Sir Henry Havelock, died 1858.	Here rest the mortal remains of Henry Havelock, Major-General in the British Army, Knight Commander of the Bath, who died at Dilkusha, Lucknow, of dysentery produced by the hardships of a campaign, in which he achieved immortal fame, on the 24th November 1857. He was born on the 5th April 1795, at Bishops County, Durham, England. Entered the Army 1815, came to India 1823, and served there with little interruption till his death. He bore an honourable part in the wars of Burmah, Afghanistan, the Maharatta Campaign of 1843, and the Sutlej of 1845-46. Retained by adverse circumstances during many years in a subordinate position, it was the aim of his life to prove that the profession of a Christian is consistent with the fullest discharge of the duties of a soldier. He commanded a Division in the Persian Expedition of 1857. In the terrible convulsion of that year his genius and character were at length fully developed and known to the world. Saved from shipwreck on the Ceylon coast by that Providence which designed him for yet greater things, he was nominated to the command of the column destined to relieve the brave garrison of Lucknow. This object, after almost superhuman exertions, he, by the blessing of God, accomplished. But he was not spared to receive on earth the reward so dearly earned. The Divine Master, whom he served, saw fit to remove him		NOTE.—The life of Havelock had been a life devoted to his profession: he had made the strict performance of duty his polar star. Gifted with military abilities of a high order, and conscious that he possessed those abilities, he had borne without repining the sapping torment of slow promotion and its inevitable results—employment in positions below his capacity. But every trial of Fortune had found him cheerful, resolute and devoted. To the smallest office he gave his best abilities, and, whilst thus labouring he had wisdom also to prepare himself for the eventualities which were to follow. When the opportunity did come, he used it in a manner which electrified his contemporaries, which gained for him the confidence and devotion of his soldiers. The statue which adorns Trafalgar Square, London, while it will show his outward form to the generations which shall have known him not, will whet their curiosity to inquire regarding the early training and later deeds of one who, in a short and glorious campaign, illustrated all the qualities which combine to form a commander of the first rank.

List of Christian Tombs or Monuments in the Lucknow Division possessing historical or archæological interest—(continued).

Serial number.	Name of cemetery, churchyard, or church.	Where situated (giving exact situation as far as possible).	District.	Tomb or Monument to the memory of—	Inscription on Tomb or Monument.	Inscription on slabs or pillars placed in churches or chapels.	Remarks. Tombs on roadsides, or battlefields (furnishing information as in columns 3, 4, 5 and 6).
1	2	3	4	5	6	7	8
482	Alam Bagh Cemetery.	In the Alam Bagh, about 5 miles out of Lucknow, on the Cawnpore road.	Lucknow...		from the sphere of his labours in the moment of his greatest triumph. He departed to his rest in humble but confident expectation of greater rewards than those which a grateful country was anxious to bestow. In him the skill of a commander, the courage and devotion of a soldier, the learning of a scholar, the grace of a high bred gentleman, and all the social and domestic virtues of a husband, father and friend, were blended together and strengthened, harmonized and adorned by the spirit of a true Christian: the result of the influence of the Holy Spirit on his heart and a humble reliance on the merits of a crucified Saviour. I have fought a good fight; I have finished my course; I have kept the faith: henceforth there is laid up for me a crown of righteousness which the Lord, the Righteous Judge, shall give me that day, and not to me only, but to all those that love his appearance. His ashes in a peaceful urn shall rest, His name a great example stands to show, How strangely high endeavours may be blest, Where piety and valour jointly go. This monument is erected by his sorrowing widow and family.		
483	Ditto ...	Ditto ...	Ditto ...	Tomb of Major Perrin, Lieutenants Grahame, Nunn and Preston, killed 1857.	Sacred to the memory of Major J. Perrin, Lieutenants V. Grahame, J. J. Nunn and M. Preston, 90th Light Infantry, who were killed in action near this spot, 24th September 1857. Erected by their comrades.		

Ditto ...	Tomb of Captain C. W. McDonald, killed 1858.	Sacred to the memory of Captain Charles William McDonald, 93rd Highlanders, who was killed in the assault on the Begam's Palace on the 10th day of March 1858, in the 23rd year of his age. This simple inscription is erected by his sorrowing relations in memory of his simple virtues as a Christian and his noble conduct as a soldier.		
Ditto ...	Tomb of Lieutenant W. Paul, killed 1857.	Here lie the remains of Lieutenant W. Paul, of the 4th Panjáb Rifles, who was killed in the attack upon Secundra Bagh with the relieving force under Major-General Sir Colin Campbell, K.C.B., on the 16th of November 1857. Erected by the officers of the 4th Panjáb Rifles.		
Ditto ...	Tomb of Lieutenant C. K. Dashwood, died 1857.	In memory of Charles Keith Dashwood, Lieutenant, 18th Regiment, B. N. I., third son of Lieutenant-Colonel A. W. Dashwood. He died at Dilkusha, Lucknow, November 22nd, 1857, aged 19 years.		
Ditto ...	Tomb of Lieutenant C. W. Sergison, killed 1858.	Sacred to the memory of Charles Warden Sergison, Lieutenant in Her Majesty's 93rd Regiment (Highlanders), who fell in the attack on the Begam's Palace, Lucknow, on the 10th March 1858, in the 24th year of his age. This simple monument has been erected by his heart-broken surviving parent as a testimony of his deep regard and admiration of his son as a brave and noble soldier.		
...	Tomb of Major the Hon'ble B. Pellew, died 1858.	Sacred to the memory of Major the Hon'ble Barrington R. Pellew, 2nd Battalion, Rifle Brigade, who died at Lucknow on the 6th of December 1858. This stone is erected by his brother-officers.		*Note*.—See entry No. 510.
Ditto ...	Tomb of Lieutenant L. E. Cooper, died 1858.	Sacred to the memory of Lieutenant Lovick Emilius Cooper, 2nd Battalion, Rifle Brigade, who died on the 15th March 1858 of wounds received before Lucknow, aged 20 years.		NOTE.—There are two inscriptions on this tomb, and there is a difference of a day in the date of death as given in the second inscription which runs as follows:— "Sacred to the memory of Ensign L. E. Cooper, 2nd Battalion, Rifle Brigade, who died of wounds received at the siege of Lucknow, 16th March 1858."

List of Christian Tombs or Monuments in the Lucknow Division possessing historical or archæological interest.—(continued).

Serial number.	Name of cemetery, churchyard, or church.	Where situated (giving exact situation as far as possible).	District.	Tomb or Monument to the memory of—	Inscription on Tomb or Monument.	Inscription on slabs or pillars placed in churches or chapels.	Remarks. Tombs on road-sides, or battle-fields (furnishing information as in columns 3, 4, 5 and 6.)
1	2	3	4	5	6	7	8
490	...	On the 6th mile of the Lucknow-Sultanpur road, to the north, not far from the bridge known as Arjun-ka-Pul.	Lucknow...	Tomb of Lieutenant P.C. Smyth, killed 1858.	Sacred to the memory of Lieutenant Percy C. Smyth, of Her Majesty's 97th Regiment, who died on the 4th of March 1858 of a wound received at the attack on the Fort of Dhowrara, on the morning of that day.		
491	...	On the 3rd mile of the Lucknow-Fyzabad road, to the south.	Ditto ...		Sacred to the memory of Captain William Frederick Thynne, 2nd Battalion, Rifle Brigade, killed in action before Lucknow on the 11th of March 1858, aged 23 years. Sacred to the memory of Captain W. F. Thynne, 2nd Battalion, Rifle Brigade, who was killed at the siege of Lucknow, 11th March 1858. This stone was erected by his brother-officers.		Note.—There are two stones and two inscriptions as given in column 6.
492	...	Near the 4th mile of the Lucknow-Fyzabad road, to the south.	Ditto ...	Tomb of Captain C. Sandford, killed 1858.	Beneath this monument rest the mortal remains of Charles Sandford, late Captain of the 3rd Bengal Light Cavalry, who, when gallantly leading a body of dismounted Punjab Cavalry in an assault on a fortified place near Lucknow, 10th March 1858, met a soldier's death. Strangers, respect the lonely resting-place of the brave. Re-erected 1877.		Note.—In the wall enclosing this tomb there is a tablet bearing the following Inscription:—"Consecrated by the Right Revd. Edward Ralph, Bishop of Calcutta, 17th January 1878."
493	...	Near the 5th mile of the Lucknow-Fyzabad	Ditto ...	Tomb of Major J. P. Smith, killed 1858.	Sacred to the memory of Major John Percy Smith, 2nd Dragoon Guards (Queen's Bays), who was killed in action near the Kokrail Bridge, on the 15th March 1858.		

		road, about a mile north of the road, in the vicinity of the village of Ghazipur.			This tablet is erected by his brother-officers.		
494	...	At Lotan Bagh, north of the road to Malihabad, between the Músa Bagh and the road.	Ditto ...	Tomb of Major J. G. Price, died 1858.	Sacred to the memory of Major John Griffith Price, 2nd Dragoon Guards (Queen's Bays), who died of fever at the Músa Bagh on the 12th of May 1858. This tablet is erected by his brother-officers.		
495	...	In the Músa Bagh, close to the main building.	Ditto ...	Tomb of Captain F. Wale, killed 1858.	Sacred to the memory of Captain F. Wale, who raised and commanded the first Sikh Irregular Cavalry, killed in action at Lucknow on the 21st March 1858. This monument is erected by Captain L. B. Jones, Acting-Commandant, 1st Sikh Irregular Cavalry, as a token of regard for his officer, whom he admired both as a friend and a soldier. Captain Wale lived and died a Christian soldier.		
496		To the south-east of the 5th milestone of the Lucknow-Cawnpore road, on the outskirts of the village Bargawan.	Ditto ...	Memorial column to the officers and men of the 5th Fusiliers, who fell during 1857-58.	This column is erected by the officers, non-commissioned officers and privates of the 5th Fusiliers, to their undermentioned comrades who fell during the occupation of the Alam Bagh Camp, under Sir J. Outram, K.C.B., 1857-58. Lieutenant J. Brown. Armour-Sergeant H. Whitworth. Sergeant W. Walters. Private W. Anderson. " W. Baldry. " T. Hill. " D. McEvoy. " H. Wright. " I. Baker " I. Martin. " W. Chamberlain. Private I. Cleary. " J. Kelly. " T. Mairs. " I. Monaghan. " W. Connolly. " D. Donnolly. " R. Preston. " I. Doughty. " W. Pottle. " W. Moran. " W. Messenger.		
497	Protestant and R. Catholic Cemetery, Lucknow.	Near Shah Najaf.	Ditto ...	Tomb of Lieutenant James Samuel Swinton, died 1858.	Sacred to the memory of James Samuel Swinton, Lieutenant, Bengal Infantry, who died here on the 29th October 1858, aged 19, in consequence of severe fatigue and exposure at Cawnpore and Lucknow. He fought the good fight of faith and trusted in his Redeemer.		

List of Christian Tombs or Monuments in the Lucknow Division possessing historical or archæological interest—(continued).

Serial number.	Name of cemetery, churchyard, or church.	Where situated (giving exact situation as far as possible).	District.	Tomb or Monument to the memory of—	Inscription on Tomb or Monument.	Inscription on slabs or pillars placed in churches or chapels.	Remarks. Tombs on Roadsides, or Battlefields (furnishing information as in columns 3, 4, 5 and 6).
1	2	3	4	5	6	7	8
498	Protestant and R. Catholic Cemetery Lucknow.	Near Shâh Najaf.	Lucknow ...	Tomb of W. E. Lynch, Esq., Assistant Surgeon, 7th Hussars, died 1859.	W. E. Lynch, Esq., Assistant Surgeon, 7th Hussars, died at Lucknow, 24th January 1859.		
499	Ditto ...	Ditto ...	Ditto ...	Tomb of Lieutenant R. Foster Melliar, H.M's. 20th Regiment, died 1859.	Sacred to the memory of Lieutenant R. Foster Melliar, H. M's 20th Regiment, who died at Lucknow on the 15th of April 1859, aged 19 years and 10 months.		
500	Ditto ...	Ditto ...	Ditto ...	Tomb of Herbert Thomas William Lawrence, died 1857.	In memory of Herbert Thomas William Lawrence. Born at Hooshyarpore, Punjâb, 2nd July 1851. Died of cholera on the 15th August 1857, within the besieged position of the British Residency at Lucknow. His remains were exhumed on the 13th August 1858 and placed under this stone.		
501	Cantonment Church, Lucknow.	On the left side of entrance door.	Ditto ...	Tablet to the memory of 48 soldiers of No. 3 Company, 8th Battalion, R.A., who fell during 1857-58.		In memory of the soldiers of No. 3 Company, 8th Battalion, Royal Artillery, who were killed or died in India during the campaigns of 1857-58. *Dulce et decorum est pro patria mori.*	
502	Ditto ...	On the right side of entrance door.	Ditto ...	Tablet to the memory of Lieut. F. J. MacDonnell, killed 1858.		Sacred to the memory of Lieutenant F. J. MacDonnell, Adjutant of 2nd Punjâb Cavalry, who was killed in action at Courci, near Lucknow, on 23rd March 1858, *æt.* 23, while gallantly charging at the head of his men; beloved and respected by all who knew him. This stone has been erected over his mortal remains by the officers and men of his regiment to mark their grief for his early death and to record their lasting sense of his many good qualities as a soldier and a man.	NOTE.—Lieut. F. J. MacDonnell is buried in the Cantonment Cemetery at Mariaon, *see* No. 505.

503	Ditto ...	In south transept wall.	Ditto ...	Tablet to the memory of Lieutenant J.E.H. Sullivan and others killed by the great landslip at Naini Tal in 1880.		In memory of Lieutenant J. E. H. Sullivan, 2nd-Lieutenant Colin J.L. Halkett, Privates H. Brown, T. Chisholm, T. Kennedy, W. Turner, of the 73rd Perthshire Regiment, who were killed by a landslip at Naini Tal on the 18th September 1880, while employed with a working party endeavouring to rescue some of their fellow-creatures. This tablet is erected by the officers of the regiment as a tribute to their heroism and devotion to duty.	*Note*—See entry No. 403.
504	Old Cantonment Cemetery at Mariaon.	About 3 miles from the Iron Bridge on the Lucknow-Sitapur road.	Ditto ...	Tomb of Lieutenant H. E. Richards, died 1858.	Sacred to the memory of Lieutenant H. E. Richards, 3rd Battalion, Rifle Brigade, who was mortally wounded in the attack on the fort of Birwah on the 21st October 1858. He died at the Old Cantonment, Lucknow, on the 8th December 1858.		
505	Ditto ...	...	Ditto ...	Tomb of Lieutenant F. J. MacDonnell, killed 1858.	Sacred to the memory of Lieutenant F. J. MacDonnell, Adjutant, 2nd Punjab Cavalry, who was killed in action at Conrci, near Lucknow, on 23rd March 1858, *æt.* 23, while gallantly charging at the head of his men, beloved and respected by all who knew him. Erected by his brother-officers.		*Note*.—See entry No. 502.
506	Christ Church, Lucknow.	Civil Lines.	Ditto ...	Tablet in memory of James Grant Thomason, B.C.S., killed 1857.		To the memory of James Grant Thomason, B. C. S., Deputy Commissioner of Mohumdi, murdered by the mutineers at Aurangabad in Oudh, 5th June 1857. This tablet is erected by George E. L. Cotton, D. D., Bishop of Calcutta, formerly his tutor in Rugby School, in thankful recollection of his character in boyhood and in the sure confidence that he is now with Christ.	
507	Ditto ...	Ditto ...	Ditto ...	Tablet in memory of the officers and men of the 2nd Dragoon Guards (Queen's Bays), who were killed or died in 1857-1859.		In memory of Brigadier-General William Campbell, C. B., Major John Percy Smith, Major John Griffith Price, Captain Orlando Frederick Cavendish Bridgeman, Captain Robert Blair, V. C., Cornet William Agnew Riding Master Israel Kirk. 1 Regimental Sergeant-Major, 1 Trumpet-Major, 2 Troop Sergeant-Majors,	

Civil Lines,	Lucknow,			8 Sergeants, 7 Corporals, 1 Farrier, 90 Privates, of the 2nd Dragoon Guards (Queen's Bays), who were either killed in action, died of their wounds or of disease or exposure during the campaigns of 1857, 1858 and 1859 in India. This tablet is erected by the officers of the regiment.
Ditto ...	Ditto ...	Tablet in memory of George Sackville Benson, B. C. S., died 1857.		Sacred to the memory of George Sackville Benson, B. C. S., mortally wounded in action at Secundra Bagh, Lucknow, 16th November 1857. Died 18th November 1857, *ætas* 29 years. A time of war and a time of peace.—Eccl. III, 8.
Ditto ...	Ditto ...	Tablet in memory of Captain George Nicholas Hardinge, died 1858.		In memory of Captain George Nicholas Hardinge, late 45th B. N. I., and Commandant, 3rd Oude Irregular Cavalry. He served in the Sutlej and Punjáb campaigns; he commanded the Sikh Cavalry and acted as Deputy Assistant Quartermaster-General throughout the defence of Lucknow. From the wounds and privations endured in that memorable siege, he died at the Sandheads, March 16th, 1858. Aged 29 years.
Ditto ...	Ditto ...	Tablet in memory of Captain Wellwood George Mowbray Maclean, killed 1857.		To the memory of Wellwood George Mowbray Maclean, Captain, 7th Regiment, N. I., who fell while gallantly serving with the small body of the Oudh Volunteer Cavalry in the attack against

					the mutineers at Chinhut on the 30th June 1857. Aged 41. This tablet is erected by Nawáb Mohsin-ud-Dowlah, Bahádur, of this city, as a token of his friendship and regard.
511	Ditto ...	Ditto ...	Ditto ...	Tablet in memory of Captain R. J. H. Magness, Oudh Service, died 1856, and Mary Anne Magness, killed 1857.	Sacred to the memory of Captain R. J. H Magness, Oudh Service, who departed this life at Lucknow, 18th December 1856—and of his widow, Mary Anne Magness, who was killed at Lucknow by rebels in June 1857.
512	Ditto ...	Ditto ...	Ditto ...	Tablet in memory of Alexander Bryson, killed 1857.	To the memory of Alexander Bryson, a Volunteer, who was killed on the 9th July 1857, within the Residency defences, while singly building, under a deadly fire, a barricade for the safety of his post, a duty he volunteered to perform. He was honourably mentioned in the official report of that memorable defence. Aged 37 years.
513	Ditto ...	Ditto ...	Ditto ...	Tablet in memory of Thomas Henry Kavanagh, V. C., died 1883.	In honour of one whose name should never be forgotten, Thomas Henry Kavanagh, V.C., who on the night of the 9th November 1857, with the devotion of an ancient Roman taking his life in his hand, went forth from the beleaguered Residency and passing through a city thronged with merciless enemies, successfully guided Sir Colin Campbell and his army to the relief of the garrison.
514	Ditto ...	Ditto ...	Ditto ...	Tablet in memory of 7 officers and 164 n.-c. officers and men of the 93rd Sutherland Highlanders, killed or died in 1857-58.	Erected by the officers, non-commissioned officers and soldiers of the 93rd Sutherland Highlanders, in memory of their comrades who fell in action, or died of wounds or of disease caused by fatigue and exposure during the suppression of the Mutiny in India in 1857-58. Killed in action :— Officers ... ... 5 Non-commissioned officers and soldiers ... 45 Died of wounds :— Officer ... ... 1 Non-commissioned officers and soldiers ... 86 Died of disease :— Officer ... ... 1 Non-commissioned officers and soldiers ... 83

List of Christian Tombs or Monuments in the Lucknow Division possessing historical or archæological interest—(continued).

Serial number.	Name of cemetery, churchyard or church.	Where situated (giving exact situation as far as possible).	District.	Tomb or Monument to the memory of—	Inscription on Tomb or Monument.	Inscription on slabs or pillars placed in churches or chapels.	Remarks. Tombs on road-sides or battle-fields (furnishing information as in columns 3, 4, 5 and 6).
1	2	3	4	5	6	7	8
515	Christ Church, Lucknow.	Civil Lines...	Lucknow ...	Tablet in memory of Captain J. T. Lumsden and Lieutenant John Cape, killed 1857.		Sacred to the memory of Captain J. T. Lumsden and Lieutenant John Cape, both of the late 30th Regiment, B. N. I., who were killed at Lucknow in the campaigns of 1857-1858. This tablet is dedicated by their brother-officers.	*Note.*—Captain Lumsden was the first man to enter Secundra Bagh enclosure on the 16th November 1857, and was killed inside by a musket shot.
516	Ditto ...	Ditto ...	Ditto ...	Tablet in memory of Captain Alfred Parmenter Simons, died 1857.		In memory of Alfred Parmenter Simons, Captain, Bengal Regiment of Artillery, who died from the effects of his wounds during the siege of Lucknow, September 8th, 1857, aged 33 years. Also of Lucy Amelia Collingwood, older child of the above. She died at Naini Tal, August 20th, in the same year, aged nearly three years. Jesus said, I am the resurrection and the life. St. John, 11c. 25v.	
517	Ditto ...	Ditto ...	Ditto ...	Tablet in memory of Lieutenant John Swanson, died 1857.		In memory of Lieutenant John Swanson, H. M's. 78th Highlanders, who died in the Residency of Lucknow, 2nd October 1857, of wounds received on the 25th and 26th September 1857. Aged 22 years.	
518	Ditto ...	Ditto ...	Ditto ...	Tablet in memory of Colonel Isaac Henley Handscomb, killed 1857.		Sacred to the memory of Colonel Isaac Henley Handscomb, Brigadier-General, Commanding the Oudh Field Force, who was shot by the Lucknow mutineers when in the firm execution of his duty on the night of the 30th May 1857. Aged 52 years. A brave soldier, a loving kinsman, and a sincere friend; he lived and died honoured and beloved by all who knew him. This tablet is erected as a tribute of affection by his nephew, Captain H. T. Bartlett, Bengal Army.	

Ditto ...	Ditto ...	Ditto ...	Tablet in memory of Major the Hon'ble Barrington Reynolds Pellew, died 1858.	Sacred to the memory of Major the Hon'ble Barrington R. Pellew (2nd Battalion, Rifle Brigade), grandson of Admiral Viscount Exmouth, who died of dysentery at Lucknow, on the 6th December 1858, in the 20th year of his age, and rests in the burying-ground of the Dilkusha. This tablet is erected by his bereaved and widowed mother to a son greatly beloved and deeply mourned by his sorrowing family and friends.	*Note.*—See entry No. 488.
Ditto ...	Ditto ...	Ditto ...	Tablet in memory of the Rev. Henry Stedman Polehampton, Chaplain of Lucknow, died 1857.	In memory of Henry Stedman Polehampton, Chaplain of this station. Born February 1st, 1824, died July 20th 1857. Also of Henry Allnuth, his only child— Born December 30th, 1856. Died January 3rd, 1857. Enter thou into the joy of thy Lord.—Mat XXV, 21.	*Note.*—Mr Polehampton, the Residency Chaplain, was severely wounded on the 7th June and died of cholera on the 20th July 1854. See entry No. 444.
Ditto ...	Ditto ...	Ditto ...	Tablet in memory of Sir Henry Lawrence, K. C. B., killed 1857.	Sacred to the memory of Sir Henry Lawrence, K. C. B., the statesman who administered in successions the great provinces of India; the soldier who died in defending the garrison entrusted to his charge; the Christian who in his last hour humbly trusted that he had tried to do his duty, and committed his soul, in full assurance of faith, to the mercy of his Lord. Born 28th June 1806. Died 4th July 1857. His body rests in the burial-ground of the Residency.	*Note.*—See entry No. 419.
Ditto ...	Ditto ...	Ditto ...	Tablet in memory of Elizabeth Clark and her children, died 1857.	In affectionate memory of Elizabeth Clark, his wife, aged 26 years, Matthew Edgar, aged 1 year and 9 months, Elizabeth, aged 10 days, his children, all of whom died during the siege of the Lucknow Residency in that year of sorrow 1857. This tablet is erected by Captain Edgar Clark, Bengal Staff Corps. The Lord gave and the Lord hath taken away. *Job I. 21.*	
Ditto ...	Ditto ...	Ditto ...	Tablet in memory of Lieutenant Thomas Frankland, killed 1857.	Sacred to the memory of Thomas Frankland, Esq., Lieutenant, 48th Madras Native Infantry, and second in command of 2nd Punjáb Infantry, who fell at the head of his regiment at the storming of	

List of Christian Tombs or Monuments in the Lucknow Division possessing historical or archæological interest—(continued).

Serial Number.	Name of Cemetery, Churchyard or Church.	Where situated (giving exact situation as far as possible).	District.	Tomb or Monument to the memory of—	Inscription on Tomb or Monument.	Inscription on slabs or pillars placed in churches or chapels.	Remarks. Tombs on road-sides or battle-fields (furnishing information as in columns 2, 4, 5 and 6).
1	2	3	4	5	6	7	8
						th Alum Bogh during the relief of Lucknow, the eldest surviving son of Sir Fred- was the eldest surviving son of Sir Frederick Frankland, eighth Baronet of Thirkely, county York. I can do all things through Christ who strengtheneth me. The Lord is my strength and my shield.	
524	Sitapur Cemetery.	Between slaughter-house and Commissariat godown in Cantonment, Sitapur.	Sitapur ...	Tomb of Major W. H. Nicholetts, died 1852.	Sacred to the memory of W. H. Nicholetts, Major, 28th N. I., Commanding 1st Regiment O. L. I. This monument is erected by the officers of the 1st Regiment, O. L. I., and Major Bimbury, as a mark of their friendship and regard. Died 19th October 1852, aged 45 years.		
525		At Madhoganj, pargana Mallawan, tahsil Bilgram.	Hardoi ...	Tomb of Brigadier the Hon'ble Adrian Hope, C.B., killed 1858.	Brigadier the Hon'ble Adrian Hope, C.B., Lieutenant-Colonel, 93rd H. D. Highlanders. Born 3rd March 1821. Killed at Ruiya, 15th April 1858.		NOTE.—Adrian Hope was one of the noblest men who ever wore the British uniform; the bravest of soldiers, and the most gallant of gentlemen. His loss, uselessly sacrificed before Ruiya, was a cause for national sorrow; his death was mourned on the spot by every man in the camp. "A gentler, braver spirit never breathed a true soldier; a kind, courteous, noble gentleman, in word and deed; devoted to his profession, beloved by his men; adored by his friends: this indeed is a sad loss to the British Army." So wrote on the spot William Howard Russell. "No more mournful duty has fallen upon the Governor-General in the course of the present contest," wrote Lord Canning, "than that of recording the premature death of this gallant young commander."
526		Ditto ..	Ditto ...	Monument to the memory of the officers who fell at the attack on Fort Ruiya in 1858.	Sacred to the memory of Brigadier the Hon'ble Adrian Hope, Lieutenant Charles Douglas, 42nd Royal Highlanders, Lieutenant Alfred Jennings Bramley, 42nd Royal Highlanders, Lieutenant H. Willoughby, 4th Panjáb Infantry, Who fell at fort Ruiya on the 15th April 1858.		

527	...	At Baraman, pargana Katiari, tahsíl Bilgram.	Ditto ...	The tomb of Brevet-Major Alexander Robertson, killed 1857.	The grave of Alexander Robertson, Brevet-Major of the Bengal Artillery, and Gun Carriage Agent, Fatehgarh, who died of wounds inflicted by the insurgent mutineers on the 17th September 1857. His memory lives in the heart of his brother-officers and friends, a few of whom have erected this tomb.		
528	...	At Khasaura, pargana Katiari, tahsíl Bilgram.	Ditto ...	Tomb of the two children of Mr. William George Probyn, C. S., died 1857.	Sacred to the memory of Elliot Markillan, born 26th March 1857, died 26th July 1857; and of Lætitia Domina, born 7th February 1856, died 12th August 1857, the beloved children of William George Probyn, Esq., C.S. Suffer little children to come unto me and forbid them not; for of such is the kingdom of God. *Luke, XVIII, 16*		
529	...	At Aurangabad, in tahsíl Muhamdi, 29 miles south-west of Lakhimpur.	Kheri ...	Monument erected to the memory of a large company of fugitive Christians from Shâhjahânpur, who were murdered in 1857 by the rebels.	*North side.* TO THE GLORY OF GOD And in memory of those honoured ones who fell on this spot, The 5th of June in the year of our Lord 1857. James Grant Thomason. Charles John Jenkins. Henry Wilder Lambie Sneyd. Cornelius Lysaght. Mrs. Lysaght. Mordaunt Money Salmon. *West side.* Alexander Key. Mary Key. Colin Alexander Robertson. Charles Frederick Scott. Mrs. Scott. Miss Scott. William Wilberforce Pitt. George William Rutherford. Thomas John Hope Spens. Ensign Johnson. Ensign E. C. Scott. Quartermaster-Sergeant Grant.		NOTE.—The monument is a beautiful structure of granite and sandstone. Captain Patrick Orr alone escaped this slaughter, but was killed at Lucknow, *see* entry No. 473.

List of Christian Tombs or Monuments in the Lucknow Division possessing historical or archæological interest—(concluded).

Serial number.	Name of Cemetery, Churchyard or Church.	Where situated (giving exact situation as far as possible.	District.	Tomb or Monument to the memory of—	Inscription on Tomb or Monument.	Inscription on slabs or pillars placed in churches or chapels.	Remarks. Tombs on roadsides or battlefields (furnishing information as in columns 3, 4, 5 and 6).
1	2	3	4	5	6	7	8
529			Kheri ...		*South side.* Mrs. Bowling and child. Mrs. Grant. Lieutenant Sheils. Mrs. Sheils. Mr. Pereira and four children. Mr. Hurst. Mr. Smith. Drummer boy August Schlottauer.		

List of Christian Tombs or Monuments in the Fyzabad Division possessing historical or archæological interest.

Serial number.	Name of cemetery, churchyard, or church.	Where situated (giving exact situation as far as possible).	District.	Tomb or Monument to the memory of—	Inscription on Tomb or Monument.	Inscription on slabs or pillars placed in churches or chapels.	Remarks. Tombs on roadsides, or battlefields (furnishing information as in columns 3, 4, 5 and 6).
1	2	3	4	5	6	7	8
530	...	...	Bahraich	Tomb of Mr. Ravenscroft, murdered 1823.			At the village of Bhabharpur near Bhinga in the Bahraich district, is the tomb of Mr. Ravenscroft, a monument with no stone tablet, which is kept up by the Rája of Bhinga. This officer was murdered on the 6th May 1823 by dakaits said to have been instigated by the Rája's son.
531	...		Gonda ...	Tomb of two English officers, said to have been killed 1858.,			At the village Bithania, nine or ten miles north-east of Tulsipur in the Gonda district, is an old brick tomb stated to be the grave of two English officers who were killed in a fight with the rebels in 1858. Enquiries were made in the beginning of 1866 by Colonel Noble, the then Deputy Commissioner, as to the names of the officers, but without success. The tomb, which consists of only two small brick pillars on a low platform, is of no architecural interest, and is kept in repair by the Balrámpur estate.

[ADVERTISEMENTS.]

Archæological Survey of India.

N.-W. PROVINCES AND OUDH CIRCLE.

The Sharqi Architecture of Jaunpur,

WITH

NOTES ON ZAFARABAD, SAHET MAHET AND OTHER PLACES IN THE N.-W. P. & OUDH.

BY DR. A. FÜHRER, PH.D., AND EDMUND W. SMITH, ARCHITECT.

Edited by JAS. BURGESS, LL.D., C.I.E., *Director-General of the Archæological Survey of India.*

Illustrated by 74 Plates of the Sharqi Architecture of Jaunpur, etc. Super-royal 4to. Sewed. Price Rs. 10.

"The finely illustrated volume issued under this title forms the first of a new series of reports begun after the reorganisation of the Archæological Surveys in Upper India in 1885; and if the work is to be continued on the same scale and with the same thoroughness of illustration, we may look to see at last something like an adequate illustration of a considerable portion at least of the immense and multifarious architectural remains of the Indian peninsula. . . . . . We recommend it to the attention of all students of architecture as a book worth possessing, containing some of the best illustrations of Indian architecture that have yet appeared. It is to be hoped that similar volumes, illustrating other branches of the architectural remains in India, will appear in due course."—*The Builder.*

"This volume is an eminently business-like production, of practical value to the architect and archæologist—and possessed of many attractions from the historical and the artistic points of view, rendering the book instructive and interesting to the educated public in general . . . . . . It is the first volume of archæological reports on Upper India which is of any distinct use to the practical Englishman, whether architect, historian, or manufacturer.

"The Government may properly be urged and expected to continue this survey in the North-Western Provinces; and to utilise the architectural members of the Survey, moreover, in advising and controlling a reasonable conservation of Historical Monuments in the Indian Empire."—*Journal, R. Institute of British Architects, 19th June* 1890.

"The first volume of Dr. Burgess' new series is a scholarly and exhaustive monograph on a special and well-defined architectural period. It is published in the form of a handsome quarto. . . . . supplying a valuable and interesting record of the history and architecture of Jaunpur, a city which for nearly a century vied with imperial Delhi both in power and splendour.

"Unlike the majority of the volumes in the former series, the Report is one of which the Government has no reason to be ashamed, and it may be safely recommended to any one interested either specially in Jaunpur or generally in Indian architecture as an adequate and trustworthy source of information."—*The Pioneer.*

CALCUTTA.—Superintendent of Government Printing, India.

Super-royal 4to. Half bound, 430 pages. Rs. 10.

The Monumental Antiquities and Inscriptions in the North-Western Provinces and Oudh.

Described and arranged by DR. A. FÜHRER, PH.D., *Archæological Surveyor, N.-W. P. and Oudh.*

"In this large volume Dr. Führer has given a very full account of the remains at each place with references to all sources of information, the whole being carefully classified with complete indices."—*Memoir on the Indian Surveys*, 1875-1890.

"We have now in a handy form a series of lists of all notable antiquities of the Provinces arranged under the districts where they are found, and accompanied not only with references to all easily accessible sources of further information, but with a set of really workman-like indices."—*The Pioneer*, September 25th, 1891.

ALLAHABAD.—Government Press, N.-W. P. & Oudh.

Super-royal 4to. Stiff boards. Rs. 30.

The Moghul Architecture of Fatehpur-Sikri.

PART I.—*By* E. W. SMITH, *Architectural Surveyor, N.-W. P. and Oudh.*

Illustrated by 125 Plates, *viz.*, 10 Photo-etchings, 10 Chromo-lithographs, and 105 detail drawings of great value to the Architect, Engineer, and Art Student.

ALLAHABAD.—Government Press, N.-W. P.

"At last an adequate beginning of a fairly complete and authoritative description of the magnificent buildings at and near Agra has been made. Nothing approaching to a scientific or reasonably satisfactory description of the Taj and other great edifices at Agra exists. The notices in Cunningham's series of Archæological Reports are feeble, inane, and all but useless; and we fear that we must wait long for the costly and elaborate work which is needed to record the results of a thorough survey of the Fort, the Taj, the mausoleum at Sikandra, and the other architectural wonders which adorn Agra and its environs. Dr. Burgess, before his retirement, decided that since it was not possible to do everything, it was more advisable to begin with Fatehpur-Sikri than with Agra itself; and it was accordingly decreed that 'the wonderful and beautiful city founded by Akbar at Fatehpur-Sikri, and often likened to Pompeii, should be surveyed.

"In the course of four seasons Mr. Edmund W. Smith, the very capable officer in charge of the Architectural Branch of the Archæological Survey, assisted by a well-trained staff of native draughtsmen, has made an elaborate survey of the Great Moghul's palace city. The first instalment of the results of his work lies before us in a handsome quarto volume, illustrated by one hundred and twenty-five full-page plates, of which some are drawings and others photo-etchings.

"The size of the work prevents its publication in one volume. The first part now published deals with the *Mahál-i-Khas*, including Akbar's bed-room, the *Panch Mahál*, the *Diwan-i-Khas*, and a few other buildings. The second part deals with Raja Bir Bal's house and the palace of Jodh Bai; the third will treat of Salim Chishti's shrine, the Turkish baths and many other edifices; and the fourth part will be devoted to the Great Mosque. Both the third and fourth parts will be enriched with coloured illustrations of the mural decoration and inlaid work. The volume now issued contains ten coloured plates, reproducing fresco paintings and ornaments, which have been executed by Messrs. Griggs and Son with their usual skill. These frescoes attract little attention from the ordinary visitor, and are now so damaged as scarcely to repay the cost and trouble of reproduction. One of the best executed and most intelligible fragments is that on the north wall of Akbar's bed-room, which represent some passengers of distinction taking their pleasure in a sailing boat, apparently on the Jumna. The figures are well drawn in the style affected by the miniature painters. In all the drawings the perspective is very bad. Some of the paintings exhibit distinct and unmistakable traces of Chinese influence. Others seem to be imitations of Japanese motives, and several offer clear evidence of the influence exercised on Akbar's eclectic taste by Christian religious art.

"The best known of the frescoes, that on the western façade of Miriam's House, which the guide points out as a picture of the Annunciation, may possibly be intended to represent that event. But the guide's theory that Miriam, or Mary, was a Christian wife of Akbar, is unsupported by any evidence, and is opposed to the evidence that exists. The queen of Akbar who enjoyed the title of *Maryam uz-Zamani*, or 'the Mary of the age,' was really the daughter of a Hindu Raja. Akbar's mother was known by a similar title, *Maryam Makani*, and there is no more reason for believing Akbar's queen, who bore the court title of *Maryam-uz Zamani*, to have been a Christian, than there is for believing in the Christianity of his mother. In short, Akbar's Christian queen seems to be the creature of the imagination of guides greedy for *bucksheesh*. But errors fed by *bucksheesh* die hard, and Akbar's Christian queen is bound to reappear frequently for the next hundred years. The Roman Catholic priests insist on believing in her existence, and their congregations, of course, are of the same opinion.

"The celebrated throne-pillar in the *Diwan-i-Khas* is perhaps the most curious of the many marvels at Fatehpur. It is adequately illustrated by a dozen well-selected plates. We are by no means disposed to accept Mr. Keene's suggestion that the little building occupied by the throne-pillar is the *Ibadat Khana*, or hall, in which Akbar used to amuse himself with listening to set debates by the professors of rival creeds. The building is far too small for such a purpose, and does not agree well with the recorded description of the *Ibadat Khana*. It is more probable, as Mr Smith observes, that the hall lay just outside the private buildings of the palace, than inside their precincts, and ruins of an important building exist near the Record Office in a position which would have been very suitable for a hall such as is described by the contemporary historian.

"We must not linger longer over the beauties of Akbar's magnificent, though singularly uncomfortable, palace. We can recommend Mr. Smith's book as an excellent piece of work, thoroughly well done; and can assure our readers that merely as a picture book it is good value for twenty rupees. The printing and paper are first rate. The binding, alas, is of the worst possible quality, and not even fit for a report by a Board of Revenue. When the next part comes out the local Government should follow the example of Bombay and treat its pretty pictures to safe and decent covering."—*The Pioneer*, July 12th, 1896.

ADDENDA.

	Dehra Dún	Tomb of Mrs. M. Evans, died 1847.	Sacred to the memory of Mary Evans, the affectionate wife of Major F. R. Evans, Commanding Sirmoor Battalion, aged 26 years 1 month and 16 days, beloved and respected by all who knew her. Dehra Dún, February 22nd 1847. While sorrow weeps o'er virtue's sacred dust, Our tears become us, and our grief is just. Such were the tears he shed, who grateful pays This last sad tribute of his love and praise; Who mourns the best of wives and friends combined, Where female sweetness met the accomplished mind; Mourns, but not murmurs, sighs but not despairs, Feels as a man, but as a Christian bears.
'o the north-west of Lal Tiba.	Ditto	Tomb of Major W. Blundell, died 1834.	Sacred to the memory of Major William Blundell, XI. Dragoons, who was killed by falling with his horse on the south side of the Landour Hill, on the 12th November 1834, aged 54 years. "*It is a faithful saying and worthy of all acceptation that Jesus Christ came into the world to save sinners.*"—In Him alone is our hope of salvation for this our dear brother, whose kind and affectionate heart endeared him as a son and as a brother, and whose departure hence is severely felt, and deeply mourned by his family and by many friends.
...	Meerut ...	Tomb of Lieutenant R. Maxwell, died 1825.	Sacred to the memory of Robert Maxwell, Esquire, Lieutenant H. M.'s XI. Light Dragoons, who died on 27th August 1827, aged 27 years and 10 months. This tablet is erected as a tribute of the esteem in which he was held while living, and sorrow for his premature fate, by some of his brother-officers, who intimately knew and deeply ap-

		preciated the many excellences of his head and heart. Alas !! Poor Maxwell !!!		
Ditto ...	Tomb of Mrs. M. M. Blackney, died 1825.	Sacred to the memory of Mrs. M. M. Blackney, wife of Lieutenant-Colonel Blackney, who departed this life, 11th January 1825, aged 24 years. This monument is erected in testimony of her worth and of his unfeigned grief by her affectionate husband. Here also resteth John, son of Colonel Blackney, deceased on 20th July 1825, 7 months.		
Ditto ...	Tomb of W. F. Neville, died 1836.	Sacred to the memory of W. F. Neville, Paymaster, H. M.'s 11th Regiment of Light Dragoons, who departed this life on 3rd February 1836. This tablet is erected by his brother-officers as a tribute of esteem for his sterling worth and uniform kindness of heart, and a memento of grief for his departure.		
Ditto ...	Tomb of Captain Thomas Warlow, died 1837.	Sacred to the memory of Captain Thomas Warlow, Bengal Engineers, who departed this life on the 2nd February 1839, aged 41 years. He lived beloved and died lamented.		
Aligarh ...	Tomb of Lieutenant John Thurton, killed 1803.	To the memory of Lieutenant John Thurton, 1st Battalion, 4th Native Infantry, who was killed at the assault of Aligarh, on the 4th September 1803, *aetatis suae* 25. This monument, the tribute of affection, was erected by a friend.		NOTE – This officer's name is not mentioned on the monument at Aligarh, see entry No. 80.
Ditto ...	Tomb of Lieutenant J. H. Young, killed 1807.	Lieutenant J. H. Young, who fell before Comonah, 14th November 1807, aged 25 years.		
Ditto ...	Tomb of Lieutenant F. E. B. Bennet, died 1830.	Sacred to the memory of Francis Edward Burton Bennet, Lieutenant, Bengal Engineers, who died at Aligarh, 17th August 1830, aged 21 years.		

541	Aligarh Fort Cemetery.	...	Aligarh ...	Tomb of Sergeant Samuel Low, died 1830.	In memory of Sergeant Samuel Low, of the Engineer Department, who died on the 12th June 1830, from the immediate effects of exposure to the sun, in the zealous performance of his duty. This tomb has been erected by his commanding officer.		
542	Ditto ...		Ditto ...	Tomb of Lieutenant F. W. Clement, died 1830.	Sacred to the memory of Lieutenant Francis William Clement, of the Bengal Engineers, who departed this life on the 4th June 1830, aged 21 years. As a mark of esteem and regret, this tomb has been erected by his sincere friends. Henry and Jane DeBude		
543	Ditto ...	...	Ditto ...	Tomb of Lieutenant H. Apperley, died 1838.	To the memory of Herbert Apperley, Esq., Lieutenant, 6th Regiment, Bengal N. I., who died at Aligarh on the 7th November 1838, deeply and sincerely regretted, aged 32 years and 6 months. This tomb was erected by the officers of his regiment as a testimony of their regard and esteem.		

List of Christian Tombs or Monuments in the Agra Division possessing historical or archæological interest.

Serial number.	Name of cemetery, churchyard, or church.	Where situated (giving exact situation as far as possible).	District.	Tomb or Monument to the memory of—	Inscription on Tomb or Monument.	Inscription of slabs or pillars placed in churches or chapels.	Remarks. Tombs on road-sides, or battle-fields (furnishing information as in columns 3, 4, 5 and 6).
1	2	3	4	5	6	7	8
544			Muttra...	Tomb of B. F. Wroughton, died 1834.			(3) About four furlongs from the tahsili at Sadabad in the Muttra district is a tomb with the following inscription:— (6) To the memory of Bartholomew Francis, fifth son of Captain Robert Wroughton, 69th Regiment, N. I., Revenue Surveyor of the Agra Division, and Sophia, his wife. Born 17th January 1830, died 17th March 1834, aged 4 years and 2 months.
545	Old Protestant Cemetery, Civil Lines, Agra.	To the south of St. Paul's Church.	Agra ...	Tomb of an English merchant (*name lost*), died 1627.	.........of Justinian of L.........C......... was chief merchant in Agra Fo......... he deceased.........April 1627.		NOTE.—The tombs (Nos. 545—581) are situated on the left hand side of the gateway leading into the cemetery. The platform as well as the tombstones are of red sandstone. It appears from these inscriptions that during the reign of Shâhjahân and Aurangzeb there were at Agra a number of English and Dutch traders.
546	Ditto ...	Ditto ...	Ditto ...	Tomb of John De Boeck, died 1627.	Her leyt begraven Ioan DeBoeck van Amsterdam, in syn leven Adsisten. Obyt 19th September Anno 1629, out 35 yaren.		
547	Ditto ...	Ditto ...	Ditto ...	Tomb of John Drake Slaine, died 1649.	Here lye the body of John Drake Slaine ....Anno Domini 1637.........A. Domini 1647.		
548	Ditto ...	Ditto ...	Ditto ...	Tomb of Elizabeth Tack, died 1649.	Hier leyt begraven Elizabet, in haer leven housvrow van den Opercoopman Yohan Tack, obit ten 19th October, Anno 1649, out 30 yaren.		
549	Ditto ...	Ditto ...	Ditto ...	Tomb of George Purchas, died 1651.	Here lye the body of George Purchas, who deceased in Agra, the 14th July 1651, *ætatis suæ 24*. *Memento mori.*		

List of Christian Tombs or Monuments in the Agra Division possessing historical or archæological interest—(continued).

Serial Number.	Name of cemetery, churchyard or church.	Where situated (giving exact situation as far as possible).	District.	Tomb or Monument to the memory of—	Inscription on Tomb or Monument.	Inscription on slabs or pillars placed in churches or chapels.	Remarks. Tombs on road-sides or battle-fields (furnishing information as in columns 3, 4, 5 and 6).
1	2	3	4	5	6	7	8
550	Old Protestant Cemetery, Civil Lines, Agra.	To the south, of St. Paul's Church.	Agra ...	Tomb of John Tack, died 1663.	Hier leyt begraven Joan Tack van Amboyna, oudt 56 yaren, in syn leven Opercoopman, obyt 11th Januari 1663.		
551	Ditto ...	Ditto ...	Ditto ...	Tomb of Peter De Liem, died 1679.	Hier leyt begraven Pieter De Liem van Randerhuysen, in syn leven Boeckhoder, obyt 29th Maert, Anno 1679, out 35 yaren.		
552	Old R. Catholic Cemetery, Agra.	Near Civil Courts.	Ditto ...	Tomb of Father Manuel Garcia, who died in prison for the faith on the 23rd March 1634.	Aquis iazo Padre Mel. Garcia, clerigo, morto no carcere pe la fe a 23 de Marco 1634.		NOTE.—Fathers Manuel Garcia and Manuel Danhaya were made war-prisoners at the capture of Hughli in 1631 by the Moghals and sent to Agra, where they died in prison in consequence of their fatigues and sufferings. The two tombstones are at present in the Mortuary Chapel called by the Native Christians *Padri Santos*, evidently a corruption of the Portuguese *Padre Santo*. Its floor is made of tombstones bearing in Portuguese the names and dates of the deaths of the following 22 Catholic priests:— Padre Manuel Garcia ... 1634 " Francesco Lanfranki ... 1634 " Antonio da Fonseqa ... 1634 " Manuel Danhaya ... 1635 " Francesco Corsi ... 1635 " Antonio Machado ... 1636 " Joseph da Castro ... 1646 " Antonio Sequre ... 1656 " Francesco da Souza ... 1657 " Alberto de Reville ... 1662 " Paulo de Mattos ... 1664 " Henrico da Veron ... 1666 " Joseph da Costa ... 1685 " Marco Antonio Santucci ... 1689 " Joseph da Padua ... 1706 " Efoiso Posfado ... 1706 " Antonio Demagosque ... 1707 " Anton Gabelsberger ... 1741 " Francesco da Cruz ... 1742 " Mattheeus Rodrigues ... 1748 " Abel Sperger ... 1761 " Francesco Xavier ... 1767
553	Ditto ...	Ditto ...	Ditto ...	Tomb of Father Manuel Danhaya, who died in prison for the faith on the 2nd August 1635.	Aquis iazo Padre Mel. Danhaya, clerigo, morto pe la fe ena prisao a 2 Agosto 1635.		

							Some of the tombstones in this chapel bear epitaphs in Armenian and record the deaths of the following priests:— Episcopus Zachar from Tabrez ... 1618 Presbyter Johannes ... 1669 " Patros ... 1682 " Pagdasar ... 1684 " Arratun ... 1776 *See also* Note to entry No. 74.
554	Ditto ...	Ditto ...	Ditto ...	Tomb of Khoja Mortenepus, Armenian merchant, died 1611.	Here lies the holy Khoja Mortenepus, Armenian, who was a professed disciple of Christ, and who was a righteous man; whatever he had, he gave in charity to the poor, in token of fidelity to his Divine Master, in the year one thousand six hundred and eleven from the birth of Christ.		NOTE.—The epitaph of Khoja or Khwaja Mortenepus is in Persian, a literal translation of which is given in column 6. The tombstone is in the Mortuary Chapel. The date of the epitaph, the high opinion of holiness in which Mortenepus was held, his wealth and the conspicuous place occupied by his tomb, seem to show that the chapel was originally erected as a funeral monument to his memory. About 60 paces from the north wall of the enclosure of the tomb of Mir Abdulla, a poet of Jahangir's reign are lying on a low mound in the fields seven Christian tombstones, with Portuguese epitaphs, two of which are dated Anno Domini 1736 and 1758, respectively. The former records the death of the wife of one Mirza Gulzar.
155	Cantonment Cemetery, Agra.	Ditto ...	Ditto ...	Tomb of Lieutenant-Colonel Joseph Taylor, B. E., died 1835.	To the memory of Lieutenant-Colonel Joseph Taylor, Bengal Engineers, who departed this life, 20th April 1835, aged 45. The Taj and Akbar's tomb were repaired and restored to beauty by this officer.		NOTE.—Lieutenant Joseph Taylor arrived in India in 1808, and was posted to Agra as Assistant to Captain Steele, the Garrison Engineer, to whose appointment he eventually succeeded, retaining it till 1826, between which period and 1830, when he returned to Agra as Superintending Engineer of the N.-W. Provinces, he successfully filled the appointments of Executive Engineer at Dinapore, Garrison Engineer and Civil Architect of Fort William, and for a short period that of Acting Chief Engineer. In the early part of his service at Agra Lieutenant Taylor was frequently employed in the reduction of the numerous small forts in the vicinity of this station, at that time occupied by refractory zamindárs, whom the recollection of successful resistance to the attempted collections of former native governors and ignorance of our power occasionally led to vain opposition to the British revenue authorities, or an endeavour to protect the hordes of freebooters with which the Agra district was then infested. The cool and determined courage of Lieutenant Taylor was manifest in all these affairs, and opportunity was not wanting for its conspicuous display on more than one occasion. In the year 1810, Lieutenant Taylor was selected by the Government to repair the Taj, and when the limited sum granted for repairs, as compared with the extent of work executed is considered, the praise bestowed by his superiors, on completion of his duty,

List of Christian Tombs or Monuments in the Agra Division possessing historical or archæological interest—(continued).

Serial number.	Name of cemetery, churchyard or church.	Where situated (giving exact situation, as far as possible).	District.	Tomb or Monument to the memory of—	Inscription on Tomb or Monument.	Inscription on slabs or pillars placed in churches or chapels.	Remarks. Tombs on roadsides or battlefields (furnishing information as in columns 2, 4, 5, and 6).
	2	3	4	5	6	7	8
555	Cantonment Cemetery, Agra.	Near Civil Courts.	Agra ...	Tomb of Lieutenant-Colonel Joseph Taylor, B. E., died 1835.			most meet with general assent. The repair of Akbar's Mausoleum at Sikandra was another of his duties, and although many years have elapsed since the task was completed, the structure bears full evidence of his zealous exertions. Many other public works of beauty and utility might be instanced at Agra, as well as at Calcutta, in proof of his taste and ability in this branch of his profession. But it was not in the execution of his civil duties alone that this gallant officer merits our notice. He was found a volunteer at Hâthras in 1817, and was present during the siege and reduction of that fortress, the last and strongest of the forts of this class that had occasionally defied our power since the province of Agra and the Doab had become subject to the British rule. He was promoted to the rank of Captain on the 1st September 1818, and in this rank was among the most distinguished of the officers of his corps. At the siege and capture of the fortified town of Bhartpur in 1825-26, having been severely wounded in an attempt to blow up a gallery made by the enemy into the ditch, which greatly impeded the operations of th attacking force, he received the personal and written thanks of the Commander-in-Chief for his gallantry. His services at Bhartpur were further acknowledged by his promotion to a Brevet Majority from the date of the fall of that fortress. His promotion to the rank of Lieutenant-Colonel took place on the 18th June 1831, and he died at the early age of 44 at Agra, on the morning of the 24th April 1835, from an apoplectic attack, leaving behind him a general feeling of respect for his memory and of sympathy with those by whom his loss was severely felt.
556	R. Catholic Cathedral, Agra.	In Padritolah	Ditto ...	Tablet in memory of Father Francis, O. C., killed at Moodki, 1845.		Sacred to the memory of the Rev. Father Francis of St. Etienne, Apostolic Missionary of the Capuchin Order, who during the performance of his sacred duties towards the Catholic soldiers of	

						the British Army, fell a victim by the sword of the enemy in the field of Moodki, on the 18th December 1845, aged 34 years. A martyr of charity whom no danger could deter from attending to his flock ; a vigilant, a faithful shepherd. He attended the Kabul troops at Firozepore, was present with them at Mahárájpore, administering to their spiritual wants when cholera was afflicting Agra in 1843, and raging in Meerut in 1845. He was seen day and night in the hospitals, venerated and beloved by Catholics, esteemed and admired by those of a different creed. Friend to all, and enemy to none, zealous for the honour and glory of God, unaffected in his piety and devotion, compassionate to the widow, orphan and poor. He sealed his glorious course with his blood for the sake of those whom Christ had redeemed.	
857	Fort Cemetery, Fatehgarh.	On the banks of the river Ganges.	Farukhabad	Tomb of Major Charles Hay Campbell, B. A., died 19th May 1832.	[The inscription tablet was destroyed in the Mutiny.]		NOTE.—Major Campbell was the third son of William Campbell, Esquire, of Fairfield, North Britain. He entered the Bengal Artillery in 1808, and early rose to distinction for his zeal as an officer. He served with the army under Lord Lake, and on subsequent occasions, on actual service ; was early brought on the staff, first as Adjutant and Quartermaster of his corps in 1810, and since that time he has filled many situations on the General Staff of the Army until 1819, when he was appointed Deputy Secretary to Government in the Military Department ; and in 1821 he was nominated Agent for the supply of Gun Carriages at the Bengal Presidency, first at Cossipore, and afterwards at Fatehgarh, which he held until his death. As an officer, Major Campbell's professional attainments placed him in the highest rank of a corps pre-eminent for science and ability ; and the kindness and generosity of his disposition endeared him to all who had the happiness to partake of his friendship. Devoted to the public services and to the interests of his profession, he was ever actively employed in what could benefit the first or promote the last. His papers in the *British Indian Military Repository*, particularly those containing the *History of Sieges in Bengal*, are models of good writing on professional subjects and display a genius and talent which shone conspicuously in whatever he attempted.

List of Christian Tombs or Monuments in the Agra Division possessing historical or archæological interest—(concluded).

Serial number.	Name of Cemetery, Churchyard or Church.	Where situated (giving exact situation as far as possible.	District.	Tomb or Monument to the memory of—	Inscription on Tomb or Monument.	Inscription on slabs or pillars placed in churches or chapels.	Remarks. Tombs on roadsides or battlefields (furnishing information as in columns 3, 4, 5 and 6).
1	2	3	4	5	6	7	8
558	Fort Cemetery, Fatehgarh.	On the banks of the Ganges river.	Farukhabad	Tomb of Lieutenant W. Briggs Garret, died 1833.	Sacred to the memory of William Briggs Garret, Lieutenant in the H. C. Bengal Artillery, who departed this life on 25th July 1833, aged 29 years, deeply and sincerely regretted.		
559	Ditto ...	Ditto ...	Ditto ...	Tomb of Ensign J. William Tomkyns, died 1834.	To the memory of Ensign John William Tomkyns, 1st Regiment, N. I., who departed this life on the 31st May 1834. Erected by his brother-officers and friends at the station in testimony of their esteem and regard for his many amiable qualities.		
560	Ditto ...	Ditto ...	Ditto ...	Tomb of Lieutenant James Fisher, died 1835.	Sacred to the memory of Lieutenant James Fisher, Interpreter and Quartermaster, 1st Regiment N. I., who departed this life at Fatehgarh on the 3rd January 1835. Erected by his brother-officers and friends in testimony of their esteem and regard.		
561	Ditto ...	Ditto ...	Ditto ...	Tomb of Major R. Bell Fulton, died 1836.	Sacred to the memory of Major Robert Bell Fulton, of the Regiment of Bengal Artillery, who departed this life on 11th May 1836, aged 48 years. He was an upright, honourable man and a sincere Christian, possessing high professional abilities and distinguished for those private virtues which endear men to society. This monument is erected by his brother-officers and friends in testimony of their regard and esteem.		
562	Ditto ...	Ditto ...	Ditto ...	Tomb of Captain Goodwin Warner, died 1812.	To the memory of Captain Goodwin Warner, 2nd Battalion, 22nd Regiment N. I., who departed this life on the 2nd of January A.D. 1812, aged 32 years.		

563	Ditto ...	Ditto ...	Ditto ...	Tomb of Captain W. H. Royle, died 1806.	Herein was deposited the remains of William Henry Royle, late Captain in the H.C.'s Service, which he served 25 years with fidelity, bravery and honor; he died October 29th, 1806, in his 40th year. This is erected to his memory by his afflicted wife, who, after nine years of uninterrupted felicity, now, with four children, is left to mourn his tender goodness of heart and many amiable qualities.		
564	Ditto ...	Ditto ...	Ditto ...	Tomb of Major Francis Hudson, died 1797.	Sacred to the memory of Major Francis Hudson, who departed this life on April 27th, 1797.		
565	Ditto ...	Ditto ...	Ditto ...	Tomb of Lieutenant-Colonel Leonard Simpson, died 1806.	To the memory of Lieutenant-Colonel Leonard Simpson, 2nd Battalion, 2nd Regiment, who died on the 1st June 1806, in the 49th year of his age. As a commanding officer he was esteemed and respected, and in his death all the officers of his corps lament the loss of a most sincere friend.		
566	Ditto ...	Ditto ...	Ditto ...	Tomb of Lieutenant H. C. O'Dowda, died 1858.	Sacred to the memory of H. C. O'Dowda, of the 48th B. N. I., Acting Adjutant of the 4th Punjab Rifles, who, having been preserved by God's mercy through the whole of the memorable siege of Lucknow in the year 1857, died at Fatehgarh on the 20th January 1858, at the early age of 18 years 8 months and 17 days.		

List of Christian Tombs or Monuments in the Rohilkhand Division possessing historical or archæological interest.

Serial number.	Name of Cemetery, Churchyard, or Church.	Where situated (giving exact situation as far as possible).	District.	Tomb or Monument to the memory of—	Inscription on Tomb or Monument.	Inscription on slabs or pillars placed in churches or chapels.	Remarks. Tombs on roadsides, or battlefields (furnishing information as in columns 3, 4, 5 and 6).
1	2	3	4	5	6	7	8
567	Old Cemetery, Bareilly.	...	Bareilly ...	Tomb of Judge James Charles Dick, died 1831.	To the memory of James Charles Dick, Judge and Magistrate of Zillah Bareilly, 4th son of Dr. Dick of Tullymet, Pertshire, North Britain, born 23rd August 1792, died 17th November 1831, deeply regretted by his friends and relations.		
568	Moradabad Cemetery.		Moradabad,	Tomb of R. Grote, C.S., died 1829.	Sacred to the memory of Robert Grote, Esquire, of the Civil Service, 7th son of George Grote, Esquire of Badgemore in the County of Oxfordshire, who departed this life on the 23rd February 1829 at Jeypore near Moradabad, aged 20 years and 6 months.		
569	Shâhjahânpur Cemetery.	...	Shâhjahânpur.	Tomb of Lieut. H. Montague Barwell, died 1837.	Sacred to the memory of Henry Montague Barwell, Lieutenant in the 69th B. N. I., second son of E. R. Barwell Esquire, H. C.'s Service, who died 8th of August 1837 in the 26th year of his age. In ever relation of life, whether as a Christian, soldier, son, brother or friend, he commanded the love and esteem of all who knew him. This tablet is erected by his afflicted parents as a frail memorial of his worth and their affection.		

List of Christian Tombs or Monuments in the Allahabad Division possessing historical or archæological interest.

Serial number.	Name of cemetery, churchyard, or church.	Where situated (giving exact situation as far as possible).	District.	Tomb or Monument to the memory of—	Inscription on Tomb or Monument.	Inscription on slabs or pillars placed in churches or chapels.	Tombs on road-sides or battle-fields (furnishing information as in columns 2, 4, 5 and 6).
1	2	3	4	5	6	7	8
570	Kacheri Cemetery, Cawnpore.	To the north of the Collector's office.	Cawnpore	Tomb of Lieutenant-Colonel Harry Stark, died 1830.	Sacred to the memory of Lieutenant-Colonel Harry Stark, of the Bengal Horse Artillery, who departed this life on the 26th September 1830, aged 55 years. He lived universally respected as an honest man and gallant soldier.		NOTE.—Mr. Stark arrived in India in September 1794 and joined the Bengal Artillery as Lieutenant Fireworker. In 1795 he was present with the army under General Stuart at the conquest of the Dutch settlements on the island of Ceylon. From 1799 to 1802 Lieutenant Stark was in Egypt with a detachment of artillery; in December 1803, he joined Lord Lake's army, with which he served during the remainder of the campaigns of the Maratha War, and was present at the sieges of Dig and Bhartpur. Accompanied Major-General John Smith's detachment into Rohilkhand, and was present at the battle of Afzalgarh, and afterwards at that of Fatehgarh under Lord Lake. Present at the sieges of Commonah and Gannauri, at the former of which Lieutenant Stark was wounded. Served under Colonels Martindell and Adams in Bundelkhand and Rewah in 1813 and 1814; under the latter officer Major Stark commanded the artillery at the attack of the Fort of Entauri in Rewah. He served with the first Division of the Grand Army under the Marquis of Hastings in 1817-18. Lieutenant Colonel Stark was present with Lord Combermere's army at the siege and capture of Bhartpur on the 18th January 1826, and it fell to his lot to be the field officer on duty in the batteries on the day of the storm. Such were the services of this officer, marked throughout by a degree of zeal and energy which could not be surpassed.
571	Ditto ...	Ditto ...	Ditto ...	Tomb of Lieutenant-Colonel Nation, C.B., died 1828.	Sacred to the memory of Lieutenant-Colonel Commandant Nation, C. B. This monument is erected as a tribute of respect, affection and regret by the European, Native Commissioned and Non-commissioned officers of the 9th Regiment, Native Infantry, in which he rose from the rank of an Ensign to that of a Lieutenant-Colonel. When proceeding to the charge of a Brigadier's command at Dehli, he died at Cawnpore on the 2nd August 1828, ætat. 49 years.		

Kache-i Cemetery, Cawnpore.	To the north of the Collector's office.	Cawnpore	Tomb of Brigadier, G. Home Murray, C.B., died 1833.	This monument is erected by the officers of Her Majesty's 16th Lancers as a token of respect and regard to the memory of Brigadier George Home Murray, C. B., Lieutenant-Colonel of Her Majesty's 16th Lancers, in which corps he served with the utmost gallantry and distinction for a period of nearly...years. Died in command of the Cawnpore station on the 15th December 1833, aged 59 years.
Ditto ...	Ditto ...	Ditto ...	Tomb of Lieutenant E. Aston McMurdo, died 1829.	The sorrow, esteem and love of his brother-officers are fully displayed by this monument raised to the memory of Edward Aston McMurdo, Lieutenant, 33rd Regiment, Native Infantry, in whose amiable character the rarest and most endearing qualities were combined; manly, intelligent and generous; the integrity of his conduct, the gentleness of his manners, his noble spirit and feeling heart caused him to be valued and beloved in life, in death most deeply lamented. He was born at Edinburgh, and died at Cawnpore on the 25th January 1829, aged 25 years.
Ditto ...	Ditto ...	Ditto ...	Tomb of Major H. E. Peach, died 1833.	Underneath rest the remains of Major Henry Edward Peach, of the 16th Regiment, Native Infantry, and Deputy Commissary-General of the Bengal Army, *obiit*, May 3rd, 1833. His brother-officers and friends have erected this monument as a last tribute of respect to his memory and in testimony of their esteem, affection, and regret.

575	Ditto ...	Ditto ...	Ditto ...	Tomb of Lieutenant-Colonel W. Worsly Davis, died 1833.	Sacred to the memory of the late Lieutenant-Colonel William Worsly Davis, Bengal Army, who departed this life on the 15th September 1833, aged 49 years.		
576	Ditto ...	Ditto ...	Ditto ...	Tomb of Lieutenant George Crofton, died 1833.	Sacred to the memory of George Crofton, Esquire, Lieutenant, Her Majesty 16th Lancers, youngest son of the late A. B. Crofton, Esquire, of Roebuck Castle, County of Dublin. *Obiit* 24th August 1833, *ætat.* 26 years.		
577	Ditto ...	Ditto ...	Ditto ...	Tomb of Lieutenant P. T. R. White, died 1833.	Sacred to the memory of P. T. R. White, Esquire, Lieutenant, H. M.'s 31st Regiment of Infantry, second son of W. B. White, Esquire, Surgeon, H. M.'s 16th Lancers. *Obiit* 1st September 1833, *ætat.* 26 years.		
578	Ditto ...	Ditto ...	Ditto ...	Tomb of R. Foley, died 1827.	Sacred to the memory of Richard Foley, who departed this life on the 3rd August 1827, aged 45 years and 11 months. He was gifted with an excellent heart, an urbanity of manners and a benevolence of disposition which seldom becomes to the lot of one man, and his virtues had so truly endeared him to his friends, that it is only when memory shall fail to record them, that they can cease to regret his loss. This monument is erected by his affectionate wife, in testimony of respected esteem for the many eminent and excellent qualities he possessed as a husband, a father and a friend.		
579	Fatehpur Cemetery.	...	Fatehpur ...	Tomb of Edward Smyth, C. S., died 1833.	Sacred to the memory of Edward Smyth, Esquire, of the Civil Service, eldest son of Edward Smyth, Esquire, of the Fence, near Macclesfield, Cheshire. Born 22nd July 1808, and died 14th September 1833. This tomb is erected by his affectionate brother W. M. S.		
580	Bánda Cemetery.		Bánda ...	Tomb of Brevet-Captain the Hon'ble P. C. Sinclair, died 1834.	This stone is sacred to the memory of the Honorable Patrick Campbell Sinclair, Brevet-Captain in the 70th Regiment N. I., who died at this place on the 13th March 1834, in the 34th year of his age. Erected in grateful affection by his afflicted widow.		

List of Christian Tombs or Monuments in the Allahabad Division possessing historical or archæological interest—(concluded).

Serial number.	Name of cemetery, churchyard, or church.	Where situated (giving exact situation as far as possible).	District.	Tomb or Monument to the memory of—	Inscription on Tomb or Monument.	Inscription on slabs or pillars placed in churches or chapels.	Remarks. Tombs on road-sides, or battle-fields (furnishing information as in columns 3, 4, 5 and 6.)
1	2	3	4	5	6	7	8
581	Kydganj Cemetery, Allahabad.		Allahabad,	Tomb of W. Scott, Assistant Surgeon, died 1844.	Sacred to the memory of Walter Scott, Esquire, Assistant Surgeon, E. I. Company's Service, second son of Walter Scott, Esquire, of Wauchpol, Roxburghshire, N. B., who died at Allahabad 17th August 1844, aged 27 years.		
582	Kalpi Cemetery.	Near the Fort	Jalaun ...	Tomb of Thomas Moodie, died 1824.	To the memory of Thomas Moodie, Esquire, Officiating Political Agent in Bundelkhand, who departed this life on April 27th, 1824, aged 3[illegible] years.		

List of Christian Tombs or Monuments in the Benares Division possessing historical or archæological interest.

rial ber.	Name of cemetery, churchyard, or church.	Where situated (giving exact situation as far as possible).	District.	Tomb or Monument to the memory of—	Inscription on Tomb or Monument.	Inscription on slabs or pillars placed in churches or chapels.	Remarks. Tombs on roadsides, or battlefields (furnishing information as in columns 3, 4, 5 and 6).
.	2	3	4	5	6	7	8
583	Old Civil Cemetery, Benares.	At Chauka-ghat.	Benares...	Tomb of Captain George Snodgrass, died 1825.	Sacred to the memory of Captain George Snodgrass, 23rd Regiment, N. I., Deputy Paymaster, Benares, who departed this life on the 11th January 1825, sincerely regretted by his friends, aged 43 years.		
584	Ditto ...	Ditto ...	Ditto ...	Tomb of William Lowther, died 1833.	Sacred to the memory of William Lowther, Esquire, Judge of the Court of Appeal at Benares, who died on the 2nd March 1833, in the 50th year of his age.		
585	Ditto ...	Ditto ...	Ditto ...	Tomb of W. Augustus Brooke, died 1833.	Sacred to the memory of William Augustus Brooke, Senior Judge of the Court of Appeal, and Agent to the Governor-General at Benares, who died on the 10th July 1833, in the eighty-first year of his age. His amiable character endeared him alike to the Hindu, the Musalman and the Christian inhabitants of this city.		
586	Ditto ...	Ditto ...	Ditto ...	Tomb of Major-General Clements Brown, C. B., died 1838.	Sacred to the memory of Clements Brown, Companion of the Most Honorable Military Order of the Bath, Colonel in the regiment of Bengal Artillery, and Major-General on the staff of the army. A soldier from his youth, he delighted in his profession, and after an uninterrupted career of more than half a century of gallant and honorable service, and while still in the active and zealous discharge of his duties, departed this life 25th April 1838, aged 72 years.		

List of Christian Tombs or Monuments in the Benares Division possessing historical or archæological interest—(continued).

Serial number.	Name of cemetery, churchyard or church.	Where situated (giving exact situation as far as possible.	District.	Tomb or Monument to the memory of—	Inscription on Tomb or Monument.	Inscription on slabs or pillars placed in churches or chapels.	Remarks. Tombs on roadsides or battlefields (furnishing information as in columns 3, 4, 5 and 6).
1	2	3	4	5	6	7	8
587	Mirzapur Cemetery.	Near Post-office.	Mirzapur...	Tomb of Ensign J. R. Piercy, died 1827.	Sacred to the memory of Ensign J. R. Piercy, 6th Extra Regiment N. I., who departed this life on the 17th November 1827, aged 17 years. This monument is erected by his brother-officers as a mark of their esteem.		
588	Ditto ...	Ditto ...	Ditto ...	Tomb of Lieutenant Coaly Burrowes, died 1829.	To the memory of Lieutenant Coaly Burrowes, 46th Regiment N I., who died December 9th, 1829.		
589	Ditto ..	Ditto ...	Ditto ...	Tomb of Mrs. E. E. Neville Skene, died 1828.	Sacred to the memory of Emma Eliza Neville Skene, wife of Major W. Skene, 5th Extra Regiment N. I., who departed this life on the morning of the 8th September 1828, aged 37 years and 10 months. This monument is erected by her disconsolate husband as a tribute of affection and regard for one who had for nearly 22 years fulfilled her duties as an affectionate wife with true Christian piety and virtue. The Lord gave and the Lord hath taken away, blessed be the name of the Lord.		
590	Old Cemetery, Chunar.	Below the Fort.	Ditto ...	Tomb of John Lawrence, died 1828.	Sacred to the memory of Mr. John Lawrence, Assistant Commissary of Ordnance, who departed this life on the 10th February A.D 1828, aged 52 years. This tomb is erected by his afflicted widow.		
591	Ditto ...	Ditto ...	Ditto ...	Tomb of Lieutenant-Colonel J. F. Paschoud, died 1814.	Sacred to the memory of John Francis Paschoud, late Lieutenant-Colonel in the Bengal Artillery, who departed this life on the 18th January 1814, aged 47 years.		

			This monument is erected by his sons F. and C. Paschoud, as a lasting testimony to the ashes of an affectionate parent.		
...	Ditto ...	Tomb of Captain B. Maltby, died 1829.	Sacred to the memory of Captain B. Maltby, Bengal Artillery, who departed this life on 2nd November 1829, aged 37 year.		
...	Ditto ...	Tomb of Captain R. Menzies, died 1826.	Sacred to the memory of Captain R. Menzies, of the Invalid Establishment, died 22nd April 1826.		
...	Ditto ...	Tomb of Rev. Charles Friend, died 1829.	Sacred to the memory of Rev. Charles Friend, who died June 12th, 1829. He was both an indefatigable minister and a genuine missionary of the Church of England.		
...	Ditto ...	Tomb of Captain W. B. L. Faithful, died 1836.	Sacred to the memory of Captain W. B. L. Faithful, of the Bengal Artillery, who died on the 18th November 1836.		
...	Ditto ...	Tomb of Lieutenant-Colonel W. Bensley Walker, died 1839.	Sacred to the memory of Lieutenant-Colonel William Bensley Walker, Commanding the European Invalids, who died 19th September 1839, aged 58 years and 9 months.		
...	Ditto ...	Tomb of Colonel Charles Poole, died 1843.	Sacred to the memory of Colonel Charles Poole of the Invalid Establishment, Commanding this garrison, who departed this life on 24th November 1843. This monument is erected as a tribute of affection and regret for the best and kindest of relations by his two surviving sisters, M. J. and L. Poole.		
...	Ditto ...	Tomb of Henry Shinks, died 1839.	Sacred to the memory of Henry Shinks, Apothecary, General Hospital, Chunar, born 25th July 1809, died 10th July 1839. Thy wife, dear Henry, o'er thy mouldering earth, Erects this tribute to departed worth. Thy faith and virtue, gifts of Grace Divine, Mark'd thee for bliss, then why should I repine? But yet, thy love, to my remembrance dear, Exacts the rising sigh, the gushing tear. O may thy wife and babes, life's wandering o'er, Meet thy lov'd shade! in heaven to part no more.		

List of Christian Tombs or Monuments in the Benares Division possessing historical or archæological interest—(concluded).

Serial number.	Name of CEMETERY, CHURCHYARD, OR CHURCH.	WHERE SITUATED (giving exact situation as far as possible).	DISTRICT.	Tomb or Monument to the memory of—	INSCRIPTION ON TOMB OR MONUMENT.	INSCRIPTION ON SLABS OR PILLARS PLACED IN CHURCHES OR CHAPELS.	REMARKS. TOMBS ON ROAD-SIDES, OR BATTLE-FIELDS (furnishing information as in columns 3, 4, 5 and 6).
1	2	3	4	5	6	7	8
599	Old Cemetery, Chunar.	Below the Fort.	Mirzapur	Tomb of D. W. Taylor, died 1834.	Sacred to the memory of Daniel William Taylor, late Asst. Apothecary, H. C. Service, who departed this life on 30th August 1834, aged 29 years and 22 days. That blameless virtue, which adorned thy bloom, Lamenting Sarah, now weeps o'er thy tomb, What neither wealth could buy, nor power decree, Regard and pity unite sincere on thee, While soft remembrance drops a willing tear, And thy dear Sarah sits chief mourner here. This tomb was erected by his truly affectionate widow, Sarah Taylor.		

INDEX TO THE LIST

OF

Christian Tombs and Monuments

of Archæological or Historical Interest

AND THEIR INSCRIPTIONS

IN THE

NORTH-WESTERN PROVINCES AND OUDH

BY A. FUHRER, Ph. D.
ARCHÆOLOGICAL SURVEYOR, N.-W. P. AND OUDH.

(Index compiled in the P. W. D. Secretariat, N.-W. P. and Oudh.)

ALLAHABAD:
Printed at the North-Western Provinces and Oudh Government Press.
1899.

A.

Page.

Abbots, J., *Sergeant* 11
Adams, *Sir John W., Major-General* 29
Adams, T. 40
Agnew, W., *Cornet* 159
Aitken, R. H. M., *Colonel, V.C.* 145
Alcock, *Captain* 36
Alexander, A. H., *Lieutenant* 81
Alexander, D. C., *Lieutenant* 137
Alexander, Mr. 84
Alexander, Mr. 55
Allan, R. D. B., *Assistant Surgeon* 49
Allen, J. W. 60
Allen, R., *Private* 85
Allen, T., *Private* 83
Allnutt, A., Mrs. 143
Allnutt, L. E., Miss 143
Almond, *Sub-Conductor* 76
Alone, Mr. and Mrs. 38
Alone, Mr. 51
Ammaun, S., Mrs. 127
Amos, G., *Private* 124
Amos, W., *Private* 85
Anderson, A., *Corporal* 85
Anderson, J., *Sergeant* 85
Anderson, J. C. 51
Anderson, Mr. 35
Anderson, R. 48
Anderson, W., *Private* 157
Andrews, C., Miss 111
Andrews, F., *Captain* 16
Andrews, Mr. 87
Andrews, *Quarter-Master-Sergeant* 48
Andrews, R. 87
Andrews, T. 87
Angelo, F. C., *Lieutenant* 58
Anne, Julia, *Her Highness Bahu Begam,* 13
Apperley, H., *Lieutenant* 172
Applegate, T. G. B., *Ensign* 59
Archer, H. 82
Archer, H. 83
Armitage, H., *Private* 16
Armstrong, A., *Lieutenant* 103
Armstrong, G. C. 120
Armstrong, H. B., *Captain* 10
Armstrong, H. H., *Lieutenant* 48
Armstrong, J. 121
Armstrong, W., *Corporal* 25
Arnold, R., *Lieutenant-Colonel* 10
Arnold, R. E., Mrs. 143
Arnold, W. B., *Lieutenant* 134
Arratun, *Revd.* 175

Page.

Arthur, L. A., *Lieutenant* 139
Ashburner, B., *Lieutenant* 47
Ashe, St. G. 47
Ashern, *Conductor and Mrs.* 35
Ashern, J., *Conductor* 32
Aspinall, Mr. and Mrs. 39
Aubin, F. Wm. St., *Lieutenant* 24
Augustin, J. 120
Aubiol, J., *Lieutenant-Colonel* 106
Ayton, H., *Lieutenant* 135

B.

Backer, G., *Private* 65
Bailiff, T. L., *Ensign* 81
Baily, T., *Private* 88
Baines, J. C. 51
Baines, P. 51
Baker, E., *Lieutenant* 106
Balderston, A., *Captain* 129
Baldry, W., *Private* 157
Balfour, M., *Lieutenant* 48
Banks, J., *Major* 137
Banmount, M. 88
Barber, G. D., *Lieutenant* 86
Barber, J., *Lieutenant* 99
Barkley, R. 86
Barlow, Mr. 61
Barnard, P. D'A. 75
Barnes, J. 41
Barnett, J., *Private* 23
Barnster, R., *Major* 135
Barrett, J. 82
Barrett, J. B. 84
Barton, C., *Captain* 99
Barwell, E. W., *Lieutenant* 187
Barwell, H. M., *Lieutenant* 180
Barwise, J. S. 116
Batavia, Martha 51
Battine, C., *Lieutenant* 49
Bax, C. J., *Lieutenant* 40
Bayne, J. C 60
Beale, W. T., *Lieutenant* 12
Beatson, S., *Captain* 57
Beatson, S., *Captain* 66
Beaumount, E. E., *Ensign* 81
Beele, J. 38
Beer, G., *Sapper* 148
Beestal, Mrs. 51
Belcher, J., *Sergeant* 11
Bell, J. 42
Bell, J., *Sergeant-Major* 49
Bell, W. 129

Page.

Bellington, Mr. 35
Bellon, Mr. 21
Belson, H., *Captain* 48
Belson, Miss 48
Bemustenfh, M., Mrs. 102
Benn, W. S. 61
Bennet, F. E. B., *Lieutenant* 171
Bennett, A., *Private* 11
Bennett, E., Miss 51
Bennett, Mr. 87
Benson, G. S., B. C. S. 160
Berkeley, C. A. F. H., *Colonel, C. B.* 66
Berkelly, H. N. L., *Lieutenant* 107
Berrill, W., *Conductor* 49
Besher, A., *Captain* 138
Best, *Sergeant* 34
Bhalbhadra Singh Thápa 3
Bhawani Bux Chowbe, *Jamadar* 146
Billington, Mr. 55
Birch, T. C. H., *Captain* 81
Birch, Y. Z. M., *Lieutenant* 44
Birch, Y. Z. M., *Lieutenant* 105
Bird, F. M. 120
Bird, J. G., Mrs. 122
Bissett, Miss 51
Biver, B., *Gunner* 92
Black, A., *Lieutenant* 101
Blackie, R. 40
Blackney, M. M., Mrs. 171
Blair, Mrs. 50
Blair, R., *Captain, V.C.* 159
Blake, G., *Lieutenant-Colonel* 110
Bleak, J. 85
Blundell, W., *Major* 170
Blyth, D. D. 87
Blyth, Mrs. 87
Boilard, J. 82
Boileau, G. E., Miss 144
Boley, J. 39
Bolton, G., *Captain* 2
Bolton, T., *Major* 44
Bolton, T., *Major* 105
Bonning, C., *Lieutenant* 80
Boodie, *Sepoy* 111
Booth, G., *Private* 85
Bosco, Mr. and Mrs. 34
Bothwick, Mrs. 51
Boulton, A. J., *Lieutenant* 48
Bowley, W., *Revd.* 105
Bowling, H. H., *Surgeon* 45
Bowling, J. P., *Assistant Surgeon* 49
Bowling, Mrs. 45
Bowling, Mrs. and Child 166
Boyd, W., *Lieutenant* 28
Boyes, W. R., *Surgeon* 48
Boyle, J. 85

Page.

Brackenbury, J., *Lieutenant* 56
Brambly, A. I., *Lieutenant* 42
Bramley, A. J., *Lieutenant* 164
Brannan, J. 81
Brates, J., *Private* 41
Brenan, J., *Private* 85
Brett, H. 51
Bridgeman, O. F. C., *Captain* 159
Bridges, O. S. 48
Brien, M., *Private* 85
Brierly, E. 51
Brierly, J. 55
Brierly, Mr. and Mrs. 34
Brierly, Misses 55
Brierly, R. 55
Bright, W. 66
Brightman, Miss 50
Britton, J., *Private* 88
Brodie, A. 42
Brooke, *Sergeant* 60
Brooke, W. A. 185
Brown, C., *Major-General, C.B.* 185
Brown, H., *Private* 159
Brown, J., *Lieutenant* 24
Brown, J., *Lieutenant* 157
Brown, J. C., *Lieutenant* 136
Brown, P., *Private* 85
Brown, *Private* 129
Brown, W., *Private* 124
Browne, *Captain* 86
Browne, Mrs. 86
Browne, Miss 86
Brownlow, E. P., *Lieutenant, Bengal Engineers.* 148
Bruere, C. F., *Major* 136
Bryce, J. H., *Lieutenant* 137
Bryson, A. 161
Buchanan, A. 42
Buck, Dr. 38
Bulbudder, 4
Bumgardt, A. M., Mrs. 81
Bumgardt, J. G., *Captain* 81
Bunney, Mr. 51
Bunting, J., *Sapper* 148
Burbon, J. P. 30
Burgess, A. 41
Burgess, *Lieutenant* 66
Burlton, F. H. M., *Captain* 30
Burlton, P. H. C., *Lieutenant* 29
Burlton, W., *Colonel* 30
Burn, Misses 51
Burnes, C. J. H., *Lieutenant* 149
Burney, F. W., *Lieutenant* 47
Burney, G. J. D. 115
Burnham, T., *Private* 85
Burrington, G., *Colonel* 44

	Page.
Burrington, G., *Colonel*	105
Burrowes, C., Mr.	23
Burrowes, C., *Lieutenant*	186
Burrowes, M.	23
Burrowes, M. A., Miss	23
Bury, E.	125
Butler, W., *Captain*	106
Byers, J. L., *Lieutenant*	75
Byjenant, *Sepoy*	111
Byran, P., *Private*	85
Byran, R., *Private*	11
Byrne, *Ensign*	84
Byrne, J., *Private*	85
Byrne, R. S., *Ensign*	55
Byrne, T.	60

C.

Caley, *Two boys*	51
Calie, B. M., *Captain*	56
Callaghan, H., *Sergeant*	93
Cameron, H., *Private*	85
Cameron, H. S., *Ensign*	106
Cameron, Mr.	39
Cameron, R., *Captain*	24
Cameron, *Sub-Conductor*	39
Campbell, A. C., *Lieutenant*	24
Campbell, *Captain*	3
Campbell, C. H., *Major, B.A.*	177
Campbell, D., *Ensign*	109
Campbell, D. E., *Revd*	55
Campbell, H. D., *Captain*	64
Campbell, J., *Lieutenant*	101
Campbell, *Lieutenant*	87
Campbell, Mr. and Mrs.	33
Campbell, Mr.	50
Campbell, R. P., *Colonel, C. B.*	135
Campbell, W., *Brigadier-General, C.B.,*	159
Canavan, T., *Private*	85
Cannon, W., *Private*	85
Cannors, J.	86
Canway, *Captain*	90
Cape, J., *Lieutenant*	162
Carew, G. P.	149
Carguist, S. C., Miss	75
Carleton, W. H. L., *Lieutenant*	135
Carmichael, J. B. H., *Second-Lieutenant,*	129
Carmoody, *Sergeant*	50
Caronan, J.	41
Carroll, Mrs.	51
Carshore, Mrs.	87
Carshore, W. S.	87
Cartby, J., *Corporal*	11
Carter, Mr.	51
Carter, W. M., *Captain*	136
Carty, J., *Private*	85
Case, W., *Lieutenant-Colonel*	56
Casey, J., *Private*	16
Cassie Deen, *Sepoy*	111
Catania, Mr. and Mrs.	35
Catania, Mr.	55
Cates, J., *Ensign*	106
Cathcart, J.	86
Cawood, Mr. and Mrs.	35
Cawood, Mr.	55
Chequers, A.	31
Chalmers, W. A., *Lieutenant*	49
Chalwin, E. C.	59
Chalwin, E. C., *Veterinary Surgeon*	48
Chalwin, L., Mrs.	59
Chamber, R. W., *Captain*	9
Chamberlain, W., *Private*	157
Chamberlayne, C. H.	93
Chambers, C., Mr.	9
Chandler, E., Miss	51
Chapman, R., *Private*	23
Charlton, J. W., *Lieutenant*	56
Chatterton, J., *Captain*	83
Chawner, T., *Lieutenant*	103
Cheap, J., *Lieutenant*	102
Cheek, A. M. H., *Ensign*	81
Cherry, G. F.	90
Childs, R., *Sergeant*	11
Chisholm, *Private*	129
Chisholm, T., *Private*	159
Chisholm, T. A., *Lieutenant*	68
Christie, J., *Corporal*	85
Christie, Misses	51
Christie, Mr.	51
Churcher, T. H.	34
Chute, A., *Ensign*	135
Chute, P., *Lieutenant*	135
Chuters, Mary	51
Clancy, J.	142
Clark, Agabel, Miss	121
Clark, E., Miss	163
Clark, Elizabeth, Mrs.	163
Clark, M. E.	163
Clarke, H.	88
Clarke, J., *Captain, R. E.*	148
Clarke, J., Miss	126
Clarke, T., *Private*	83
Clarke, W., *Corporal*	59
Clayburn, W., *Private*	124
Claydon, E., *Captain*	32
Clayton, E. M., Mrs.	102
Cleary, J., *Private*	157
Clement, F. W.	172
Clivet, T., *Private*	85
Clooney, *Drummer*	51
Cockerell, H. E.	73

	Page.
Cockey, H. E., *Revd.*	70
Cockey, *Revd.*	50
Codd, P. S., *Ensign*	81
Coldie, *Colonel and Mrs.*	38
Coleman, G., *Conductor*	82
Colgan, Miss	51
Collins, J., *Colonel*	132
Collins, M., Mrs.	82
Collins, P., *Private*	153
Collins, R. J.	51
Collins, T., *Private*	124
Collyer, N., *Surgeon*	49
Colvin, J. R.	80
Comb, A., *Private*	158
Connell, J.	143
Connell, P., *Private*	124
Connolly, W., *Private*	157
Convay, Miss	51
Cook, R. B.	51
Cook, V.	115
Cooke, R. B.	58
Copeland, Master	51
Copeman, Mrs.	51
Cooper, H. R.	51
Cooper, L. E., *Lieutenant*	155
Cormack, A., *Private*	41
Cornwallis, C., *Lord, Governor-General and Commander in Chief in India*	118
Corsi, F., *Revd.*	174
Cosgrave, M., *Private*	85
Cosser, W., *Private*	23
Cosserat, J. F., *Captain*	138
Cousins, J.	51
Cox, Mr.	51
Cox, W., *Private*	85
Coxen, E., *Captain*	6
Crab, Mrs.	51
Cracklow, G., *Captain*	116
Crady, J., *Private*	85
Craig, T., *Private*	85
Craw, D., *Sergeant*	11
Crawford, D. H.	28
Crawford, E., *Private*	124
Crawford, J., *Captain*	88
Crawford, Mr.	87
Cripps, Miss	51
Crofton, G., *Lieutenant*	183
Crommelin, C. B.	120
Cross, *Quarter-Master*	38
Cruisor, Mr.	39
Cuise, Mr. and Mrs.	34
Cummings, A., *Lieutenant*	44
Cummings, A., *Lieutenant*	105
Cummings, T., *Sergeant*	85
Cummins, Mr.	51
Cunliffe, F. J., *Lieutenant*	187
Cunliffe, F J., *Second-Lieutenant*	139
Cunningham, *Lieutenant*	3
Cupola, L.	113
Curran, A., *Trooper*	123
Currie, A. P.	94
Currie, E., *Captain*	66
Currie, E., *Captain*	135
Currie, L. E., Mrs.	123
Currie, S., Mrs.	122
Cussen, F.	60
Cusson, C.	104

D.

	Page.
Dachey, Mrs.	51
DaCastro, J., *Revd.*	174
DaCosta, J., *Revd.*	174
DaCosta, L., *Captain*	152
DaCruz, F., *Revd.*	174
DaFonseqa, A., *Revd.*	174
Dallas, Mrs.	51
Dalton, P., *Sergeant*	11
Dalton, T.	86
Daly, Mrs.	51
Daly, M., *Sapper*	148
Daly, P., *Private*	85
Daniell, M. G., *Lieutenant*	48
Darby, Mrs.	51
Darcy, S., *Private*	85
Daring, P., *Private*	16
Darlay, G.	86
Darling, Mrs.	51
Dashwood, A. J., *Lieutenant*	139
Dashwood, C. K., *Lieutenant*	155
Dashwood, H. J. G.	139
Dashwood, T. J.	99
DaSouza, F., *Revd.*	174
Dauhaya, M., *Father*	174
Davis, J., *Corporal*	85
Davis, J., *Lance-Corporal*	148
Davis, Mr.	51
Davis, Mr. and Mrs.	36
Davis, R. G.	114
Davis, W. W., *Lieutenant-Colonel*	183
Dawson, A., *Ensign*	49
Dawson, C. J.	5
Dawson, E., *Captain*	102
Dawson, Eliza, Mrs.	5
Day, H. H., *Captain*	57
D'Castro, G.	82
DeBosse, J.	173
DeCastro, J.	81
DeCruz, Miss	82
DeGama, J. K.	32
DeL'Etang, C. A.	119
DeL'Etang, E.	119
Demaghsque, A., *Revd.*	174

Page.

DeMattos, P. 31
DeMattos, Paul 174
Demine, J. 100
Dempsey, B., *Private* 85
Dempster, C., *Lieutenant* 47
Denison, H., *Captain* 135
DeRussett, Mr. 52
Devory, J., *Color-Sergeant* 83
Dhoukal Pershad 34
Dibdin, F., *Lieutenant* 27
Dick, J. C. 180
Dickens, J., *Private* 11
Dickens, R. M., *General* 27
Dickson, J. 42
Diddea, A., Mrs. 82
Diddea, C., Miss 82
Diddea, G. 82
Dingwall, A. F., *Captain* 28
Dobbs, F., *Lieutenant* 134 & 153
Dodd, E., Mrs. 113
Donaghey, E., *Private* 153
Donelan, H., *Quarter-Master* 136
Donnaughey, H., *Sergeant* 64
Donnolly, D., *Private* 157
Donovan, D., *Private* 85
Doondayal Pandey, *Subadar* 146
Dougherty, J., *Private* 157
Douglas, C., *Lieutenant* 164
Douglas, C. S., Mrs. 99
Doyle, C. J., *Captain* 37
Doyle, P., *Private* 42
Doyle, P., *Private* 85
Drake, J. 173
Drew, J. 129
Duane, J., *Private* 85
Duncan, D. 52
Duncan, J. 52
Dundas, W. 52
Dunlop, *Captain* 87
Dunn, J. 42
Dunn, J. 85
Dunn, W., *Private* 85
Dutton, Mrs. 52
Dyce, G. A. D., *Colonel* 13, 15
Dyce, J. A., Mrs. 15
Dyson, J., *Private* 28
Dyson, J., *Sergeant* 11
Dyson, J. C., *Lieutenant* 38

E.

Eastwood, A., *Private* 23
Eaton, C., *Private* 85
Edgall, H., *Color-Sergeant* 83
Eckford, *Ensign* 34
Eckford, J. A. H., *Lieutenant* 47
Eddy, G., *Paymaster* 136
Edmond, A., *Private* 18
Edwards, C., *Sergeant-Major* 106
Edwards, W. I., *Brigadier-General* 10
Eggington, H., *Private* 85
Elliot, T., *Sergeant-Major* 79
Elliott, E., Mrs. 112
Elliott, Mr. 55
Elliott, Mr. 87
Elliott, Mrs. 87
Elliott, Mr. and Mrs. 34
Ellis, *Ensign* 3
Ellison, F. C., *Lieutenant* 27
Elms, E. J., *Captain* 46
Emmor, W. A. 47
Endicott, W., *Corporal* 11
Ereth, T. W. 142
Erskine, C., *Lieutenant* 77
Evans, J., *Corporal* 11
Evans, J., *Corporal* 85
Evans, J., *Private* 85
Evans, Mrs. 51
Evans, M., Mrs. 170
Evans, M., *Quarter-Master* 57
Evans, R. 90
Evans, W. 73
Ewart, J., *Lieutenant-Colonel* 48
Ewart, J. H. C., *Lieutenant* 48
Excell, J., *Bombardier* 93

F.

Fagan, H., *Lieutenant* 48
Fagan, Mr. 58
Fairburn, Mrs. 52
Fairhurst, P., *Revd.* 141
Fairlie, E. 99
Fairservice, A., *Sapper* 148
Faithful, W. R. L., *Captain* 187
Falkner, A. 85
Farmer, Mr. 52
Farrance, *Private* 129
Farrington, Sir Charles H. 3
Faulkner, Mr. 34
Faulkner, *Pensioner* 55
Fayrer, R. W. 36
Frade, *Lieutenant* 80
Feddon, C., *Color-Sergeant* 56
Fenn, Mrs. 52
Fenwick, A. 38
Fernando, A. 82
Ferrell T., *Private* 85
Ferrier, J. 117
Finlay, J., *Private* 85
Finlay, Miss 33
Finlay, Miss 55
Finlay, Mr. 35
Finlay, Mr. 55
Finnis, J., *Colonel* 5
Firebrace, W. J., *Lieutenant* 36

Page.

Fisher, J., *Lieutenant* ... 178
Fisher, Revd. & Mrs. ... 33
Fitles, J., *Private* ... 85
Fitzgerald, J. ... 52
Fitzgerald, J. F., Miss ... 144
Fitzgerald, Lieutenant & Mrs. ... 34
Fitzgerald, N., *Private* ... 25
Fitzpatrick, B. ... 64
Flanagan, H. ... 93
Fleming, M. B., *Lieutenant* ... 24
Flemming, Mr. ... 87
Flinn, J., *Private* ... 85
Flood, *Sergeant* ... 129
Foley, R. ... 183
Foley, T., *Sergeant-Major* ... 81
Ford, J., *Sapper* ... 148
Ford, S., *Private* ... 85
Forester, Lord G. C. ... 14
Forman, T. W., *Ensign* ... 49
Forsyth, W. ... 52
Forsyth, W. ... 60
Fothergill, *Ensign* ... 3
Francis, Mr., *infant son of—* ... 129
Francis, R. R., *Captain* ... 136
Francis, Revd. Father ... 176
Francis, T. M. ... 130
Fraser, A., Miss ... 58
Fraser, *Captain* ... 42
Fraser, *Captain* ... 75
Fraser, G. ... 41
Fraser, G. W., *Captain* ... 58
Fraser, J., *Sergeant* ... 40
Fraser, Mrs. ... 51
Frankland, T., *Lieutenant* ... 163
Fraser, H., *Major-General* ... 26
Frederic, P. ... 31
Freeman, J. E., *Revd.* ... 56
Freeman, Mr. ... 52
Freeman, Mr. and Mrs. ... 33
Friend, C., Revd. ... 187
Frith, R., *Brigadier-General* ... 27
Frith, W., *Colonel* ... 119
Frost, E., Miss ... 52
Frost, M., Mrs. ... 52
Frost, R., Mrs. ... 52
Fryer, T., *Sergeant* ... 11
Fullerton, E. ... 141
Fullerton, J. ... 141
Fulow, J. ... 82
Fulton, G. W. W., *Captain* ... 137
Fulton, R. B., *Major* ... 178
Fulton, S., Miss ... 52
Fulton, W., Master ... 52

G.

Gadkiaseeroke, A., Revd. ... 174
Gainty, S. J., *Private* ... 16
Gale, C., *Captain* ... 107
Gall, F. H. ... 79
Gall, W. H. ... 103
Galway, Mr. ... 52
Garcia, M. Father ... 174
Gardner, A. ... 37
Garret, Mr. ... 52
Garret, W. B., *Lieutenant* ... 178
Garvey, H. P. ... 149
Gates, C. ... 43
Gee, J., *Private* ... 64
Gee, Mr. ... 52
Gee, W. ... 71
George, R. ... 82
Georanjee Singh, *Sepoy* ... 111
Gerrard, G., *Lieutenant-Colonel* ... 12
Gibaut, A., *Lieutenant* ... 135
Gibbins, *Lieutenant* ... 70
Gibbs, F., *Sergeant* ... 11
Gibson, Mrs. ... 58
Gibson, Mr. and Mrs. ... 33
Gifford, A., *Captain* ... 123
Gill, *School Master* ... 50
Gillespie, *Lieutenant* ... 89
Gillespie, Sir R. R. ... 3, 7
Gilpin, Mr. ... 52
Gladwell, H., *Sergeant-Major* ... 48
Glanville, C. J., *Lieutenant* ... 47
Glanville, *Lieutenant* ... 67
Glasgow, Misses ... 50
Glynn, J. ... 88
Golaub Singh, Naik ... 111
Goldie, A., *Colonel* ... 55
Good, G. R., *Lieutenant* ... 49
Goodridge, T., *Captain* ... 129
Goodwin, Mr. ... 52
Gordon, A. ... 126
Gordon, *Captain* ... 86
Gordon, H., *Ensign* ... 135
Gordon, J., *Captain* ... 59
Gordon, W., *Quarter-Master-Sergeant* ... 49
Gosling, *Lieutenant* ... 3
Graham, G. M. L., Miss ... 140
Graham, F. J., Miss ... 140
Graham, J. ... 140
Graham, J. R., *Captain* ... 2
Graham, N., *Lieutenant* ... 135
Graham, R. ... 90
Grahame, V., *Lieutenant* ... 154
Grant, A. P. ... 140
Grant, C. J., Miss ... 108
Grant, J. W. ... 121
Grant, L., *Lieutenant-Colonel* ... 106
Grant, M., Miss ... 107
Grant, Mrs. ... 166
Grant, *Quarter-Master-Sergeant* ... 165
Grant, W. H., Master ... 107

	Page.
Gray, H., *Private*	153
Gray, J., *Quarter-Master-Sergeant*	11
Gray, W. S.	129
Green, G. W., *Lieutenant*	136
Green, *Pensioner*	50
Greene, Mrs.	149
Greenhill, J., *Lieutenant*	95
Greenway, E. F.	51
Greenway, S.	51
Greenway, T.	51
Greig, J., *Private*	83
Grier, J., *Ensign*	65
Grier, L. J., *Ensign*	59
Griffin, W.	83
Grinsey, Mr.	52
Groom, W. J., *Lieutenant*	134
Grote, R.	180
Grover, *Sergeant*	129
Guise, H. J., *Captain*	92
Guise, I. H., *Captain*	45
Guise, Mr.	45
Gun, Mr.	52
Guthrie, *Lieutenant-Colonel*	35
Guthrie, Mr.	53
Gwitt, E. B., *Lieutenant*	12

H.

Hackett, R., *Sergeant*	17
Haig, E. J., *Lieutenant*	138
Hale, F. E.	142
Hale, H. G. F., Miss	142
Hale, K. C. S., Miss	142
Halket, C. I. L., *Second-Lieutenant*	129
Halkett, C. J. L., *Second-Lieutenant*	159
Halliday, W. L., *Captain*	49
Hamilton, J., *Lieutenant*	113
Hamilton, T.	35
Hammerton, J., *Corporal*	11
Hammond, *Sergeant*	55
Hampton, Miss	52
Hamulin, J., Mons.	23
Handcock, W., *Sergeant*	11
Handscomb, I. H., *Colonel*	162
Handyside, C. E., *Lieutenant*	97
Hankeman, W., *Lieutenant*	43
Hanna, R.	60
Hannah, J. B., A.M. D., *Staff Surgeon*	129
Hannah, J. B., *Surgeon-Major*	129
Hannah, Mr.	52
Hansbrow, Dr.	88
Harding, G.	76
Harding, J., Mrs.	76
Hardinge, G. N., *Captain*	160
Hardy, W. N.	56
Hardyman, B., *Major-General*, C. B.	7
Harkness, Mr.	52

	Page.
Harrington, *Lieutenant*	8
Harris, H. P., *Assistant Surgeon*	49
Harris, J., *Private*	85
Harris, *Lieutenant*	59
Harrison, J., *Private*	85
Harrison, J. H., *Lieutenant*	47
Hart, M., *Sergeant*	86
Harth, *Lieutenant-Colonel*	108
Hasted, G. H.	94
Hastings, J., *Private*	85
Hathord, H. B., *Captain*	38
Haugh, J., *Sergeant*	11
Havelock, C. W., *Lieutenant*	116
Havelock, Sir H.	57
Havelock, Sir Henry, *Major-General*	153
Hawes, G. H., *Lieutenant*	81
Hawkins, *Lieutenant*	76
Hawkins, M., Mrs.	76
Hay, J. D.	52
Hay, J. M., Dr.	88
Haycock, Mr.	52
Haycock, Revd.	50
Haycock, W. H., Revd.	70
Hayes, F. F. C.	36
Hayes, J., *Private*	85
Hayes, *Private*	129
Haynes, H. S. F., *Captain, R. E.*	129
Haynes, W.	43
Hayter, J. H.	92
Healy, W., *Private*	85
Hearsey, A. W., *Lieutenant-Colonel*	80
Heathcote	55
Heathcote, Dr. and Mrs.	33
Heffernan, W.	47
Helderson, G. C.	50
Helderson, Mrs.	50
Helmuth, *Private*	129
Hempland, G., *Captain*	49
Henderson, D., *Lieutenant*	55
Henderson, D. H., *Lieutenant*	8
Henderson, E.	52
Henderson, J. W., *Lieutenant*	49
Henderson, *Lieutenant*	34
Henderson, R. W., *Lieutenant*	49
Hennessey, D.	42
Hennessey, M.	86
Hennessey, M., *Corporal*	85
Henry, *Quarter-Master*	38
Hensley, A. P., *Lieutenant*	59
Hepburn, J., *Private*	41
Heberden, A. C.	60
Heberden, M. C.	52
Hern, O., Mr.	56
Heron, *Sergeant-Major*	50
Hessing, J. W., *Colonel*	30
Hiddle, J.	40

Page.

Hiddus, J., *Sergeant* 41
Hiles, R. 86
Hill, E. C., *Ensign* 47
Hill, E. C., *Lieutenant* 56
Hill, Mrs. 57
Hill, T., *Private* 157
Hillersdon, W. R., *Major* 48
Hilling, C., *Sergeant-Major* 48
Hilton, W., *Captain* 10
Hinde, H., *Major* 98
Hinkeman, W., *Lieutenant* 105
Hitchcock, J., *Private* 85
Hodgson, J. 60
Hodson, W. S. R., *Captain and Brevet Major* 152
Hogan, Mr. 52
Hogg, E. H., Mr. 97
Hogg, F. H. 97
Holans, *Lance-Corporal* 42
Hollier, M., Mrs. 115
Hollier, M., Miss 115
Hollings, *Captain* 51
Holmes, E. Miss 52
Holmes, J. 61
Home, D. C., *Lieutenant* 17
Hooper, *Assistant Surgeon* 89
Hope, *Hon'ble A., Brigadier, C. B.* 164
Hope, H. 98
Horan, B. 17
Horne, J., *Corporal* 11
Horsford, Sir J. 68
Howard, R., *Private* 85
Howe, Lucy 117
Hubbard, A. R., Revd. 70
Hudson, C., *Private* 85
Hudson, F., *Major* 179
Hudson, J., *Lieutenant* 23
Humphray, R., *Lieutenant-Colonel* 80
Humphreys, E., *Major* 101
Humphreys, Miss 34
Hunter, J., *Captain* 9
Hunter, J., *Captain* 41
Hurd, J. H., *Lieutenant* 24
Hurst, P. 86
Hurst, Mr. 166
Hutchinson, W. H., *Captain* 140
Huxham, E. F. 144

I.

Incha, *Sepoy* 111
Ingle, H., *Lieutenant* 113
Inglis, *Sir J., Major-General* 147
Inglis, R. L., *Ensign* 136
Irons, W., *Private* 11
Ives, J. 55
Ives, Mr. and Mrs. 33

Page.

J.

Jack, A., *Colonel* 61
Jack, A. W. T. 61
Jack, *Brigadier-General* 46
Jack, Mrs. 46
Jack, W., Revd. 61
Jackford, Mrs. 53
Jackson, J. A., Mrs. 58
Jackson, Miss 149
Jackson, P. H., *Lieutenant* 49
Jackson, P. H., *Lieutenant* 58
Jackson, Sir M., *Bart.* 149
Jackson, T., *Private* 85
Jacobi, F. 52
Jacobi, H. 53
James, E. 34
James, M., *Captain* 45
James, W. 52
Jellicoe, F. G., *Lieutenant* 48
Jemmison, W., *Lieutenant* 75
Jenkins, C. J. 165
Jenkins, R., *Captain* 67
Jenkins, R. W., *Captain* 47
Jennings, M. J., Revd. 70
Jermyter, E., *Sergeant* 11
Jervis, Hon'ble Mary Anne 14
Jervis, S. C., *Lieutenant* 47
Jewerarity, D., *Lieutenant* 10
Jipps, B., *Private* 11
Johnson, A. E., *Captain* 136
Johnson, A. O., Revd. 55
Johnson, E. 86
Johnson, *Ensign* 168
Johnston, A. R. 53
Johnston, Mr. and Mrs. 83
Johnston, *Private* 45
Joly, E. Del., *Lieutenant* 56
Jones, E. S. 111
Jones, F. Miss 82
Jones, J. M. 32
Jones, Mr. 53
Jones, Mr. and Mrs. 35
Jones, Mr. and Mrs., J. M. 34
Jones, P., *Sergeant* 59
Jones, W. H., *Captain* 124-25
Jordon, E., *Ensign* 65
Jordon, E., *Lieutenant* 59
Jordon, P., Miss 77
Joyce, J. 55
Joyce, Mr. and Mrs. 34
Juhannas, Revd. 175
Juliana, *Lady* 30
Jybookh Deenah, *Sepoy* 111

K.

Kalford, W. H., *Colonel* 138
Kalka Tewari 164

Page.

KAVANAGH, T. H., V. C. 161
KEARNEY, J. 88
KEELER, MRS. 53
KELLY, J., *Private* 157
KELLY, J., *Sergeant* 64
KELLY, *Sergeant* 50
KEMP, C. M. 111
KEMPLAND, L. G. 104
KEMPLAND, MISS 49
KENNA, J. *Private* 85
KENNAULTY, H., *Private* 85
KENNEDY, *Private* 129
KENNEDY, T., *Private* 159
KENNY, H., *Ensign* 186
KENNY, T., *Private* 158
KERR, G., *Private* 11
KERR, W., *Lieutenant* 27
KEW, J. B. 56
KEW, MR. AND MRS. 33
KEW, MISS 33
KEW, MISS 56
KEY, MRS. 45
KEY, A. 165
KEY, A., *Lieutenant* 45
KEY, A. M., *Captain* 104
KEY, M., MRS. 165
KING, J., *Private* 11
KING, W., *Ensign* 67
KINLESIDE, MRS 53
KIRK, I., *Riding Master* 159
KIRK, *Lieutenant* 180
KIRK, MR. 53
KIRK, MRS. 53
KIRPATRICK, J. 53
KIRPATRICK, T., *Captain* 100
KIRWAN, H., REVD. 141
KNIGHT, G. A. 129
KNIGHT, G. A., *infant daughter of*— 129
KNIGHT, G. A., *Sergeant* 129
KNIGHT, MRS. 53
KNOSE, R. T., *Brevet Captain* 108
KOCH, L., *Catechist* 70
KOINE, G., *Major* 14
KUNDSON, C., *Colonel* 103

L.

LAIRD, T., *Private* 85
LAKE, LORD 23
LAMB, J. K. H., *Lieutenant* 30
LANCASTER, W. 82
LANDLES, A. 41
LANFRANKI, S. J. 30
LANFRANKI, F., *Father* 174
LANG, NANCY 33
LANG, N., MISS 55
LANKHAM, J., *Corporal* 64
LARKINS, C., *Major* 47
LA TOUCHE, C. 78
LA TOUCHE, C. 119
LA TOUCHE, F. 78
LA TOUCHE, H. 53
LA TOUCHE, W. D. 60
LAWRENCE, SIR H. M. 133, 168
LAWRENCE, H. T. W. 158
LAWRENCE, J. 58
LAWRENCE, J. 186
LAWRENCE, MR. 39
LAWRENCE, SIR HENRY, *Major-General, K. C. B.* 146
LAWRIE, E. T. 76
LAWSON, D. 43
LAYAN, C. 43
LEAK, T., *Quarter-Master Sergeant* 49
LEARY, MR. 53
LEATH, MISS 53
LEFEVRE, ANNE, MRS. 15
LEFEVRE, L. A., *Captain* 18
LEHANE, J., *Private* 17
LEIGH, D. D. 40
LEIGH, G. 126
LEITCH, A. 40
LEMAISTRE, J. R. 46
LEPPINGS, E. G., *Captain* 47
LESTER, *Lance-Corporal* 186
L'ESTRANGE, J. W., *Captain* 186
LEVING, P. 26
LEWELLYN, J. L., *Lieutenant* 107
LEWIN, E. P., *Lieutenant* 187
LEWIN, E. S., MISS 189
LEWIS, B., *Sergeant* 11
LEWIS, J. 53
LIEW, PETER, DR. 174
LIMUEL, C. 73
LINDSAY, C., *Ensign* 46
LINDSAY, MRS. 46
LINDSAY, M. MRS. 94
LINDSAY, W., *Major* 46
LITTLE, J., *Lieutenant* 58
LITTLE, MR. 53
LIVINGSTONE, W., *Sergeant* 11
LLOYD, A., MRS. 101
LLOYD, C. H., *Lieutenant-Colonel* 106
LOCKWOOD, B., *Private* 83
LODER, H. M., MRS. 77
LODER, J. W., *Major* 77
LODER, J. W. S. 77
LOW, S., *Sergeant* 172
LOWIS, MR. AND MRS. 84
LOWIS, R. U. 56
LOWTHER, C. O., MISS 114
LOWTHER, R. O. 114
LOWTHER, W. 185
LUCAS, F. D., *Captain* 189

	Page.
LUGGET, L.	88
LUID, A. F.	97
LUMSDEN, J. T., *Captain*	162
LUMSDEN, *Major, Deputy Commissary-General*	8
LUSHINGTON, M., MRS.	131
LUXFORD, *Lieutenant*	39
LYALL, L., MISS	53
LYNCH, W. E.	158
LYNDON, *Ensign*	65
LYSAGHT, MRS.	45
LYSAGHT, C.	165
LYSAGHT, MRS.	165
LYSAGHT, O., *Captain*	45

M.

	Page.
MACCALLAM, J., REVD.	45
MACDONALD, A., *Colonel*	95
MACDONALD, D., *Colonel*	5
MACDONALD, L. S., MRS.	5
MACDONALD, MR.	35
MACDONALD, MRS.	55
MACDONNELL, F. J., *Lieutenant*	158,159
MACDOWELL, C. J. M., *Lieutenant*	32
MACFIE, T., *Lieutenant*	33
MACHADO, A.	80
MACHADO, A., REVD.	174
MACKENNA, *Lieutenant*	70
MACKENZIE, J. H., *Surgeon*	77
MACKENNES, J.	60
MACKIE, ANT., *Lance-Corporal*	41
MACKILLOP, J.	50
MACKILLOP, J. R.	61
MACKINNON, MRS.	53
MACKINTOSH, C.	53
MACKINTOSH, C.	71
MACKINTOSH, D. C., MRS.	71
MACKINTOSH, E.	71
MACKINTOSH, I.	71
MACKINTOSH, J. A.	71
MACKLIN, MR	55
MACKLIN, MR. AND MRS.	35
MACLANDERS, *Sergeant*	50
MACLEAN, MR.	55
MACLEAN, MRS.	34
MACLEAN, W. G. M.	160
MACLEOD, A. F. E., *Captain*	77
MACLEOD, N., *Captain*	43
MACLEOD, N., *Captain*	43, 105
MACMORAN, MISSES	53
MACMULLEN, MR. AND MRS.	33
MACPHERSON, D.	40
MACQUEEN, A., *Surgeon*	83
MADDEN, J., *Private*	85
MADDEN, J. R.	55
MADDEN, MR. AND MRS.	35
MADDEN, MISSES	56
MADDOCK, T., *Lieutenant-Colonel*	8
MAGNESS, M. A., MRS.	161
MAGNESS, R. J. H., *Captain*	161
MAGRATH, J., *Sergeant*	67
MAGRATH, R. A., *Captain*	83
MAGUIRE, T.	117
MAHAN, P., *Private*	85
MAINWARING, C., *Cornet*	48
MALING, C. S., *Colonel*	97
MALING, G. W.	53
MALING, J.	53
MALING, N., MRS.	98
MALONEY, *Pensioner*	50
MALTBY, *Assistant Surgeon*	55
MALTBY, B., *Captain*	187
MALTBY, DR. AND MRS.	34
MANDERSON, W. J., *Lieutenant*	47
MANNION, M., *Sergeant*	83
MANSFIELD, J., *Lieutenant*	28
MANSFIELD, J. W., *Captain*	56
MANTELL, R. N.	60
MAPELTON, F. M. M., *Lieutenant*	57
MARCH, J.	41
MARK, E., MISS	53
MARLEY, H., MISS	107
MARSHALL, W.	141
MARSHELL, W., MRS.	53
MARTHA, *Native Christian servant*	130
MARTIN, C., *Major-General*	150
MARTIN, H. B.	144
MARTIN, I., *Private*	157
MARTIN, J., *Private*	47
MARTIN, J. N., *Lieutenant*	59
MARTIN, J. R. B.	144
MARTINDELL, N. MISS	58
MASTER, G. A.	48
MATTHEWS, W., *infant daughter of—*	117
MAUBEY, J., *Captain*	44
MAUBEY, J., *Captain*	44, 105
MAULDU, J., *Private*	11
MAUVILE, C. H., *Officiating Sub-Conductor,*	49
MAXWELL, H., *Major*	106
MAXWELL, MR.	50
MAXWELL, R., *Lieutenant*	170
MAY, J.	86
MAYBURY, R., *Lieutenant*	136
MAYNE, A. O., *Lieutenant*	152
MCAULEY, D., *Assistant Surgeon*	47
MCCORMACH, C., *Private*	85
MCCREA, *Captain*	70
MCCULLEN, *Master*	53
MCCULLOCK, G., *Sergeant*	40
MCDONALD, C. W., *Captain*	155
MCDONNALD, A., *Private*	42

Page.

McDougal, P., *Colonel* 102
McEgan, Dr. 87
McEgan, Mrs. 87
McEkan, P., *Private* 85
McEvoy, D., *Private* 157
McEwan, A., *Sergeant-Instructor* 128 9
McGower, S., *Ensign* 108
McGregor, A., *Quarter-Master Sergeant* ... 79
McInnes, D. 42
McIntyre, D., *Private* 42
McKane, W. 42
McKay, A., *Private* 41
McKay, R., *Private* 42
McKenzie, H. 41
McLardy, D., *Corporal* 42
McLaruk, T., *Private* 85
McMahon, *Sergeant-Major* 49
McManns, J., *Lieutenant* 75
McMillan, J., *Lieutenant* 40
McMullen, J., *Revd.* 55
McMurdo, E. A., *Lieutenant* 182
McNair, J. 42
McNair, R. 41
McPherson, E. 41
McPherson, W., *Sergeant* 16
Melliar, R. F., *Lieutenant* 158
Memorial Tablet recording the events of the siege and the defence of the Lucknow Residency in 1857 147
Menth, W., *Lieutenant* 24
Menzies, R., *Captain* 187
Mercer, M. E., Mrs. 133
Messenger, W., *Private* 157
Millard, Mrs. 87
Millard, *Sergeant* 87
Miller, A. M. 50
Miller, A. M. M. 60
Miller, C., *Private* 85
Miller, J. S. 77
Miller, R., *Lieutenant* 57
Mitchell, A., *Surgeon* 109
Mitchell, F. M., *Ensign* 57
Mitchell, F. M. 71
Moira, T., *Private* 157
Monaghan, I., *Private* 157
Monckton, *Lieutenant and Mrs.* 33
Moncrieff, E. J. R., *Revd.* 50
Monckton, P. 122
Monkton, J. R., *Lieutenant* 55
Monro, R., *Major* 55
Monteath, C., *Lieutenant* 101
Monteith, L. F., Mrs. 133
Monteith, T. 42
Montgomery, *Major* 25
Montgomery, S. 86

Page.

Monument to the memory of the Native Officers and sepoys who fell in the defence of the Residency, Lucknow, 1857. 146
Monument to the memory of the Officers, Non-Commissioned Officers and men of the 78th Highland Regiment who fell in 1857 and 1858 145
Moodie, T. 184
Moore, A., *Ensign* 28
Moore, J., *Captain* 47
Moore, J., *Captain* 56
Moore, J., *Corporal* 17
Moore, Mrs. 56
Moore, S., *Assistant Surgeon* 9
Moore, S., Mrs. 133
Moore, W., *Private* 85
Moore, W. R. 96
Moorson, W. R., *Lieutenant* 139
Moran, W., *Private* 157
Mordaunt, J. 44
Mordaunt, J., *Captain* 105
Morfett, J., Mrs. 53
Morgan, C. 128, 9
Morgan, C. R. J. 145
Morgan, E. 128
Morgan, F., *Corporal* 148
Morris, J., *Lieutenant* 28
Morris, *Lieutenant* 89
Morris, W. L. G., *Lieutenant* 49
Morrison, A., *Drummer* 43
Morrison, D., *Private* 43
Morthemphur, *Khoja* 175
Morton, *Sergeant-Major* 149
Moss, E. T. 128, 9
Motherall, R. 109
Moultrie, A., *Lieutenant* 135
Mowtiobu, J. E. V. 112
Mudge, F. L. 61
Muir, D. 64
Muir, M. F. 79
Muir, C. D., *Lieutenant* 81
Munro, G. L., *Ensign* 81
Munro, *Major* 34
Munrow, Mr. 87
Murphy, *Captain* 70
Murphy, S., Mrs. 128
Murphy, M., *Major* 128
Murphy, Mr. 53
Murray, *Drum Major* 50
Murray, H., *Brigadier-General, C. B.* ... 182
Murray, Infant son of Mr. and Mrs.— 117
Mutlow, Mr. 87

N.

Nairn, R., *Major* 21

	Page.
Napier, J., *Private*	41
Nation, *Lieutenant-Colonel, C. B.*	181
Neill, J. G. S., *Brigadier-General*	134
Nelson, Mr.	53
Nelson, R., *Assistant-Surgeon*	135
Neville, W. F., *Paymaster*	171
Newal, T. R. A.	125
Newenham, A. W. R., *Surgeon*	48
Newman, S., *Sergeant*	149
Newton, Mrs.	87
Newton, *Quarter-Master Sergeant*	87
Nice, *Lieutenant*	75
Nicholas, S. G.	38
Nicholetts, W. H., *Major*	164
Nichols, G., *Corporal*	85
Nichterlein, J., Mr.	22
Nichterlein, S. A., Mr.	22
Nixon Reid, *Pensioner*	50
Noad, G. H. Carden	128
Nobilis, Joanna	13
Noble, G., *Ensign*	97
Norris, Mrs.	53
North, W.	53
Northam, S.	114
Northwood, D., *Sapper*	148
Nugent, G., *Captain*	107
Nunn, J., *Lieutenant*	123
Nunn, J. J., *Lieutenant*	135
Nunn, J. J., *Lieutenant*	154
Nye, J., *Private*	85

O.

Oballo, M. P., *Captain*	15
O'Brien, J.	53
O'Brien, J. L.	53
O'Brien, L., *Corporal*	85
O'Brien, L. R., *Lieutenant-Colonel*	104
Ochterlony, Sir D., *Major-General*	7
O'Connor, Miss	53
O'Crady, P., *Sergeant*	85
Odell, W., *Lieutenant*	43
Odell, W., *Lieutenant*	105
O'Dowda, H. C., *Lieutenant*	179
Offley, J.	173
Ogle, M.	53
O'Hara, *Lieutenant*	3
O'Meagher, J., *Sergeant*	16
Ommanney, M. C.	115-137
O'Neil, P.	17
Orr, P., *Captain*	149
Osborne, J., *Private*	85
Osborne, Mrs.	53
O'Shea, A., *Captain*	95
Ouseley, E. A., Mrs.	143
Ouseley, G.	143
Ouseley, R.	143
Outerson, W., *Sapper*	148

P.

	Page.
Pace, J., *Cornet*	76
Padua, da.- J., Revd.	174
Paethod, L. C., *Colonel*	15
Paodasch, Revd.	175
Pakenham, R., *Captain*	135
Palfreyman, Mr.	87
Palmer, J.	56
Palmer, Mr. and Mrs.	33
Palmer, Messrs. F. and H.	53
Palmer, Susanna	147
Palmer, S., *Private*	85
Pantan, T., *Private*	85
Pareira, Mr., and Four children	168
Parker, Lady	6
Parker, *Sergeant*	50
Parker, Sir G., *Captain*	6
Parker, Sir G., *Captain*	47
Parker, Sir G., *Captain*	67
Paschoud, J. F., *Lieutenant-Colonel*	166
Passanah, R.	80
Patros, *Revd.*	175
Pattle, W., *Lieutenant*	8
Patton, S., Mrs.	132
Paul, J., *Private*	85
Paul, W., *Lieutenant*	155
Peach, H. E., *Major*	162
Peake, C. H.	53
Pearson, H. C., *Major*	38
Peel, G.	53
Peel, Sir W.	60
Pellew, Hon'ble B. R., *Major*	155, 163
Penny, N., *Major-General, C. B.*	6
Pennyng, T., *Major*	103
Peppe, W.	123
Percy, W., *Private*	85
Perkins, H. G., *Lieutenant*	17
Perons, *General*	32
Perrin, J., *Brevet-Major*	135
Perrin, J., *Major*	164
Perrin, J. R., *Ensign*	57
Perry, F., *Private*	85
Peters, A., *Assistant Apothecary*	49
Petworth, W., *Private*	83
Phellan, Mr. and Mrs.	38
Pheroo Singh, *Sepoy*	111
Phillips, John, *Veterinary Surgeon*	5
Phillomore, *Captain*	34
Philloft, *Major*	34
Phillott, J., *Major*	55
Piercy, J. R., *Ensign*	186
Pinkney, F. W., *Major*	34
Pistol, H.	53
Pitt, W. W.	45

Page.

Pitt, W. W. 165
Pitts, Foster, H., *Lieutenant*.............. 97
Platt, W., *Lieutenant* 95
Plumer, J., *Lieutenant* 44
Plumer, J., *Lieutenant* 105
Plumer, S., Mrs.. 109
Plunket, T., *Captain*............................ 81
Pogson, *Lieutenant-Colonel* 92
Pogson, Mrs... 53
Polehampton, H. A. 141, 63
Polehampton, H. S., Revd...............141, 63
Poole, A. B. 77
Poole, C., *Colonel*................................ 167
Poole, W., *Lieutenant* 135
Pooran Bahader Caubi, *Sepoy*.......... 111
Pottle, W., *Private*.............................. 157
Powell, T. S., *Colonel* 72
Power, W., *Captain* 56
Powis, *Lieutenant* 86
Powis, Mrs. 87
Preston, M., *Lieutenant* 154
Preston, N., *Lieutenant* 135
Preston, R., *Private* 157
Price, J. G., *Major* 157
Price, J. G., *Major* 150
Price, *Pensioner* 50
Pringle, G. S., *Ensign*.......................... 81
Probett, Mr. 53
Probyn, E. M. 165
Probyn, L. D., Miss 165
Prole, W. G. 48
Prout, W. R., *Major*.............................. 40
Purfada, E., Revd. 174
Pulding, T. 86
Pulfit, J., *Private*.................................. 11
Punchoo-Golandauze, *Gun Laskar* 111
Purcell, G. 87
Purcell, J. 87
Purcell, Mr. 53
Purchas, G.. 173
Purton, F., *Private*................................ 83

Q.

Quin, C. W., *Lieutenant* 47
Quin, R. O., *Lieutenant*........................ 47
Quinlan, W. 86
Quirk, P., *Private* 16

R.

Radcliffe, C. W., *Captain*.................... 138
Raikes, G. D. 38
Raikes, G. D. 39
Raikes, S. M., Mrs. 2
Raikes, T. A., *Lieutenant*.................... 49
Raker, I., *Private* 157
Ralph, R., *Lieutenant-Colonel* 80
Ram Pershad, *Subadar*........................ 146

Page.

Ramsay, Mr. 53
Ranjit Singh 4
Rankin, G.. 41
Ravenscroft, E. W., *Lieutenant* 106
Ravenscroft, Mr. 167
Ray, Misses 84
Ray, Misses 56
Redman, F., *Lieutenant*........................ 48
Redman, *Sergeant*................................ 64
Reed, J., *Private* 63
Reed, J., *Sergeant* 46
Reid, G. 68
Reid, J., *Sergeant* 42
Reid, *Sergeant* 50
Reilly, Mr.. 53
Reilly, N., *Assistant Commissary* 49
Reinhardt, W. 80
Reinhardt, W., *alias* Scrumers or Sombre 12
Renand, G. C. S., *Major* 134
Reparey, *Lieutenant* 102
Reville de A. 174
Reynaud, L.B., *Nawab Muzaffar-ud-daulah* 13
Reynell, Sir T., *Major-General* 13
Reynolds, J., *Private*............................ 85
Reynolds, J. H., *Captain*...................... 48
Reynolds, M., *Captain* 48
Reynolds, W., *Sergeant*........................ 11
Richard, R., Revd.................................. 106
Richards, H. E., *Lieutenant*.................. 159
Richards, T., *Private*............................ 73
Richardson, G. 61
Richardson, J., *Lieutenant* 43
Richardson, J., *Lieutenant* 105
Richardson, J. A., *Lieutenant*.............. 134
Richardson, T. C., *Captain* 38
Richie, R., Mr. 39
Ricketts, F. F. 132
Ricketts, M. 45
Ricketts, Mr. 54
Ridley, T. 40
Riley, J. 17
Rivett, J. 89
Roach, Mr. 54
Roach, Mr. 56
Roach, *Sergeant and Mrs.* 33
Roberts, Mrs. 54
Robertson, A., *Brevet-Major* 165
Robertson, C. A., *Lieutenant* 45
Robertson, C. A. 165
Robertson, D 38
Robertson, *Major and Mrs.* 34
Robertson, T., *Private* 65
Robinson, A., Revd. 128
Robinson, Mr. 54
Robinson, R. S. P., *Second-Lieutenant*...... 128
Robinson, W., *Sapper*.......................... 148

Page.

Rodrigues, M., Revd. 174
Rogers, R. I., *Sergeant-Major* 128
Rohan, *Conductor and Mrs.* 85
Rohan, M., *Conductor* 55
Rommel, *Captain* 15
Rooney, J., Revd. 50
Rose, H. 100
Rose, Sir H., *Major-General* 85
Ross, J. 99
Rowland, A. M., *Captain* 122
Rowner, J., *Corporal* 11
Royle, W. H., *Captain* 179
Russell, E., Mrs. 54
Russell, L. 88
Russell, Mrs. 54
Rutherford, G. W., *Lieutenant* 45
Rutherford, G. W. 165
Ryan, *Sergeant* 50
Ryder, C., *Major* 27
Ryves, J. L., Mrs. 82

S.

Sagg, T., *Sergeant* 11
Salmon, M. M. 165
Salmon, M. M., *Captain* 45
Salmon, W. B., *Colonel* 98
Samru Begam 13
Sandford, C., *Captain* 156
Sandwith, B., *Lieutenant* 135
Sandys, D. C., Revd. 70
Sasson, Anna 141
Santos, M. A. 31
Santucci, M. A., Revd. 174
Satchwell, R. M., *Lieutenant* 48
Saunders, F., *Lieutenant* 135
Saunders, F. J. G., *Lieutenant* 47
Saunders, J. 86
Saunders, Mr. 54
Schlottaner, A. 166
Scott 45
Scott 45
Scott, A. 87
Scott, A., *Lieutenant* 91
Scott, A. J., *Ensign* 81
Scott, C. E. 45
Scott, C. F. 45
Scott, C. F. 165
Scott, E. C., *Ensign* 165
Scott, G. 40
Scott, L. C., *Captain* 57
Scott, Miss 165
Scott, Mr. 54
Scott, Mrs. 165
Scott, W. 184
Scriven, J., *Private* 16

Page.

Sequeira, A., Revd. 174
Sergison, C. W., *Lieutenant* 155
Seymour, C., *Lieutenant-Colonel* 135
Shah Alam 13
Sharp, W., *Sergeant* 85
Shaw, A. 41
Shaw, Mr. 54
Sheils, *Lieutenant* 166
Sheils, Mrs. 166
Sheils, Mr. and Mrs. 33
Sheldon, W., *Corporal* 41
Sheo Charan Singh, *Subadar* 146
Shepherd, D. 54
Shepherd, E., Mrs. 54
Shepherd, J. S., *Captain* 138
Shepherd, Miss 56
Shepherd, Mrs. 35
Shepherd, Mrs. 56
Sheridan, R. 54
Sherman, Mr. 54
Sherry, J., *Corporal* 17
Shields, J., *Private* 85
Shiels, A. 128, 9
Shiels, C. 128, 9
Shiels, I. W. 128
Shiels, *School Master* 55
Shiels, T. W. 128, 9
Shinks, H. 187
Shore, Mrs. 54
Shorn, J., Mr. 54
Showers, H., Mrs. 114
Sibbald, H., *Brigadier* 38
Simmons, J. E., *Major* 136
Simons, A. P., *Captain* 187
Simons, A. P., *Captain* 162
Simons, L. A. C., Miss 162
Simpson, E. J., *Captain, Assistant Commissary-General* 7
Simpson, H. 54
Simpson, *Lieutenant* 34
Simpson, L., *Lieutenant-Colonel* 179
Simpson, W. 54
Sinclair, H. 81
Sinclair, Mr. 54
Sinclair, Hon'ble P. C., *Brevet-Captain* 183
Siommons, E., *Private* 83
Skardon, S. 33
Skene, A., *Captain* 86
Skene, Mrs. 86
Skene, E. E. N., Mrs. 186
Slade, J., *Sapper* 148
Slaney, W. 47
Sliven, Mr. 54
Smith, A., *Captain* 126
Smith, Alfred, *Sapper* 148
Smith, A. C. 45

	Page.
Smith, *Colonel and Mrs.*	34
Smith, E., Mrs.	115
Smith, E. W., *Ensign*	81
Smith, G. A., *Colonel*	55
Smith, H. S., *Lieutenant*	48
Smith, J.	85
Smith, J., *Major-General*	26
Smith, J. P., *Major*	156
Smith, J. P., *Major*	159
Smith, *Lieutenant*	71
Smith, M. D., *Ensign*	81
Smith, Mr.	54
Smith, Mr.	166
Smith, R., *Private*	124
Smith, S., *Sergeant*	78
Smith, T.	42
Smith, T., *Captain*	18
Smith, T., *Sergeant*	11
Smith, W., *Corporal*	64
Smith, W., *Private*	85
Smyth, E.	188
Smyth, G. C., *Colonel*	5
Smyth, P. C., *Lieutenant*	156
Sneyd, H. W. L., *Captain*	45
Sneyd, H. W. L.	165
Snodgrass, G., *Captain*	185
Soane, *Head Bullockman*	111
Sombre, D. O. Dyce	13, 14
Southeby, C. M. W., *Lieutenant*	47
Southeby, C. M. W., *Lieutenant*	61
Southeby, G. H., *Captain*	70
Southeby, M. W., *Lieutenant*	70
Spence, A.	61
Spence, G., *Private*	41
Spens, T. I. H.	45
Spens, T. J. H.	165
Spesger, A.	86
Spesger, A., Revd.	174
Spiller, F. J., *Major*	104
Springate, R., *Color-Sergeant*	140
Springham, T., *Corporal*	11
Stacey, H. H.	51
Stack, Dr.	84
Stainforth, E., Mrs.	121
Stainsforth, *Lieutenant-Colonel*	69
Stalker, J., *Lieutenant*	91
Stanley, Mr.	54
Staples, *Sergeant*	88
Stapleton, Rt. Hon'ble	11
Stark, H., *Lieutenant-Colonel*	181
Staywell, G., *Private*	124
Stedman, J. F.	78
Steevens, C., *Captain*	56
Steevens, R. A., *Lieutenant*	49
Stephens, R., *Sergeant*	85
Stephenson, J. L., *Lieutenant-Colonel*	134
Sterling, *Captain*	70
Sterling, M. A., Mrs.	76
Sterling, R. G., *Major*	76
Stewart, D., *Captain*	83
Stewart, H. R., *Lieutenant*	38
Stewart, J., *Private*	124
Stewart, R., *Lieutenant*	81
Stewart, W. M., *Major*	109
Stirling, W. A., *Cornet*	48
Stoke, Lucy	54
Stoke, W.	54
Stowell, M., Miss	84
Strachey, Hon'ble Sir John	29
Strangways, M. H. D., Miss	145
Stuart, E., *Lieutenant*	103
Stuart, Miss	33
Study, W. H., *Lieutenant*	56
Sturgess, W.	85
Sullivan, J., *Private*	85
Sullivan, J. E. H., *Lieutenant*	128
Sullivan, J. E. H., *Lieutenant*	159
Supple, J. C., *Ensign*	48
Sutherland, Mr. and Mrs.	83
Sutherland, R., *Colonel*	28
Sutton, J., *Private*	124
Swanson, J., *Lieutenant*	162
Swanson, W.	41
Swetenham, C. W., *Lieutenant*	55
Swetenham, H. D., *Lieutenant*	10
Swetenham, *Lieutenant*	34
Swinton, J. S., *Lieutenant*	157
Swinton, Mrs.	51
Sym, G.	121
Symes, J., *Lieutenant*	91
Symes, P., *Corporal*	11
Synge, R. D., *Lieutenant*	135

T.

Tablet in memory of 7 Officers and 164 Non-Commissioned Officers and men of the 93rd Sutherland Highlanders, killed or died in 1857-58	161
Tablet to the memory of 48 soldiers of No. 3 Company, 8th Battalion, R.A., who fell during 1857-58	158
Tack, Elizabeth	173
Tack, J.	174
Taffingham, E.	88
Tandy, J. O.	25
Tapley, *Lieutenant*	130
Taylor, C. B.	60
Taylor, D. W.	168
Taylor, E. E.	100
Taylor, F. S., *Brevet-Colonel*	128
Taylor, F. S., *Colonel, R.E.*	130
Taylor, J., *Lieutenant-Colonel, B.E.*	175

	Page.
Taylor, L.	128
Taylor, *Lieutenant*	87
Taylor, R.	115
Taylor, W., *Corporal*	85
Taylor, W., *Gunner*	92
Taylor, W., *Sergeant*	43
Taynes, Mr.	39
Tebnant, D.	42
Thomas, C. E., Mrs.	143
Thomas, D.	82
Thomas, M., Mrs.	82
Thomas, W., *Sergeant*	11
Thomason, J.	40
Thomason, J. G.	165
Thomason, J. G., B.C.S.	159
Thompson, J.	47
Thompson, J. D., *Lieutenant*	56
Thompson, R.	40
Thompson, W. A. F., *Captain*	123
Thompson, W. F.	61
Thomson, Miss	34
Thomson, M. G., Miss	103
Thomson, W. T., *Ensign*	59
Thorne, J., *Private*	83
Thornhill, J. B.	140
Thornhill, M., Mrs.	63
Thornhill, M. B.	55
Thornhill, M. C. B.	140
Thornhill, Mr. and Mrs.	33
Thornhill, R. B.	63
Thornton, H. M., Mrs.	89
Thornton, J., *Private*	93
Threipland, M. A., Mrs.	115
Thurton, J., *Lieutenant*	171
Thynne, W F., *Captain*	156
Tibbets, Mrs.	54
Tieffenthaler, J., Fr.	32
Tilfer, F. J., *Lieutenant*	105
Tilfer, J., *Lieutenant*	44
Tillbock Singh	111
Tod, A., *Captain*	78
Todd, F. K., *Captain*	100
Todd, J.	41
Todd, Mr.	54
Tof, *Captain*	101
Tomb of two English Officers said to have been killed in the Gonda district in 1858,	157
Tombs, H., *Colonel*	17
Tomkins, Mrs.	54
Tomkinson, F. H., *Lieutenant*	40
Tomkyns, J. W., *Ensign*	178
Tomminson, D., *Private*	16
Tooth, W., *Corporal*	85
Toun, G., *Private*	85
Trampton, H., *Private*	23
Travers, A., *Private*	83
Tregear, E. H., Mrs.	8
Tregear, V.	8
Tresham, Mrs.	54
Tress, F., *Quarter-Master Sergeant*	48
Trition, Mr.	54
Trout, *Captain*	13
Trout, H. B., *Lieutenant*	124
Tucker, C., *Sapper*	148
Tucker, *Colonel and Mrs.*	34
Tucker, Miss	34
Tucker, Mrs.	55
Tucker, R. G., *Ensign*	38
Tucker, R. T.	72
Tucker, T., *Lieutenant-Colonel*	32
Tucker, W. F.	128
Turnbull, A.M., *Captain*	49
Turnbull, A. M., *Captain*	137
Turnbull, L. J., Mrs.	116
Turnbull, *Lieutenant*	86
Turnbull, S. K., Mrs.	128
Turner, A., *Captain*	48
Turner, *Private*	129
Turner, R.	80
Turner, T., *Private*	11
Turner, W. D., *Captain*	112
Turner, W., *Private*	159

U.

Urquhart, C. L., Mrs.	76
Urquhart, G. T.	76
Urquhart, R., *Conductor*	79

V.

Vaughan, Mr.	54
Venables, E. F.	125, 26
Venables, G. H., *Ensign*	95
Vergin, Mr.	54
Verga de H., Revd.	174
Vibart, *Captain*	34
Vibart, E., *Major*	47
Vibart, E., *Major*	62
Viscardi, Mr.	54
Vyse, S., *Lieutenant*	23

W.

Wade, F. L., Mrs.	51
Wainwright, F., *Lieutenant*	47
Wainwright, F., *Lieutenant*	56
Wainwright, Miss	57
Wainwright, Mrs.	57
Waitt, J., *Private*	11
Wale, F., *Captain*	157
Walker, A., Mrs.	71
Walker, Mr.	54
Walker, W. B., *Lieutenant-Colonel*	187
Wallett, Miss	54
Walsh, D., *Riding Master*	48

Page.

Walsh, J. E., *Ensign* ... 105
Walsh, Mr. ... 54
Walters, W., *Sergeant* ... 157
Walton, D. C. ... 87
Walton, Mrs. ... 87
Ward, V. L., *Lieutenant* ... 95
Warde, H. J. G., *Lieutenant* ... 49
Warden, Mr. ... 54
Wardlow, G., *Captain* ... 23
Wardrop, D. ... 86
Warhaw, Mrs. ... 56
Warlow, T., *Captain* ... 171
Warner, G., *Captain* ... 178
Warrell, *Sergeant* ... 38
Warren, *Sergeant* ... 50
Watkins, C. R., *Quarter-Master-Sergeant*, ... 79
Watkins, G., *Quarter-Master-Sergeant* ... 81
Watson, J., *Private* ... 85
Watson, L. S., *Captain* ... 57
Watsons, T., *Sergeant* ... 11
Watt, J. ... 114
Watts, Miss ... 38
Watts, Mr. ... 38
Wauchope, J. ... 74
Way, C. G., *Ensign* ... 81
Wayatt, G. ... 38
Webb, P. C., *Lieutenant* ... 56
Wells, E., *Lieutenant* ... 44
Wells, E., *Lieutenant* ... 105
Wells, H., *Private* ... 11
Wells, Mr. ... 54
West, E., Mrs. ... 54
West, G., *Private* ... 85
Weston, W., *Sergeant* ... 11
Westroys, C. S. L., Mrs. ... 22
Westroys, E., Miss ... 22
Whalley, C. F. E. ... 103
Wharton, M. E. M. F., Mrs. ... 119
Whelan, *Sergeant* ... 50
Wheeler, Sir H. ... 67
Wheeler, Sir H., *Major-General* ... 46
Wheeler, O. R., *Lieutenant* ... 46
Wheeler, J., *Color-Sergeant* ... 83
Wheeler, Lady ... 46
Wheeler, W., *Private* ... 85
Whinyat, C., *Colonel* ... 101
White, C. S., Mrs. ... 90
White, I., Miss ... 50
White, J., *Colonel* ... 108
White, M., *Captain* ... 101
White, P. T. R., *Lieutenant* ... 183
Whitelock, *Major-General* ... 73
Whiting, F., *Captain* ... 47
Whitworth, H., *Armour-Sergeant* ... 157
Wideep, Jane ... 54
Wideep, Katharine ... 54

Page.

Wideep, T. ... 54
Wiggens, E., *Lieutenant-Colonel* ... 46
Wiggens, Mrs. ... 46
Wilcox, J., *Colonel* ... 133
Wilford, *Lieutenant-Colonel* ... 90
Wilkins, L., *Assistant Surgeon* ... 101
Wilkinson, Mr. ... 54
Wilkinson, W., *Private* ... 85
Williams, E., Mrs. ... 55
Williams, B., *Colonel* ... 49
Williamson, *Captain* ... 47
Williamson, Mrs. ... 47
Willis, Mrs. ... 54
Willoughby, H., *Lieutenant* ... 164
Wilson, A. ... 42
Wilson, T., *Private* ... 124
Wilson, M., *Colonel* ... 65
Wilson, W. T., *Captain* ... 109
Wollaston, L. H. ... 100
Wood, J., *Sergeant* ... 85
Wood, R., *Colonel* ... 27
Wood, T. W., *Private* ... 83
Woodford, C. J., *Lieutenant-Colonel* ... 63
Woods, L., *Sergeant* ... 11
Woods, R., *Sergeant* ... 11
Woolcar, Mrs. ... 56
Woollaston, J. ... 85
Wren, F. S. M., *Lieutenant* ... 47
Wright, H., *Private* ... 157
Wright, J. ... 41
Wrixen, (*Junior*) ... 34
Wrixen, (*Senior*) ... 34
Wrixon, C., Miss ... 55
Wrixon, R. B. ... 55
Wrixon, W. M ... 55
Wroughton, B. F. ... 173
Wybrow, F., Revd. ... 122
Wylde, C. V., *Lieutenant* ... 132
Wynne, *infant sons of R. O. and Sarah*— ... 113

X.

Xavier, F., Revd. ... 174

Y.

Yates, Mrs. ... 55
Yeo, J., *Sapper* ... 148
Young, D., *Private* ... 85
Young, G. ... 87
Young, J. ... 87
Young, J., *Captain* ... 64
Young, J. H., *Lieutenant* ... 171
Young, Mrs. ... 87

Z.

Zachar, E. ... 30
Zachar, E., Revd ... 175
Zeb-un-nissa, J., Her Highness, or Sumru Begum ... 12, 13

www.ingramcontent.com/pod-product-compliance
Lightning Source LLC
Chambersburg PA
CBHW031829230426
43669CB00009B/1280
* 9 7 8 3 3 3 7 3 8 5 0 1 9 *